MY DARLEY AND BEYOND:
THE JOURNEY OF A LIFETIME
YESTERDAY'S AND TODAY'S PEOPLE AND INDUSTRIES

LEWIS R. JACKSON

COUNTRY BOOKS/ASHRIDGE PRESS

Published by Country Books/Ashridge Press
Courtyard Cottage, Little Longstone, Bakewell, Derbyshire DE45 1NN
Tel/Fax: 01629 640670
e-mail: dickrichardson@country-books.co.uk

ISBN
978 1 898941 86 6
1 901214 72 9

© 2006 Lewis R. Jackson

The rights of Lewis R. Jackson as author has been asserted by him
in accordance with the Copyright, Designs & Patents Act 1993

All rights reserved. No part of this publication may be reproduced,
stored in a retrieval system or transmitted in any form or by any means,
electronic, mechanical, photocopying recording or otherwise,
without the prior permission of the publisher.

*The photographs of the submarines appear
by kind permission of the RN Naval Museum, Gosport*

By the same author:
DARLEYS IN THE DALE

Printed and bound by: Cromwell Press Ltd.

Contents

Acknowledgements	4
Prologue	5
Chapter 1: Darley Dale	8
Chapter 2: Family and Forebears	19
Chapter 3: Vineyard Terrace and the Broad Walk gang	36
Chapter 4: Work, Bikes and Romance	78
Chapter 5: The Building Trade	126
Chapter 6: Lewis Jackson (Builders) Ltd	199
Chapter 7: Inventions, Patents and Manufactures – IDC and TDI	248
Chapter 8: Life has not been all work	264

ACKNOWLEDGEMENTS

Ron Slack
Harold Allen
Peter Naylor
Clifford Wright
John Wildgoose
Keith Taylor
Tod Dakin
Dick Richardson
My wife, Barbara, daughters Lesley and Beryl,
for typing, proof reading and patience,
sons, Andrew and Russell,
and many other people
who have shared their knowledge
and memories with me.

Prologue

This is the story of my life and times, also of the people I have met and worked with on my journey through life. I have been well blessed, with my wife and family, parents, relatives, workmates and pets all contributing to my great adventure. Memories of times of joy, times of sorrow, times long past, from first hearing a radio to watching men land on the moon. The thrill of first travelling on a bus to a nearby village to jetting off to distant lands. When I was a child in 1934 it was an event when a plane went over. Twenty years later going through the sound barrier was an event. Twenty years after that in 1974 the sound barrier was being broken every day by Concorde, and men had actually flown to the moon and landed on it. We had the privilege of watching them thanks to the progress that had been made since I first listened to our Mac Michael wireless in 1934. Knowing and working with people from the Victorian age to the youth of today. Witnessing a way of life now gone for ever, seeing the zenith of the British Empire and its descent.

I have observed a huge decline in self-sufficiency, paralleled with a huge increase in the standard of living and a much longer life expectancy coupled with personal freedoms. I seem to have lived through a lifetime of wars. Worldwide, people are their own worst enemies, yet at the same moment can be your greatest friend. We all have a time to live and a time to die. There are no exceptions. Some lives are short, some are long, some happy and some sad. I have been very fortunate in my life time journey, always looking over the fence to see what it is like on the other side. Over the last one thousand years four basic industries have dominated our civilisation, agriculture, construction, manufacturing and transport. These industries, along with the marketing side of them, have not only provided a living to countless millions over the centuries, they have provided the essential basics of life, food, shelter, manufacturing and communication. In my long and varied journey through life I have been involved in all these activities.

Darley Dale, and its people, have changed. Darley has grown from a series of small hamlets into a conglomeration of large housing estates. The large open fields between Broad Walk and Two Dales are now covered with dwellings. The main A6 road through our valley is overloaded with traffic. Quarry and railway men have become practically extinct, along with nurserymen and lead miners. In 1968, one hundred and twenty years since it was laid, the railway line through the valley was taken up, the railway sidings were dismantled, and the engine sheds demolished - the end of an era and an industry. However the sound of steam engines has once more returned to the valley with Peak Rail's four miles of single track, a mere shadow, however, of the glory days of yesteryear.

There are not so many people out and about nowadays. People seem to either stay at home watching the latest electronic miracle, or firmly ensconce themselves in their cars, isolated from their neighbours, travelling to the nearest town for shopping and leisure purposes. Most of them are so busy and have so many TV programmes to watch that they have no time to explore physically and historically the beautiful, mysterious and historic valley we live in.

On the other hand we are fortunate in having several local well-supported shops. People still congregate together in large numbers for social and leisure activities, like the Carnival, car boot sales etc., which seem to have lost none of their attraction. We still have two well-attended primary schools in Darley Dale and one in South Darley. Children over eleven years go to either Lady Manners School at Bakewell, or Highfield School at Matlock by bus. We had our own comprehensive school of four hundred and fifty pupils from 1964 to the early 1980s when the Derbyshire County Council closed and sold it, with its lovely playing fields, for house-building. Schools are the young vibrant beating heart of a community. People of my age who went to school before the Second World War were all naive children until after we left school. Today's children seem to have been stripped of a large slice of our simple childhood pleasures and security. A way of life may have changed but the valley is enduring, still full of wonderful nooks and crannies, and treasures unknown to some of today's commuters.

My life with my wife Barbara has been idyllic. Our family of four children and four grandchildren, our pets and friends, have been a joy and comfort to us. We have had a fairy-tale life. I still sincerely believe that one's wealth should be measured in leisure and contentment. Contentment equals happiness, leisure is doing what you want to do with your time. If one's work is also one's pleasure and hobby, and you have the right partner, every day is a pleasant adventure. I have been well blessed and am in a better position than most to reflect on our mortality as I have undertaken the funerals, laid out and put to rest so many of my friends, workmates and relatives. My motto has always been – make the most of every day, do anything you like so long as it does not trouble your conscience. This can help turn yesterday's dreams into today's realities. Whatever you want to do, do it now, for everyone there is a tomorrow that we shall not see so make the most of today and every day.

I started work on Whit Monday, 31st May 1941, a few days before my fourteenth birthday, and spent the next 60 years on the move, rarely spending more than six months in one workplace. I loved the excitement of travelling to new locations, meeting with new characters, and new things to do. Every day an adventure.

Chapter 1: Darley Dale

Geography

Seventy-nine wonderful years have flown by since I was born at number 3 Vineyard Terrace on Darley Hillside. Vineyard Terrace, a name to conjure with, visions of grapevines basking in the sun, on the south-facing side of our section of the Derwent Valley. Sheltered from the bitter east wind by the 1,000 ft (320 metres) high moors to the north and east, warmed by the sun from dawn till dusk, over-looking the lovely river Derwent which flows peacefully along the broad green valley bottom.

The birthplace of the author, 3 Vineyard Terrace, Darley Dale Hillside

Darley Hillside, because of its south-west facing situation, was a very sunny place with green fields, placid cattle and a few horses. Breath-taking sunsets, with shades of red, blue and purple are seen at their best from our hamlet, the trees and fields taking on a rosy glow as the sun sinks down to the horizon. In the winter snow stays longer on the steep dark slopes on the opposite side of the valley.

Darley Hillside to me is the perfect place to live. Except for a relatively short time of fifteen years when I lived lower down the hillside slope adjacent to the A6, Darley Hillside has always been my home. I have been privileged to know it intimately, its nooks and crannies, trees, buildings, streams, stone walls, roads and paths, the different moods, its people and pastimes, some now long gone. To me it is more than a home, a place to live, Darley Hillside is a treasure chest of memories overlaid with an aura of peace and tranquillity. It always gives me a sense of belonging, and being firmly rooted in its soil.

Darley Hillside must always have been a glorious place in which to live. Unbeknown to most of today's inhabitants Bronze Age men lived and died here. Several of their remains have been found over the years. Their camp with its burial mound near the top of what was Stancliffe Tor was only destroyed by quarrying in the last two centuries. This area was included in the Doomsday Book. I am so fortunate to have spent the majority of my time on earth here, contributing to and witnessing the many changes that have taken place over time.

Our Darley valley is about four miles long, perhaps two miles wide, bisected by the river Derwent on its journey from the Peak District's heather-clad, wild gritstone uplands, to the river Trent in the south of the county. The northern slopes of the Derwent Valley are the most populated, taking full advantage of the warmth and light of the sun and shelter from the bleak north winds. Our Darley valley is typical of this scenario, divided into several hamlets nestling in sheltered locations. Darley Hillside is central to the valley and has been inhabited since recorded history began.

Darley Hillside hamlet is mostly situated on the spring line. Ample pure water, which has filtered down through the gritstone-capped moorlands, emerges around the 200 metre (640 ft) elevation. Slightly below the spring line and central to the hamlet stands Vineyard Terrace, built in the late 1800s out of the famous Stancliffe gritstone, with a welsh slate roof. The terrace of weathered stone snuggles unobtrusively into the landscape. Scattered in the vicinity of the one hundred years old terrace are several other old dwellings, some dating back to the 1700s. There are a few 1920s spec. bungalows and some present day dwellings, probably about forty or so dwellings in all.

HISTORY

When I was young Darley Dale was a great place to live in. The economic slump that encompassed so much of Britain in the early 1930s passed Darley Dale by. Most of the men worked on the railway, approximately five hundred and fifty, the Stancliffe gritstone quarry and estates two hundred and eighty, the nurseries approximately forty and the Millclose lead mine and smelter around five hundred men. Darley Dale had no steel industry, textile mills or coal mines. Other men worked in agriculture and transport. In the 1930s most of these workers lived in Darley Dale. It was thanks to nature providing abundant, easily got raw materials, ie stone and lead, and excellent agricultural and horticultural conditions. Darley Dale flourished from 1850 to 1950. The railway was the icing on the cake, providing work for over 600 people at its peak. The railway arrived in Darley Dale in 1848 and closed in 1968.

Darley Dale, with South Darley and Little Rowsley was a very large parish until recently. Darley Dale has no real centre. It is composed of a series of hamlets stretching along both sides of the river Derwent between Matlock and Rowsley. History abounds, from stone circles, bronze age burial mounds, old halls, old hamlets listed in the Domesday Book, ancient trackways and old lead mines and quarries. Roman remains have been found on Oker Hill, which dominates the centre of our valley. In the early 1900s spiritual needs were well catered for, with three churches and eleven chapels scattered around our valley.

HOUSES AND SHOPS IN THE 1930S

In the year of my birth Darley Hillside had a delightful mixture of dwellings of all types, some from the early 1600/1700s with stone slate roofs, to 1920s bungalows with pink asbestos roof tiles. All these buildings were built of stone, from the nearby Stancliffe Quarry, as were the boundary walls which divided the fields. Darley Hillside had four farms and several small-holdings. These, and the approximately 40 dwellings, are all interlinked by a confusing network of roads and paths, all seemingly leading to nowhere in particular. At least eight stone troughs, fed by springs, were dotted about the various roads for communal use. They were usually covered with a lid made from hardwood. Several of the troughs had an adjacent, uncovered one, for use by horses and droving cattle. Incongruously, a standard-gauge railtrack ran diagonally across the steep hillside just below the hamlet, transporting stone from the Hall Dale Quarry to the Stancliffe Stone Company's works situated next to the Grouse Inn on the main London to Carlisle A6 trunk road of 1831.

At the start of the second war there was an abundance of shops in central Darley on the A6 between the junction of Church Lane and Station Road. In a space of three-quarters of a mile there were seventeen shops. Window shopping was a pastime for young and old alike. Young lads gazing in awe and envy at the latest bicycle or toy, children spending hours deciding which sweets to have if they had any money, women looking at clothes, fabrics and accessories. Almost every household then had a sewing machine. The Broad Walk shops were the children's favourite place to congregate. All the shops except Wilson's Fish and Chip shop shut around 6 p.m. At night there were no lights to be seen. North to south on the A6 from the Church Lane junction on the south side were Price's general provisions shop first, then dear old Daisy Woolliscroft's shop which was also the home of the Silver Service Bus Company. One could also buy tickets for a Sunday afternoon or night Mystery Trip, usually going to somewhere like Castleton, Buxton or Dovedale. Next door was Nellie Boam's paper shop. I remember in the winter it was a very cold shop. Picking up comics before one purchased them was strictly forbidden.

Across Green Lane was Darley Dale Post Office run by Ada Siddall, who also sold such diverse things as electric light bulbs, cakes, cards and stationery. The shop next door again was a shoe sale and repair shop. Footwear was displayed in the window and shop. Mr Fielding, who repaired boots and shoes in the cellar beneath the shop always wore a leather apron. He personally dealt with customers' repairs, proffering advice, and I spent many happy hours watching him at work. A more chaotic shop than the next, run by Pa Fearn, would have been hard to find. I never did know his real name as everyone called him Pa. He sold clothes, materials, accessories, wools and cottons. Darley Co-op at the top of Crowstones Road was next. There were two completely separate shops – the Provisions one managed by Albert Shimwell from Youlgrave, and a Draper's shop run by Martha "Dolly" Wall. Across the A6 was Orme's shop, an upmarket provision shop. Both the Co-op and Orme's delivered customers' orders, which one of the staff travelled for once or twice a week. Just below the Co-op on Crowstones Road was the hairdressing shop of Robert Allsop, always known as Bob, which kept open until around seven o'clock. There were no more shops or houses on the south side of the A6 between Crowstones Road and Station Road B5057. The north side more than made up for this as there were five shops at the bottom of Broad Walk. The first was Wilson's fish and chip shop, who also sold green grocery and had a green grocery round with a horse and dray. Mr Wilson always seemed to be at work both with the horse and dray in the daytime, and late at night in the chip shop. Dorothy Cartledge kept the chemist's shop next door. My uncle Fred Jackson kept the baker's shop between the

Top of Dale Road and Church Road looking south, Darley Dale

Dale Road looking north Grouse Inn and Stancliff crane

Dale Road looking south from The Grouse

Broad Walk shops, looking north

chemist and Hayto's sweets and tobacco shop. Last but not least was Chapman the butcher, who also ran a horse and trap delivery service. I almost forgot to mention that my uncle Fred delivered bread and cakes via a handcart. The cart was a large tall box on two huge spoked wheels. It was pushed by a young man called Allen who became known as "Buns". After them there were no more shops and only eight houses before Station Road on the north side of the A6. At the top of Station Road there were three shops, a bicycle shop, a cobbler's shop and I cannot remember what the third shop was, perhaps a ladies' hairdresser.

1960 was the beginning of the end for this wealth of diverse shops. Today, 2006, there are only nine original ones, plus four new ones, a small Supermarket/Petrol Station, the old Westminster Bank, now a chemist, a new ladies' hair dresser opposite the subway to Oker Avenue, and a household goods shop at Broad Walk. One shop that I, and I am sure many other central Darley natives remember above all others, is Mrs Rogers's sweet shop next to Churchtown School. It was full of all types of sweets and chocolate which could be purchased for a penny or a half-penny. However she made a living I do not know but her shop was a bright light on a dull school day. The sheer joy of looking and deciding were moments to be savoured. Growing old and looking back at those far-off days of the small shops, each with its own character, and the personalities who ran them, brings back many memories, not only of them but of the many small local Co-ops I worked in.

THE DARLEY FAMILY

Ernest Paulson, neighbour, friend and my ex-teacher, was doing some research into the family who came over with William the Conqueror and adopted the name of Darley when they came to live in our Darley valley. I helped Ernest with his research and took him to a place called Butter Cranby in Yorkshire to visit a man who was a descendant of the original 1066 Darleys. I decided not to go in my Jaguar in order not to appear ostentatious, so we went in a Fiat 850. When we arrived there we found to our amazement that he lived in a place like a young Chatsworth House. His father had been a Viscount. We knocked on the front door, which was one of two, about nine feet high and four feet wide. A footman, or butler type person, asked us our business. We explained, he asked us in, and we waited in a vast hall with marble columns until Mr. Darley was ready to see us. When at last we were ushered into his presence he was very icy. To break the ice I asked him why he had a set of stage coach harness in the hall. "How do you know what it is?" he asked me. I told him that I had a friend who ran two stage coaches, and he replied that his hobby was driving a coach and four.

The ice was broken and after that nothing was too much trouble for him. He showed Ernest and me a large painting of the Darley Arabian which his family imported into Britain from Syria. Over eighty per cent of the world's race horses are descended from this horse. One of its descendants was the first thoroughbred to be imported into America. Two weeks after our visit he was here at Darley Dale, visiting Caroline Smith, of the Red House stables, my stage coach friend. A few years after our visit to Butter Cranby I was talking to the Duke of Devonshire and mentioned the Darleys. His Grace told me that he had served in the war in Italy with Mr Darley's brother Charlie in the Coldstream Guards and that he was at Charlie's side in the front line when he was seriously wounded.

DARLEY FAMILY HISTORY

When William Duke of Normandy was preparing for his invasion of England a certain Edmond of ErIe in Normandy was one of his cavalry officers and knights. Sir Edmond furnished and supervised the care and handling of William's horses. Edmond, who was born in 1034, was granted possession of the vale of Dereleie in 1066. Ernest and I were intrigued to find that over nine hundred years later several members of the Darley family still had equine connections.

William landed in England at the end of September 1066, and fought the Battle of Hastings on 14th October. November and December were spent subjugating England and dividing it among his followers whom he left with men-at-arms at strategic points to guard against uprising. William then returned to London and was crowned King on Christmas Day 1066. Edmond's wife and young son John, born at ErIe in 1066, came and joined him in Darley soon afterwards. Edmond, as was the French custom, took the name Edmond de (of) Darley. He constructed himself a manor house, probably of wood, alongside the road called Derwent Lane, 220 metres north of St. Helen's Church, Darley, on or near the site of the present day Abbey House. The present owners, whilst excavating for a swimming pool, came across what they believe to be the remains of a moat which may have surrounded the stone building that eventually replaced the wooden one. According to Glover's Derbyshire Directory, published in 1829, it was a building of considerable size. It was pulled down in 1771 on the orders of the Duke of Rutland.

In 1067, while King William was away in Normandy, there was a rebellion in the York area, led by Edgar Atheling, the last survivor of the English royal family. William returned to England and marched north to York. Edmond de Darley and his horses went with him and helped to put the rebellion down. William granted lands in the area to Edmond and asked him to guard it. Edmond and his son John took up residence at Wistow about twelve miles south of York in about 1085. Edmond's second son Richard, born at Darley in 1070, became Lord of the manor of Darley and John became Lord of the Manor of Wistow. There is another village called Darley near Harrogate, in Yorkshire.

The Yorkshire Darleys prospered. In the 15/1600s they became ship builders and merchant adventurers, building the ships that took the Pilgrim Fathers to America – the Mayflower, the Seaflower, the Abigail and the Bonaventura. Thomas Darley became an early settler in America, according to the Society of Genealogists. He was held prisoner in the American War of Independence in 1780. After the war he took up residence in South Carolina. It is also recorded that in 1624 a John Darley sailed to Virginia on the Jacob. There is no doubt, according to the records, that several Yorkshire Darleys were early settlers in America.

The Darleys of our parish are next recorded about four generations after the Richard who was alive in 1070. William was born in 1194. William's son Andrew, born in 1215, was made Lord of the Royal Forest in the King's Peak in 1249. Andrew at that time was also Lord of Bakewell. I personally wonder if there is any connection with the inscribed stone coffin lids in St. Helen's church porch and the Darleys. Andrew died in 1272 aged 57 and was succeeded by his son Hugh, who may have had a connection to Darley Abbey, at Derby. The next member of the family of whom there is any real information is Sir John de Darley, great-grandson of Andrew. In 1321 Sir John engaged master masons to build him a large Manor House on the southern end of Darley Hillside, close to the old road which ran from Darley Bridge to Hall Dale Lane. In 1790 this dwelling was superseded by the present Darley Hall, built by Richard Arkwright, who demolished the old one in 1796 and used the stone to help build his cotton millls. Digressing, I think it is amazing that Richard Arkwright and Joseph Whitworth, both of humble origin, two of the men who, in my opinion, contributed immensely to the Industrial Revolution (factories and precision engineering), should have been Lords of the Manor of Darley through their ownership of Darley Hall.

Chapter 2: Family and forebears

Jacksons and Tofts

The Jackson side of the family came down from the Hope Valley Eyre family through the female line. I was told that my several times great grandfather in the early 1800s married the sister of one of the Eyres, who I believe went to Virginia to make his fortune in the late 1700s and was never heard of again. My father, James Edward Jackson, always called Jim, was born on a lonely hill farm called Batham Gate, just north of Buxton. The farm is situated around 1,300 feet above sea level, on an old Roman road, a very bleak place in the snowy and frosty winters of the 1800s. Father had five brothers. The farm was not large enough to provide employment for all five, and in consequence Father started work at the age of 15 on the Midland Railway at Buxton. His farm upbringing, where he worked mostly with the horses helped him on his journey through life.

My mother Kate Toft, who was born in 1887, was the daughter of George Toft, builder and lead miner at Youlgrave, whose own father was born in Youlgrave in November 1804 – before the Battle of Trafalgar. George was born in 1845. He married twice and Kate, the youngest of six children of his first marriage, was just four years old when her mother died. George was in his late fifties when he married again. He had three more children, two sons and a daughter, Bill, Walter and Louisa, and died at Haddon Hall in January 1907, as a result of falling off scaffolding near the end of a several years long restoration. His second wife and her three children went back to live in her home town, Wolverhampton, after his death. Many years later, while we were living at Redlands in 1946, a knock came on the door and standing there was a man about fifty, with a trilby hat and glasses. He enquired if Kate Toft lived here. He was Bill Toft, my mother's half brother whom she had last seen in 1907. Two years later I took mother to meet her two half brothers and sister, Bill, Walter and Louisa at Wolverhampton. Louisa died in 2001 at Brownhills in Staffordshire, aged 101 years.

My grandfather, George Toft the builder, kept a diary of his life and times, though I have not had the pleasure of reading it. My family on the Toft side goes back to the early 1500s in the Youlgrave area. The Eyres and the Jacksons are both old-established families in the Peak district and, like the Tofts, have a history of occasionally producing people who are a bit different, almost to the point of eccentricity. Through the centuries the Tofts have been gifted at building, mining and engineering.

Mother, father and brothers

Mother and Father married in 1906 and came to live in Darley Dale adjacent to the A6 near Northwood Lane. By the time I was born they were living at Vineyard Terrace. My mother was forty and I had three brothers, with a big age gap between us. The eldest, John, 19 years older than me, was in the Navy. Clifford was 17 years older than me and lived at home together with Jim, 15 years older than me. In the 1930s Clifford worked at Smedley's Hydro, Matlock, in the baths. Jim had various jobs, including nurserying, stone-walling, building, concrete block making, and as a caller-up on the LMS railway. Father was an engine driver at the Rowsley Loco Depot.

My mother had, in her younger days, kept a small fish and chip shop at Dungreave Avenue, Deeley Town, the now defunct name for the area near Firth Rixson's factory. In 1935 she and my father purchased a plot of land below Redlands, the bungalow which they had bought in 1934, and built a pair of houses on it, employing my brother Jim and other builder relatives. Uncle Ezra, my mother's brother, who built most of the houses on Northwood Lane, set the houses out and gave advice. I remember all the floor joists came from Baslow Hydro which was being pulled down at that time (1936) and which my father collected with a horse and dray borrowed from farmer Dakin of Tor Farm, now demolished, on the A6 road, Darley Dale. My parents named one of the houses Pandora, after the submarine my brother John was serving on. The Pandora was based at Wei-Hi-Wei in China. Before coming to rest on the bottom of Malta's harbour, sunk in a wartime bombing raid. The other house was called Forres after the submarine depot ship, also based in China. In 1936 my brother Clifford married Gladys Greatorex from Derby who worked with him at Smedley's Hydro and they set up home at Barnard Terrace, Matlock Bank. This turned out to be a good thing as Redlands had only two bedrooms, one of which Jim and I shared.

John had joined the navy in 1928 as a boy sailor, and was serving at Plymouth when he married Bertha Fearn who lived 250 yards further along Hall Moor Road from Vineyard Terrace. Shortly after his marriage he was posted to China for about two and a half years, serving on His Majesty's submarines Pandora and Osiris. I remember it was the time of the Japanese and Chinese War. His first son, called John Geoffrey, was born in 1935 and did not see his father for almost two years. John left the Navy in 1938 and settled down on Darley Hillside with Bertha and John Geoffrey, finding work on the pumps which prevented flooding at the Millclose Mine. He was called up at the time of the Munich crisis around late 1938 and again in the second week of August 1939, at the time of the Polish crisis. He was very upset as Bertha was expecting her second child at the end of the month. I had vaguely become aware that the crisis that was occurring with Germany was very serious.

John was still away when the child was born on Friday 1st September 1939. Mother told me that I was now an uncle twice over. I was twelve years and two months old. I had no experience of babies when I went to see Bertha and her new baby on Sunday morning, 3rd September 1939. Bertha showed me the baby boy while sitting in the armchair with the wireless on, listening anxiously for any news about the crisis with

H.M.S. Submarine PANDORA
Pandora was launched in 1929 and saw service world-wide before being sunk by enemy aircraft whilst lying in Malta's harbour on 1st April 1942, with the loss of twenty-seven crew members. Pandora was raised and beached in September 1943 and was finally scrapped in 1957. Pandora's bell is on display at the R.N. Submarines Museum, Gosport.

H.M.S. OSIRIS
Osiris was launched in 1928 but not commissioned until 11th December 1933. She also served world-wide and had a very hectic war service, including sinking the Italian destroyer Palestro in September 1940. Osiris served in the Meditteranean area throughout the war with no loss of life, and was scrapped at Durban in 1946.

H.M.S. PHOENIX

Phoenix was launched in 1929 and served world-wide until she was sunk on 16th July 1940 near Augusta, Sicily, by the Italian torpedo boat Albatros. All the fifty-five crew members were lost.

To me, the dwellings which mother and I built, and were named after these submarines, are a small memorial to the one hundred and thirty-seven men who lost their lives.

H.M.S. OXLEY

Oxley was launched in June 1926 and served world-wide up to her unfortunate demise on 10th September 1939 with the loss of fifty-five lives.

All four submarines carried a crew of fifty-five, displaced around one thousand seven hundred tons, and had a surface range of eight to ten thousand miles. Brother John's naval record has the letters D.D. OXLEY, 10.9.39 written at the bottom. D.D. is the abreviation for Discharged Dead.

Germany. The announcer said that the Prime Minister, Mr. Neville Chamberlain, was to speak to the nation at eleven o'clock. We sat together in the cottage at the top of Gill Lane, near Vineyard Terrace, which had been their home for just one year, when Chamberlain announced that "As from now a state of war exists between Great Britain and Germany." I really had no idea what this would entail except that John would not be coming home for a while. Bertha had sent a telegram to him informing him of the birth of his baby son and that they were both well. John sent a telegram back saying how happy and pleased he was, and would see them both shortly. John, as we now know, then set sail in the submarine Oxley accompanied by its sister submarine Triton to patrol near to the entrance of the Baltic Sea.

WARTIME TRAGEDY: JOHN AND THE SUBMARINE OXLEY

Just over a week after war had been declared I was tinkering with my bike when our postman Wallace Young from Stanton Lees came up the path. He asked if my mother was in and I said yes. Wallace knocked on the door and mother answered it. Moments later she came out crying and saying "John is dead, John has been killed." Wallace had come to ask mother to go with him to help break the terrible news to Bertha who lived on her own on Darley Hillside with her two young sons. "Come with us Lewis" mother said. We trudged up Darley Hillside, my mother crying. The postman, who knew John, was also very upset. I was bewildered.

When we arrived at Bertha's I had never known such a scene of despair and grief, and found it all very disturbing. The telegram stated that John had been killed by an accidental explosion at sea. The grief and despair would I believe, have been even greater had we known at the time that John's submarine had been torpedoed by its sister submarine Triton on 10th September, one week after war had been declared. The cause of this was the failure of the signalling equipment. Triton sent several signals to Oxley asking her to identify herself. When no signal was received the Triton fired a torpedo at what she assumed was a U-Boat. Immediately after the torpedo was fired the Oxley's spare signalling apparatus sent the required identity signal. It was too late. Out of the fifty-five crewmen, who included John, only the Captain and the Signalling Officer were saved because they were on the conning tower. I believe the day the telegram came was the day I grew up, the most traumatic day of my life. The next few years were to be a life of hardship, rationing and anxieties. The war taught me, at an early age, to take nothing for granted. I learned that life can, and will, turn upside down in an instant. Expect the unexpected at all times.

In 1989, the fiftieth anniversary of John's death, by what we today call friendly fire, we got the full truth about what had happened. Information about this disaster was withheld at that time and was still scarce in 1989. I telephoned the ITV at Nottingham about the fifty years old tragedy and they took Barbara and me to Portsmouth and the submarine base at Gosport to make a TV film of the tragic happening.

Redland/Phoenix, Crowstones Road.
One of three Jackson dwellings named after submarines

The naval authorities and ITV made sure I was informed all about the whys and when of the tragedy and I took part in the film. Brian Collins was the producer. After the film was shown on television I received a letter from a fiancee of one of the men killed in the disaster. Another lady wrote to the newspapers saying she had never really known what had happened to her husband until she saw the TV film. I found it most moving. My brother John's son John, whom he never knew, was also featured in the film, as was my brother's widow Bertha. She had never remarried.

Flitting

My mother was a marvellous lady and an entrepreneur, always going to sales, buying and selling anything from furniture to houses. In his forty-nine years service on the railway my father became a top engine driver. In the second World War he was in the London link, driving express goods trains to Kentish Town, sometimes working through air raids. He worked very hard for which he received good pay. Mother invested it wisely in 1936 in the Redlands property and again in 1947 when she bought Sir Joseph Whitworth's old house, Highlands, at the sale of the Stancliffe Estate. Father was a well-respected person in the poultry world and won the cup for the best bird in the LMS Fur and Feather Show in 1927. I have the replica cup now. Father did well that year, won the first prize at the Show, and became my Dad. He loved to play cards; all his life he liked to spend some time at various public houses but I never ever saw him the worse for drink. I am sure he only went for the cards and dominoes. He made me stand up for myself and was never unkind or ill-treated me. I am proud of both my parents.

Father flitted us twice in 1948. Each time we borrowed the shire horse and the hay cart from the ever obliging Mr. Dakin. Father was a dab hand at horse driving thanks to his farm upbringing. After mother had purchased the Highlands in November 1947 we moved to Craven Villa opposite High Tor and then in mid-summer 1948 we moved to the

Tor Farm. Mr Dakin's farm dog at Tor Farm guarding the pigs. Tor Farm at the southern end of Firth Rixon's factory has now been demolished. The first Tor Farm was situated 300 yards further south and was demolshed in the 1870's. Its foundations are still to be seen behind Sir Joseph Whitworth's roadside wall

Highlands. It was a fine day when we did the two journeys from Matlock Dale. The dray was loaded with our belongings, including the dog and cat. I vividly remember going up the drive to the new house, the poor old horse scrabbling up the steep slope.

There are six acres of land at the Highlands, with a nine-feet high wall round it, and several internal walls about six to seven feet high, plus a building known as the Apple House. Forty to fifty fruit trees were scattered around the land. It had originally been Sir Joseph Whitworth's private garden, and the Apple House was the only portion remaining of the immense conservatory which had stood in the centre of the garden. This had been so large that a horse and carriage could be driven through it. There was also an underground tunnel (access to Stancliffe Hall grounds) alleged to be haunted by Lady Whitworth who died in 1896. I knew three people who swore to seeing her ghost near to the entrance to the tunnel! I never saw or heard anything odd but the tunnel entrance has a spooky atmosphere, not a place to visit on a dark winter's night.

Some friends of my mother's from Leicester, George Gutteridge and his wife and family, came to stay in 1949. They had first come to Darley Dale on an excursion from Leicester to the Whitworth Institute in 1918 and became firm friends with my parents. They spent at least one week's holiday with them every year from the end of the first war until the late 1970s and we still visit each other. The party in 1949 included their son and his fiancee. I told the young couple about the ghost. When they went out one night I waited in the tunnel in the dark. When I heard

The tunnel leading to Stancliff Hall grounds

them coming I made a strange wailing sound. The drive above the tunnel which was lined with yew trees was as black as a bag and they both ran off up the drive to Highlands. Worse was to come. In the middle of the night the poor girl had a nightmare about the ghosts and the tunnel. They went off me a bit the next day when I told them it was only me.

However our visitors' troubles were not over. My father and I, the young man and his father went up the orchard in the dark to dig out a wasps' nest, a job it is better to do in pitch darkness with only an occasional flash of a torch. Father and I convinced them they were in no danger of being stung. Halfway through the operation in the dark father jabbed George in the bottom with a pin. He exploded, leaping up and down shouting he had a wasp in his trousers and it was stinging him. Father reassured him it would not sting him again then gave him another jab. The results were spectacular. Moments later George had his trousers off and ran off in his underpants, whirling his trousers round and round. He burst into the house shouting and carrying on in a most alarming manner. It was two years before we dare tell him the truth.

Marriage and homes

My wife Barbara and I were married in 1951 and lived at Highlands Cottage, an old house with only primitive heating, cooking and sanitary arrangements. In 1959, twenty-three years after the house Pandora had been built, and eight years after our marriage, I bought a plot of land alongside the disused Stancliffe rail track at the bottom of Moor Lane, where father had kept his poultry, and built a bungalow for Barbara and me. We named it Osiris after one of the submarines in the China flotilla.

In 1968 Barbara and I decided to build ourselves a larger house next to Osiris. Our eldest child, Beryl, was then sixteen, Lesley fourteen, Andrew twelve and Russell five years. We had no garage at Osiris and the vehicles filled the drive. We purchased an adjacent plot of land. I

HIGHLANDS

The silence, and the summer's glare,
Hot, dozing stillness everywhere;
Old apple trees, gnarled, crumbly-green,
At ground-defying angles lean,
And pear trees, where glittering flies crawl
Still ranked along the red brick wall;
Wide grey stone steps, hot in the sun,
With lichen-spots, where spiders run;
Decaying pig-sties, broken down,
With ivy rampant, thick green gown;
The apple-house, mysterious, dim,
With cobwebbed windows, scents within
Of ancient apples, ripened, sweet,
The stone floor cold to sandalled feet.
Outside the drone of insects' sounds
And birdsong fill the peaceful grounds.
In the far orchard, scythe in hand,
The keeper of this secret land
With ancient waistcoat, cap on head,
He cuts the grass, with daisies spread,
And dreams of youth, so far away,
Through all the golden summer's day.

Lesley Brameld, Feb. 1995

*Lewis' father,
James Edward Jackson,
1950's*

had drawn the plans for this dream house when I was passing time away convalescing in Walton Hospital after a double pneumothorax in 1962. Barbara brought me the drawing materials to the hospital where I designed it down to the last detail. I carried out the excavation work for it in 1968, built it in 1969 and we moved in 1970. We called the house Isis, after another China flotilla submarine. In the year 2000 I purchased Redlands, our old home, remodelled it and renamed it Phoenix after a sister submarine to Pandora.

My father Jim died in 1968 aged 79 after working on the railway for almost 50 years. My mother phoned down in a state. "Come up quickly. I think your father is dead." Father had died in his sleep, a very peaceful end. I buried him in St. Helen's Churchyard and put on his gravestone "James Edward Jackson, Engine Driver".

Mother fell in 1972 and broke her hip and could not cope on her own so Barbara and I reluctantly sold Isis and went back to live at Highlands to look after her. When I first went to live at Highlands in 1948 my father and I had no equipment besides an axe and a scythe. Returning twenty-four years later in 1972 I had a lorry, a digger, a tracked loading shovel and lots of men. We renovated the Highlands from chimney to cellar. In the garden we downed trees, ploughed up all the grassland and scrub, planted new grass areas and fruit trees. We excavated and levelled the site of the huge old conservatory. The Cornish boiler that heated it is still in situ, in the underground boiler house, now filled in. I purchased a very old Ferguson tractor, a spring-tine cultivator, a farm roller and a gang-mower, none of them new, renovated them and put them to work. It was marvellous to see the six-acre garden being restored. The conservatory had been sold for scrap and the gardens abandoned in the early 1930s depression. Father had worked so hard at Highlands with his scythe trying to get it tidy after being derelict for seventeen years. He would have been over the moon with my JCB and the tracked excavator. Mother died in 1974 aged eighty-eight.

Children and foster children

Our eldest daughter Beryl married Chris, a soldier, in 1977 and lived at our first home, Highlands Cottage, which we renovated for her. Our son Andrew also left home in 1977, buying a house at Broad Walk. Lesley our second daughter had already married and had purchased a house in Broad Walk in 1975. Barbara and I and our younger son Russell lived at Highlands. We had two bedrooms to spare and after over twenty years of having a family at home the house seemed empty. Barbara, being a caring, compassionate person, proposed we take in short term foster children. I thought this was a good idea, we applied, were vetted, and passed. Shortly afterwards we had phone call saying two young sisters needed a home immediately and so we started what was to become a very satisfying and rewarding part of our life. How Barbara coped I do not know. She ran all the office and financial side of the business we had started in 1964, and which was very busy, and I was on the District Council, which kept me busy too.

The Social Services lady arrived with two girls whose mother had been taken into hospital, and whose father was away in the far east with the armed forces. The girls soon settled in and Barbara took them to school in the car. They became firm friends with our cats and dogs, and played in our large garden. Over twenty-five years later one of the sisters still comes to visit and writes to us from Scotland, where she lives with her husband and her seven children. When they went back home we really missed them.

Our next pair were two young boys and when they arrived we were saddened and shocked. They were cowed and silent. Apprehension hung over them like a cloud and they were both incontinent, very much in need of tender loving care which is what we gave them in abundance. We soon realised that their previous life had been a daunting experience. They had had all the spirit taken out of them. After a few months they were returning to something like normal, enjoying life with our family and pets, trusting us and establishing a relationship with our family. Out of the blue we were informed that their father had demanded they be returned to him immediately. We were very sad to see them go. We have never had any contact since, and often wonder what became of them.

The next pair were two sisters who did not appear to be remotely distressed. Settling in was no problem for them and coming from an inner city life they took to the country and the animals. The younger one thought our garden was a park. One of them came back to see us in the teens of years later, complete with husband and daughter and it was great to see them.

The last two brothers came from a colliery district and they too were very self-reliant and assured. Their mother came to see them for an hour or so, perhaps once a fortnight, and brought them small presents. They were good lads but life had matured them too quickly. Sadly these two were the last foster children we had. Our workload was too high to give the amount of attention that all foster children need.

The first two boys had been a real eye-opener to Barbara and me who had a happy, secure childhood. When one has been guardian to young children of four and six who have had all the joys of childhood taken from them at such an early age it makes you realise what a lot of unhappy children there must be in our modern world of broken homes, divorces, step parents etc., no family rock to build your life on, no home security.

Our sons Russell and Andrew both worked for the family building firm. Both passed their City and Guilds in brickwork. Andrew represented Chesterfield Technical College at bricklaying in Birmingham and was awarded a silver trowel. Barbara and I are very proud of them both, as we are of our daughters Beryl and Lesley who hold down responsible jobs for the Derbyshire County Council. Our idea was that Russell, who left school with only one O level (in Art) would learn book keeping and take over the office work from his mother and Andrew would take over from me. When aged twenty Russell got a job with the Peak Park Planning Board's Ranger Service to learn administration. He performed exceptionally well and with help from the Peak Park authorities went on to Sheffield University. He went to live at Sheffield to fulfil his own dreams. Russell now has a BA, an MA and a Ph.D. Barbara and I carried on with the business ourselves. No-one can, or should, run other people's lives for them.

Andrew, like myself, has always been a hands-on man and is very mechanically minded. He learned to drive the JCB when he was fourteen. He designed and built himself a lovely stone house on Darley Hillside, in the garden of the house my mother purchased for me at the Stancliffe sale in 1947 when I was twenty. Andrew is a master craftsman in stone and brickwork.

A farmer at Monyash whom Andrew helped in his school holidays gave him an old Wolseley car. He decided, despite the fact that he was only fourteen, and the car had no MOT, tax or insurance, to drive it home. Going round a sharp bend near Stanton Lees he lost control and crashed through a wall, and careered down a steep field. He then walked home complete with bumps and bruises, and eventually told us about the car. We went back to Stanton Lees and saw the owner of the field who said he had reported the crashed car to the police. The car was beyond repair. I contacted my friend, the late Len Marshall, scrap dealer, to remove the car. His lorry was fitted with a crane. We lifted the car on to the back of his lorry, took it back to his scrapyard, and cut it up. The police came to our house the next day and said they believed our son had crashed a car in a field at Stanton Lees. The owner of the field had given the police the registration number and they had traced the car to the farmer from Monyash. I told them the car had been scrapped. No car, no evidence, no vehicle offences, only a gap in the wall which we later built up. Andrew was summonsed for driving a car under age.

In the early 1980s Andrew took up bomber and banger racing on an oval track at High Edge near Buxton. He bought MOT-failed cars, stripped them down and prepared them for racing. I accompanied him. Andrew did this for several years and became an extremely proficient race driver and car repairer. However, he eventually had a spectacular crash and demolished the car. Barbara would not go again, she said it was too upsetting to watch him. We also went to Hednesford near Wolverhampton. The race track there is in the bottom of a disused reservoir. Our seven and a half ton Ford lorry, which was fitted with ramps, was our car transporter. Several banger and bomber car drivers told me that after a time they got used to crashing and rolling over and over up the track. I suppose one can get used to anything, even car crashes. I tried to get the police to have a banger car team. I believe they would have benefited from the subtleties of banger car racing, ie how to avoid being spun off the road whilst at the same time spinning other cars off and getting used to the stress of crashing. I believe practical experience beats theory every time.

Jim, my remaining brother, died in 2002 aged ninety-one years. He lived on Sir Joseph's Lane in a bungalow we built for him in 1985. He left a wife, a son and two daughters. I think about him often.

Chapter 3: Vineyard Terrace and the Broad Walk gang

Childhood on Vineyard Terrace

I entered the world on 6th June 1927 at 3 Vineyard Terrace, a row of eight houses divided into two blocks of four by a gennel. My first memories of Vineyard Terrace are of lying in my bed watching the hissing, flickering gas jet high on my bedroom wall, a fan-shaped oasis of blue and yellow light. My bedroom at no. 3 faced south and looked out over the Derwent Valley. At a very young age I used to stand at my bedroom window and look down the valley. I could see for miles, many animals, cows, sheep and horses dotted around the distant hills and in the valley bottom. Every day seemed to be full of sunshine and joy. I cannot remember one bad day.

The nine families who lived in the eight houses in Vineyard Terrace were a close-knit bunch of people. There were four young children living on the row and every house was an open door to us with a welcome, a drink, a bun or a biscuit, and conversation. None of the women had a job and all stayed home looking after their house and family. Two families lived at number 1, the Haytos and the Allsops. Mr Percy Allsop worked on the railway, Mr. Charlie Hayto worked for Stancliffe Estates as a blacksmith. He was my friend for many years. Stancliffe employed several blacksmiths, who could turn their hand to most jobs, from repairing the company's two steam locos, sharpening all the quarry tools, or surreptitiously making iron hoops for local children to bowl along. The Allsops had a daughter Janet, about two years older than me, and she took me to school. She went to live in

Canada after the war and I have never seen her since though I have a photograph of her. The Haytos had a son, Eric and, I believe, a daughter, Avis.

Mr & Mrs Masters lived at number 2. They seemed to me to be elderly, both grey haired. Mrs Masters was obsessed with cleaning. My shoes were examined before I was allowed in the house and newspaper was laid down for Mr Masters and any visitors to walk on. Everything was scrubbed, from the chairs to the fire shovel handle. Mrs Masters always wore a long black dress covered by an apron. Her husband was a carter, wearing leather leggings and a waistcoat as he drove his horse and cart. They had no children that I knew of.

At no. 4 lived the Hawksworths who had a son Ken who was older than me. I only knew them for a short time before they left and a family called Bunting came to live there. Mr Bunting was called Wilf and he and his wife had two children, a boy and a girl. George was about six months younger than me and Eunice about two years younger still. George and I were bosom friends. Over the gennel at no.5 were Mr and Mrs Slater. Mr Slater was a painter and decorator and had a bicycle which usually had a ladder strapped to it, and a bucket banging from the handle-bars. He always wore a dirty, paint-stained white apron at work times. The Slaters had two sons, Jess and Jim, and a daughter, Phyllis, all considerably older than me. Jim was a lead miner and our paths crossed in later life.

Mr and Mrs George Holland lived at number 6 and they had a son and a daughter, both also older than me. I don't know what Mr Holland did for a living. Their son Edward, always called Eddie, worked for the Stancliffe Estates in the masons' yard, in charge of a huge stone planing machine and a stone shaping lathe. Our paths also crossed in later life when I used to watch Eddie making stone balustrades and sections of fluted columns and marvelled how he did it. The Pearsons lived at number 7. Mrs Pearson had worked with my mother and Mrs Hallowes, from nearby Cherry Tree Farm, in Stancliffe Quarry at the time of the First World War. At number 8 lived the O'Connors who, as their name implies, came from Ireland, and who spoke with a strong Irish lilt. Mr O'Connor, who was a very tall man, worked on the railway. He and his wife had at least two grown-up daughters and were my favourite friends on Vineyard Terrace, always welcoming me, giving me drinks, a piece of cake, a warm by the blazing coal fire in winter. Later in life I had the privilege of undertaking both their funerals. I shed a few tears for them.

Our house had two bedrooms and a box-room which was my bedroom. Our front room was very sunny and light, facing south, with a front door opening on to the very small front garden. The front room was only used on Sundays and special occasions, such as when we had visitors for tea. We all sat round the large rectangular mahogany table which Mother, in later life, told me she bought at a Willersley Castle sale in the 1920s. I am now sitting at this table, with its ornate shaped legs, writing.

Facing north at the back of the house was the kitchen/dining room, dominated by the huge cast iron range which had a water boiler on one side and an oven on the other, with

The author and his mother at number 3 Vineyard Terrace in 1929

tall stone jambs each side supporting a large stone lintel which spanned the fireplace. Next to the fireplace, on the left was the round coal-fired cast iron wash boiler, about 750mm (2ft 6in) in diameter. My most abiding memory of 3 Vineyard Terrace is of wash-days, with the coal-fired clothes boiler going full blast, steaming away, and a proliferation of dolly pegs, ponches, dolly-tubs and buckets. We had a large rack suspended from the ceiling and in the winter it always seemed to be full of wet clothes. The pantry was on the opposite side of the room to the fireplace.

The floors were covered with linoleum (lino) and pegged rugs of various sizes and colours. Cutting old clothes and materials into strips about 25mm (1 inch) wide and 50mm (2 inch) long ready for pegged rug making, and placing the various colours into separate bags to make borders and patterns for the rugs, was a winter's night pastime We had a small wooden settle with several cushions on the bottom and back. The settle, along with a small pine table and four wooden chairs filled the kitchen. Looking out of the kitchen window into the back alley one could only see the coal-house and wc door, and the ashpit wall all about 3 metres (10 feet) across the yard. People constantly walked past as the back yard to Vineyard Terrace was a stone-paved thoroughfare with access from each end of the row. Everyone's kitchen window had a roller blind to provide privacy. Most blinds were of a dense, blue material which let very little light through, making the back yard quite dark in winter.

There was, of course, no bathroom or inside toilet, or hot water on the yellow pot sink. All our bedrooms had chamber pots. A trip to the wc on a winter night was an expedition. My mother escorted me across the yard, then went into the wc to light the candle. She then waited outside if it was not raining as there was very little room in the tiny wc. I was scared of the wc at night as it was not unknown for the candle to blow out. Hessian sacks were draped around the overhead water system all winter for frost protection, a haven for the largest spiders in Britain which now and then descended on a thread to have a closer look at you.

Coal was kept in a bucket near the range to save journeys across the yard at night.

Hanging from the centre of the ceiling in the front room and kitchen was a gas pipe about 500mm (1 foot 6 inches) long. Halfway down it was a circular shiny metal shield about 300mm (1ft) across. This reflected the light and helped to stop the ceiling getting hot and black. Below this was the fragile gas mantle in a glass shade. Two control chains hung down. Just lighting the gas was fraught with trouble. I was never allowed anywhere near it. First of all a match or spill was lit and held about 50mm (2 inches) below the mantle with one hand. With the other hand you gently pulled one of the chains down to turn on the gas. Too sharp a pull or not holding the match close enough to the gas mantle resulted in a mini explosion instead of a gentle pop. Gas jets, where you just turned the gas tap on and lit the burner, caused no such problems. Why so many dwellings were still standing at the end of the gas age is a mystery to me when the potential for blowing them up or burning them down abounded.

Being built on the steep hillside a flight of steps alongside the wc led up to the large back gardens. All garden produce had to be carried down these steps and manure carried up in buckets. The manure came in cart loads pulled by a horse. It was tipped at the bottom of the steps. Everyone's large vegetable garden provided all the necessities for good living. I spent a lot of time in the garden playing and eating my fill of strawberries, raspberries, black and red currants, broad beans and the odd young turnip. There were rows of cabbages, carrots, peas, parsnips and lettuce. I only remember one garden with a greenhouse This grew tomatoes.

  My mother used to make what she called fruit pies in a large basin lined with suet pastry. She filled it with elderberries, raspberries, black currants etc and small slices of pear or apple mixed with what other fruit was ripe and available at the time. She then steamed them in a double decker contrivance. When done she placed a big dish with high sides over the basin and, holding the dish firmly, she inverted the basin over the dish and gave it a sharp tap before lifting it off the pie. It was a matter of luck whether or not the fruit pie stayed intact. When it did stay in one piece we all cheered. They were wonderful mouth-watering occasions as the fruit pie sat quivering on the dish before a knife was plunged into it and all the fruit spilled out, ready to be spooned into our dishes then topped over with custard.

Father kept poultry. He was also a master poacher so we lived like royalty. Chicken, pheasant or rabbit were everyday items on mealtime menus. The times at which we had dinner varied because of father's odd working hours on the railway. My brother Clifford also worked odd hours at Smedley's Hydro. Brother Jim worked for the Stancliffe Estate at various jobs.

Vineyard Terrace had no dustbins but had an ashpit across the yard, next to the wc. About once a month the ashpit was dug out on to the back yard and the Council lorry collected it. Coal was delivered by the ton or half-ton, and also tipped on to the back yard to be shovelled into the coalhouse. On nearby Moor Lane there was a small walled enclosure known as the rubbish depot. This depot was a mecca for small children. It contained all manner of things, old chairs for the numerous dens we made, old bicycles, broken tools, household items, broken and discarded toys. It was treasure trove unlimited.

I had a small tricycle with brakes, most essential on our steep valley sides, which I rode everywhere. Cars and lorries were very few and far between. I loved my tricycle. I remember that at first it was a bit too big for me but with the seat right down I managed the pedals all right. The pedals drove the back wheels by means of a chain. A lever on the handlebar worked the one and only brake, which clamped down on the front wheel tyre. The frame was painted black and it had white tyres with shiny wheels and handlebars, and a strange bell with no lever. To make it ring you turned the middle of the bell round. It must have been very low geared because I cannot remember pushing it much. A free wheel gear was on the back axle. I do not know what happened to the tricycle; I cannot remember having it when we moved to Redlands next to the A6, in 1934. I believe the three years or so I had my tricycle, when I roamed far and wide on Darley Hillside's practically traffic-free roads, inspired my love of vehicles of all types. Having the means to roam about is lovely, be it an old tricycle, car or heavy lorry. I have been so fortunate to have had a set of wheels of some sort or another practically all my life. The freedom to roam and visit pastures new is priceless.

Most of the farmers and nursery folk had horse and traps or drays, as had many of the butchers, greengrocers and travelling men. There were a few small vans belonging to local trades-people. The pride of the road in the early 1930s were the drug horses. These magnificent shire horses pulled the timber drugs loaded with trees. It was awe-inspiring to see the immense timber drugs with four shire horses, two holding the drug back with the centre pole. There were steel slippers under the wheels, shedding cascades of sparks, and there was smoke coming from the wooden brake blocks as the drugs made their way down the steep hillside to Gregory's sawmills. Modern articulated lorries are awesome, but the drugs were majestic. In my younger days I was lucky enough to have rides on shire horses, hanging on to the chains which fitted in a kind of immense belt, around the horse's waist and neck.

Two travelling boot and shoe sellers came to our house, who both ran a so-much-a-week club. One was Miss Mills from Matlock and the other, Mr Simmons, from Two Dales. Prior to going to school Mr Simmons and my mother's brother, Ezra Toft, the builder from Youlgreave, were the only people I knew who had a car. Squires the baker from Lumb Lane had a small van, as did Stanley Wagstaffe, a Two Dales butcher. When I started school at Churchtown in 1932 the headmaster, James Charles Bartram, also had a car, a maroon and black Singer Junior. I knew the names of everyone and their pets who lived in our hamlet. Our neighbour at number 2, Mr Masters, drove a horse and cart and wore leather leggings, as did Mr Duroe also a carter, as did most of the Hillside farmers, Hallowes, Grindy, Doxey and Fearn.

Health care in those days was rough and ready compared with

today's facilities. Diptheria, scarlet fever, mumps, measles and chicken pox abounded. My wife Barbara had diptheria when she was nine years old and was incarcerated in the isolation hospital at Bakewell, near Lady Manners school, for around six weeks. Visitors were not allowed into the hospital so Barbara and her parents could only look through the windows at each other. At school we children caught a multitude of sicknesses. I vividly remember having measles, a week in bed then two weeks off school, and chicken pox. I still have the small white scars as most of the people of my age do. When I was about four or five, a cyst grew on my neck. My father sat me on the kitchen table and cut it off with his cut-throat razor while my mother held me. No National Health Service then! One person whom I disliked to see was Mr Greatorex, the travelling dentist. He had a small gladstone bag for his equipment. His visit usually occasioned another kitchen table effort, accompanied by loud groans and moans. All our family's dental needs were treated by him. Dr Meachim was our doctor and his surgery was in the front room of a house in Stancliffe View on the A6.

Friday night was the night for Youlgrave, six miles away, when mother took me with her on her weekly trips to see her sister Annie, who was the eldest of my grandfather Toft's first family, and where every other person seemed to be a relative of mine. We used to go there on a Woolliscroft's Silver Service bus which ran from Matlock via Youlgrave to Friden, a journey of about twelve miles. The last bus back was about 10.40 pm from Youlgrave. It went via Picory Corner, then over the hump-backed Fillyford bridge on the old A6 and everyone on the bus cheered as they left their seats. Today the old, small hump-backed bridge sits forlorn in lonely isolation in a field near the new bridge and dual carriageway which replaced it in 1936.

When my grandmother died, leaving a family of six, the youngest of whom was only four, Annie became mother to them. They were all, understandably, very close. Aunt Annie married one of her father's workers, Ralph Webster. As a wedding present grandfather built her a cottage down Bradford Lane and she spent the rest of her life there.

Old Fillyford Bridge on the original A6 near Picory Corner, abandoned in 1936

Aunt Annie, like my mother, was only just over five feet tall and Ralph was over six feet. Annie and Ralph built a small shop in their garden and one of her daughters, Nona, ran the shop for about thirty years. She lived at home and never married. Friday night at Youlgrave was family night. A paraffin lamp was on the table and another on the dresser and they, along with the blaze from the fire, cast a soft, warm glow in the living room. Annie's family and relatives all congregated together and filled the room to overflowing.

Annie had two sons and four daughters. My uncle Jim, another of my mother's brothers, died the year I was born leaving ten daughters. Another brother, Uncle Ezra, had six children. I believe the families all lived in Youlgrave. Many of them congregated at Annie's on Friday nights when we all had a sing-song around the piano, singing songs from the First World War time. When I was aged about six or seven I knew all the words of "Just a Song at Twilight". I could sing well and always gave a solo and everyone clapped. It made me feel so proud and gave me a lovely feeling of belonging. After supper everyone talked of yesteryear, people and happenings long gone.

Aunt Annie smoked a pipe, which did not seem in the least unusual to me as she had always done so since I could remember. Ralph died in the 1950s and Annie soldiered on. She never had hot water on tap, no bathroom, and only an outside toilet. She had electricity put in after the Second World War and never ceased to marvel over it and the wireless. When Annie died in the 1950s she took her last journey up Bradford Lane on the village bier. This was of Victorian origin with large iron spoked wheels and solid black tyres. The front two wheels were steered by means of a long handle which protruded from the front by about four or five feet and had a crosspiece to enable a man each side to pull and steer it. Bradford is a very steep lane and all the relations, sons and nephews, helped to push Annie up the lane to rest. I think, next to having a hearse drawn by a pair of black horses with plumes, this is the way to go. Annie's funeral was a great gathering of the Toft clan.

One day Father called me in out of the backyard of Vineyard Terrace "Lewis, we are going down to the henpen," he said. Little did I know that at the tender age of six it was to be the first day of a love affair that was to last for over seventy years. Father's henpen was alongside the Stancliffe Estates standard gauge rail track which ran, via two loops, from the LMS London to Manchester main line to the Hall Dale Quarry, high on the side of the Hall Dale. I had seen and admired the small tank engines, Joseph Whitworth and Henry Dawson, several times before. They made their way up via a loop system, one end of the loop in Stancliffe yard and the other end at the junction of Moor Lane and Whitworth Road. From the stop block situated there they went below Hallowes's farmhouse, now demolished, across Hall Moor Road to the Hall Dale, about one mile away. The engines with a few waggons puffed and snorted their way up to the stop block and, after resting there while the firemen changed the points, set off to climb the steep incline across Darley Hillside to the gritstone quarry about three quarters of a mile away. While the train was resting at the stop block father had a word with the driver who said he would take me up to the quarry. I could not have been more thrilled. It was one of those warm, magical moments that occur very rarely. I can only remember the chuff, chuff, chuff of the engine as it toiled up the hillside, shrouded in dirty white steam and enveloped in heat from the engine as I sat in the swaying, lurching cab. Even more wonders were awaiting me at the quarry; a giant steam crane loaded the waggons making lots of quick little puffs of steam and a huge clanking noise. There a small stone "snap" shed, where the quarrymen ate their food. I was mesmerised by it all. We returned to the stop block where father was waiting for me. I had more rides on the train later but none excelled my first unforgetable journey. The quarry and the line was closed around 1936/7, and the crane, whose boiler chimney always seemed to be smoking, was scrapped.

My father, being a railway man, had a number of free passes a year to travel anywhere by train. In 1934, when I was seven, we all went to Plymouth to my eldest brother John's wedding While at Plymouth we went to Southampton to see the big ocean liners in the docks. I was absolutely amazed at the size of them. I had always assumed that all trains were in LMS maroon and was surprised to see trains in other colours, and see out of the carriage the water troughs between the rails, which enabled steam engines to pick up water while on the move.

Every boy at Churchtown school wore boots. We were all proud of our boots. I used to pester my dad, who had an iron cobbler's hob, to put hobnails in mine. He repaired all our boots and shoes. No boys wore long trousers until they were about eleven or twelve years of age. Girls never wore trousers. When I was about six or seven I learned to ride a two-wheeled bicycle. I never had one of my own until I was about nine when I was given a lady's bike for my birthday. It was a very old bike with a string curtain affair which ran from holes in the rear mud guard to the back axle. This was to stop long dresses becoming entangled in the spokes and chain. It had a Sturmey-Archer three-speed gear. I loved it and the mobility it gave me. I had a brand new bicycle out of a catalogue called a Granby Glider for my twelfth birthday. This too had a three-speed gear, an essential in our hilly valley. I could not have been more pleased with a Rolls Royce.

THE BROAD WALK GANG

The days of close-knit relationships with other families living on Darley Hillside were about to end. I would be about seven, two years after starting school, when my mother announced we were going to move to a bunglow called Redlands (now Phoenix) on the A6 opposite the Derwent Valley Co-operative Society shop, now a supermarket. Just before we went Mrs. O'Connor called me in and gave me a compass. "This is for you Lewis, something to remember me by" she said. I still have and treasure it over seventy years later. Every time I see it I am transported back to those idyllic days of infancy on Vineyard Terrace and all those lovely friendly people who nurtured me, and in whom I had implicit trust.

The author aged seven at Redlands/Phoenix

Two or three journeys down Moor Lane and Whitworth Road, with all the furniture in Mr Dakin's dray and mother and I walking behind with Patsy the Irish Terrier, we were soon settled in. No more would I have to climb up the valley side from Churchtown School to Vineyard Terrace. It was only about one third of a mile from the bungalow to school. No more baths in the tin bath in front of the cooking range fire on Monday nights, after the washing was done, or so I thought. No more carrying a candle across the back yard to the wc, hoping it would not blow out, or a spider descend on your head. I was sad to leave the hillside and all my friends.

I soon took up with the boys who lived nearby on South Park Estate, (Broad Walk) or as we called it in those days "the new houses". They were one hundred and sixty houses, constructed from the mid 1920s to the mid 1930s by a builder from Manchester called Morton who was also the managing director of Stancliffe Estates Ltd. Three bricklayer brothers from Manchester (the Ainscoughs) were the main builders. In the 1950s I worked with two of them, Bob and Tommy. The eldest and foreman of the Broad Walk job was nicknamed Mad Harry because he worked like mad. Bob died in 2000, one of the last of the old time bricklayers. The Broad Walk boys became a gang which lasted around eleven marvellous years. They came from all sorts of backgrounds and one or two families were quite poor. One family was really poor as the father was very ill and could not work. I think there were six members of the family and when it rained they would come to school with sacks around their shoulders. All wore cast off shoes and clothes, but they were a nice honest family and have stayed that way.

I believe our gang of Darley Broadwalk boys were no better or worse than any other boys in their early teens. We all had a good relationship with one another, knew our strengths and weaknesses and stuck up for ourselves. Harmony is a word that springs to mind. The main members of the gang which flourished in the war years were Bill Allison, Brian Allwood, Sam Briddon, Billy Goodwin, Charlie Hopkinson, David Holmes, Tom Helliwell, Tom Hibbert, Dennis Hanson, Henry Mellor, Reg Parkes, Gerald Robinson, Geoffrey Sellors, Brian Taylor, Ron Waller and Trevor Wright.

No member of our gang was ever in real trouble with the police, probably because Darley Dale had a surfeit of police throughout the war. Sergeant Tansley lived at South Darley, PC Thorpe at Broad Walk. They were supplemented by around 4 or 5 Specials – no wonder we never got into serious trouble – there always seemed to be a policeman of one sort of another lurking around every corner.

Our gang of boys was subject to strict discipline at school. Our ex-army officer Headmaster laid down the rules and we all knew just how far we could go before retribution caught up with us in the form of the cane. Having the cane was a very public affair carried out in front of the class. It was always a traumatic moment, one had a few minutes to think about what was going to happen to you and how much it was going to hurt, while the Headmaster explained to you and the class of thirty or forty pupils why the cane was being administered.

Unfortunately, probably because I was not the most docile of pupils, I had more than my share of the cane. We even learned how to avoid its worse effects, relaxing the hand and at the last moment tilting the palm downwards helped. Keeping the thumb back and low saved it from becoming bruised. As I have mentioned, life was hard, we never had any money, many boys aged between 12 and 14 worked part of their summer holidays in the nurseries or helping on farms. Late summer was a very busy time on the land.

I occasionally helped on Hallowes' farm, but I had no affinity with weeding and clearing in the nurseries. Father made me work in our large garden, we also had a very large school garden where all the dreadful labour of double-digging, excavating trenches for bean and pea rows, and searching for microscopic weeds took place. As the war entered its second year, all food was rationed – sweets practically vanished.

One enterprising lad in Darley who was not a member of our gang bred rabbits, he was the same age as me. His rabbits were in great demand. When he left school he got a job close to home but the hours were long which left him little time in the winter to feed his multitude of rabbits with greenstuff, which he collected from the roadside with a scythe. Then came catastrophe – it snowed so he went to the allotments and asked if he could have any stripped brussels sprout plants, weary cabbages or anything green that was surplus. However, he could not keep up with the rabbits' demands so he purloined odd cabbages from gardens and allotments. He was warned to stop, but did not and consequently ended up in court. Our gang of boys were typical frisky teenagers getting into all sorts of scrapes but we were all aghast when for stealing a few cabbages he was sent to Borstal. To make matters worse, around the same time two other local boys were summonsed to court. One of them was a part-time errand boy for a local shop, his father worked away from home, and there were several other younger children in the family. He stole a quarter bag of potatoes, a loaf of bread and a tin of shoe-blacking to clean the family's shoes. The gang were horrified when he was sentenced to have the birch. These happenings, and the punishments inflicted on the participants, made an enormous impression on the various gangs of local lads, especially as we had a lecture from our local friendly policeman who said he had been unable to stop the severe retribution being inflicted upon them by the courts. What would be a minor episode today fostered a huge awareness of crime and punishment in the Darley gang. I believe this contributed immensely to keeping us on the straight and narrow path away from crime. However, we were still mischievous and landed in quite a few situations, but not outright crime and vandalism. The punishments handed out kept us from doing petty crimes.

Now that we lived across the road from the Stancliffe Stone yard their works hooter ran the day. Four times it sounded, in the morning, twice at lunchtime, and at knock-off time, when Stancliffe men formed a queue for the bus near the Grouse Inn. Nearly all the men wore corduroy trousers, tied just under the knee with string, yorks or yokes they called them. They all wore waistcoats and caps, and most carried small wicker lunch baskets.

Darley Dale household refuse was disposed of by two local men, Tommy Allwood and Bill Roose. Tommy drove the small grey 30 cwt lorry. Both wore overalls and a flat cap. They were cheerful, hard-working and playful men, always ready for a bit of banter with anyone or a helping hand for the less able. Darley Dale's municipal tip was situated at Lumb Lane, Northwood. It was on the same tip that took the spoil from the 1912 one mile long, two metre diameter Derwent Valley Water Board tunnel that ran deep under Darley Hillside from

Northwood to the Hall Dale. In the school holidays children used to play around the tip. It was alongside the Northwood wood which was carpeted with bluebells in the spring. Northwood Brook ran close by. It did not so much run as leap, bouncing from ledge to ledge, tinkling and sparkling, as it cascaded down the steep hillside. Several footpaths traversed the wood leading to Tinkersley, Rowsley and the valley bottom. In the 1930s a light-hearted war raged between Tommy and Bill and the children who scavenged the tip looking for discarded prams, bicycles, toys, anything that could be adapted for use as a plaything or pastime.

Looking back I now realise what a dangerous place the tip was. The valley side was very steep and the tip even more so. Rubbish slid down the almost vertical slope before being arrested by the trees at the bottom. Our most scary adventures there were to do with old bicycles and prams. Most old bicycles we found on the tip had either no tyres, or flat tyres, and a distinct lack of brakes. We used to ride them down the steep path through the wood to the valley bottom, sometimes

Entrance to the old Northwood tip and bluebell wood off Lumb Lane

inadvertently leaving the footpath and crunching our way into the wood. The ride then usually came to an abrupt halt. Old prams were a great prize, usually wheeled home to be made into a trolley. These were constructed from a piece of wood about 3 feet 6 inches long, 7 or 8 inches across, with a second piece of wood nailed or screwed to it near the back which had one pram axle screwed to it. The front crosspiece was secured to the wood by a nut and bolt, leaving enough slack so that you could steer it. A stout piece of rope was tied to each end of the front axle to enable you to steer it and pull the contraption back up the hill. Braking when going down hill was always a tricky job. We used three methods, pressing the sole of your boot on to the front tyres (not very clever, it stopped you steering), two wooden levers which when pulled back caught on the rear tyres, but the most efficient method was to fasten a piece of zinc sheet to the wooden frame which overhung the wheels; one then pressed down on it. Because the last method generated a fearsome heat blocks of wood were nailed to the zinc sheets above the tyres to stop your hands from getting burnt. The last resort was to sluther your feet on the ground, very detrimental to one's shoes and took a lot of explaining away to your parents. Crashes were commonplace.

Riding old bicycles and trolleys was all thrills and spills, definitely not a pastime for the girls or the faint-hearted. I believe the tip was in use up to the end of the second war. The tip is now completely overgrown and apart from some subsidence at the top it has completely merged in with the surrounding landscape. 1935 was the Silver Jubilee year and 1937 was, I think, the Coronation. Both events were celebrated at the Whitworth Institute which was the hub around which Darley Dale revolved, for recreation and other events, from Armistice Day to Carnivals. Every child was presented with a silver spoon in 1935 and a medal in 1937.

The Broad Walk gang of boys was not quarrelsome. We had occasional fights, with no kicking or the use of weapons. The older boys, brothers or fathers, made sure all fights were fair. I made a life-long friend, Charlie Hopkinson. He was one of a family of six children, and lived on a smallholding at Bent Lane, above our terrace. His father worked for the Council at one time and kept the hillside remarkably clean and tidy. He also grazed the grass verges with his stock, as did one or two others. They all made hay out of the verges. The grazing animals were mostly kept an eye on by either the very young or the very old. Mr Hopkinson exchanged conversation with everyone and kept an eye on everything and was the unofficial information officer. Around these times the roads were tarred and chipped. Charlie's father was an extremely hard worker, armed with a brush, shovel, wheelbarrow and billhook. Darley Hillside was better kept than some of today's parks. Charlie and I became school pals, workmates and stayed close friends for over fifty-five years. He was best man at my wedding in 1951. Sadly he died in 1988 and I as an undertaker laid him to rest.

In the spring we went bird-nesting, taking only one egg from each nest. We made a hole in each end of the egg and blew out the contents, quite a job with a pheasant egg. We all knew which species of bird the egg belonged to. We raided orchards – plum, apple and pear trees, and gooseberry, and raspberry bushes over a wide area. The gang covered a territory about two and a half miles radius from Broad Walk, which stretched from Stanton Moor to Rowsley and Darley Moors, including Two Dales, Ladygrove, Wensley and the length of the river Derwent both sides from Wensley to Snitterton. We also knew the location of every conker, walnut and sweet chestnut tree, also most hazel nut trees. Our favourite place was the Hall Dale wood and brook. We never poached fish or shot birds until we left school.

I would be about nine and a half when other my life-long friend, Geoff Sellers, came to live at Pandora, the house my father had built next to Redlands. His father had lost an eye and a hand in the First World War and worked for James Smith & Sons of Two Dales, who at their peak employed one hundred and fifty men in their famous nurseries, which covered two hundred and fifty acres (one hundred and one hectares). Geoff was three years younger than me, Charlie

MY DARLEY AND BEYOND

Hopkinson two days older, and we all went everywhere together if Charlie had not got to work on his father's smallholding. Our gang of Broad Walk boys, to which we all belonged, had very little to do with the nearby Green Lane gang outside school hours, or the Two Dales or Wensley boys who lived about a mile away. We were a large enough

Proprietors and staff of James Smith & Sons Darley Dale Nurseries

Consignment about to leave the Darley Dale Nurseries for H.I.M. the Emperor of Germany, Potsdam

gang, approximately a dozen strong, to range into their territory with impunity. Just occasionally we had small, fairly good natured skirmishes with other gangs. All the different boys knew one another well because of school.

HALL DALE DAYS

The Hall Dale is the northerly one of the two dales which gives the old Darley hamlet its name. The Brooks which flow through the two dales converge in the hamlet before flowing on to the Derwent. Geoff and I spent all our summer holidays and spare time together, exploring our Derwent Valley, taking picnics which we usually ate and drank shortly after setting forth. It was so much easier to carry them internally. We uncovered the delights and surprises of the Hall Dale bit by enthralling bit. Our first trip was along Hall Moor road to the rail crossing, then walking up the now rusty rail track to the rarely worked quarry. It was a wonderful place to explore, the steam crane which we pretended to drive, the stone blacksmith's shop and tool shed, and a snap cabin to play in.

Just below the quarry the Hall Dale Lane ran along the dale side, about one third of a mile, to Hall Dale Cottage. The road then was covered in sand, washed down from the gritstone quarry. Beyond the cottage the road turned into a cart track before crossing the Hall Dale brook another third of a mile further along. The road overlooked the James Smith Hall Dale Wheatley nursery. The brook ran along the bottom of the nursery slope which was on the north side of the dale, sheltered from the north winds and warmed by the sun. Another cart track ran down the wooded slope behind Hall Dale Cottage to a stone arched bridge over the stream. Venturing down the track we crossed the bridge (now swept away) and came across an old ruined building. Some of the building was still standing to halfway up the window opening alongside the brook. That too was a joy to explore. My mother told me it had once been a straw hat mill. It must have been deserted for many years. The roof had fallen in, bringing portions of the wall with it.

From the old mill ruins the dale side became very steep. Making our way up the fast flowing, leaping, babbling brook, with its green slippery bank, inevitably led to our feet getting wet through. Every now and then a fallen tree would span the brook, issuing a challenge to us to scramble across the dirty, moss-covered trunk. This usually became a shuffle on one's bottom, much to the detriment of our short trousers and bare legs, which became the same dirty green colour as the fallen tree. Around two hundred yards further up the brook a ten feet high waterfall cascaded over a young cliff into a deep pool surrounded by a rocky bank. In times of high water flows the fall made a lovely noise as it dropped into the pool before hurtling on its journey down stream. Spray and bubbles glistened in the sunlight and sometimes a rainbow could be seen hovering around the base of the fall. The pool was deep and mysterious. It was always a struggle to surmount the falls by the steep, wet, slippery banks each side. Once over the top the banks maintained their steepness which led to us occasionally slipping down into the stream, getting even wetter and dirtier. In places we had to detour up the banks as they became almost vertical.

Eventually we arrived at the place where the track from Hall Dale Lane crossed the brook by a large clapper type bridge, with two openings under it to let the water through. Huge stone slabs spanned from each side to a stone pillar about two feet by eight feet and about five feet high on the downstream side. On the upstream side the immense stone slabs spanning the brook were only about one foot above the stream. A large pond about twenty feet across lay immediately upstream from the bridge. Its banks were shallow and covered with sand, as was the bottom of the pool. It was easy to paddle in and make sand castles. Geoff and I christened it Sandy Beach. In later years, when our gang of boys went on a Sunday afternoon walk on the Hall Dale, it had become universally known as Sandy Beach. The bottom half of the Dale had proved to be the most adventurous natural playground one could wish for. The days were always too short. We never possessed a watch until the wartime and often got into trouble for being late.

Exploring the upper reaches of the Hall Dale above Sandy Beach we

The old road (Back Lane) at Two Dales Hill

found things that we had never dreamed of. A veritable feast of discoveries awaited Geoff and me. At Sandy Beach the track divided. The north side ascended up the Dale side, arriving at Bent Lane a couple of hundred yards before Bumper Farm. The track on the south side went to the old green lane known as Back Lane. Back Lane was the main road to Chesterfield from Two Dales prior to the new turnpike road of the 1700s called Sydnope Road, the B5057. Back Lane was then abandoned. Stone sign posts are still in position, despite being out of use for over one hundred years. It was a ridge road like so many of the really old roads. The Hall Dale Lane and track was called Jaggers Lane in the 1700s. The part which ran past the old 1321 and new 1792 Darley Halls from the river Derwent was also abandoned over one hundred years ago.

Geoff and I set forth from Sandy Beach upstream like two Doctor Livingstones. We had only travelled one hundred and fifty yards when we came across an area where the brook ran still and very quiet. On the north side the bank rose almost vertically, profusely covered with primroses, various wild flowers and ferns, and odd small bushes, all clinging to the steep bank. The south side of the brook was bounded by an old moss-draped gritstone wall about two and a half feet high. Wood sorrel with its pretty white flowers festooned the top and a few ferns grew out of the sides. Behind the wall a gentle sloping grassy bank ascended towards Back Lane. We lay on the grassy bank watching the reflections of the flowery bank shimmering in the still water. The only sounds were

Old Darley signpost, Back Lane

the odd plaintive cry of curlews. We were so taken with it that, even at that young age, the profound effect of peace and quiet that pervaded the area imposed itself upon our senses. Geoff and I christened it Quiet Place, and so it remained for many a year until some raging flood water swept the mass of boulders away that dammed the water back. The same flood also swept away the clapper bridge at Sandy Beach, destroying the pond with its wonderful sandy sides and bottom.

Another one hundred yards upstream from Quiet Place we squelched our wet way alongside the stream, only to be halted by a six feet high waterfall with tall gritstone walls on each side of it. Scrambling up the bank and over the wall we found ourselves in an abandoned nursery. The boundary wall ran as far as Bent Lane on one side and Back Lane on the south side. There were row upon row of heathers, including white heather, hundreds of rhododendron bushes with every colour of flower from yellow to crimson, avenues of cupresses and other shrubs, interspersed with weeds and brambles, an unkempt and wild travesty of the orderly, clean and tidy nurseries lower down the valley. My father told me that this area of the Hall Dale, Gritston, was part of the Stancliffe Estate nurseries, which came into being after the death of Lady Whitworth in 1896. The estate was then purchased by the Stancliffe Estates Company. The nursery side was abandoned by Stancliffe following the economic depression of 1929/30s. Geoff and I explored it thoroughly, taking home armsfull of white heather for our mothers. Gritston was eventually purchased by a local nursery man, Hugh Gregory, in 1947 when Stancliffe Estates sold up.

Continuing upstream our best discovery awaited us. The track into the old nursery from Bent Lane, about two hundred and fifty yards below Bumper Castle Farm, ran down to the brook and crossed it by a very well constructed clapper bridge capable of taking a large horse and dray. The nurseries finished here and another stone wall spanned the valley. Alongside the bridge a masonry construction enclosed the brook, about twelve feet long and seven feet wide. At the down stream end an opening about one yard wide was left with large stone piers each side. Down each pier ran a deep groove which was made to hold planks to turn the construction into a sheep wash. A few yards upstream stood a small well-built and obviously cared-for stone building. This had no windows and the door was locked. We later found this was the source of the Darley and South Darley water supply. This fact also made sense of the cast iron marker post bearing the legend DDWW. These marker posts were scattered alongside the track from Hallmoor Road to Sandy Beach. Crossing the brook by the bridge near the sheepwash the track ascended through a rough abandoned field to an old empty farm house and out-building. We approached this with trepidation. The doors were open and most of the window glass was broken. The farm yard was still walled and very overgrown. The sun shone down again. The baking stillness was only disturbed by the cries of the curlews circling overhead. We could not have been more surprised if we had found a space ship. The house and outbuildings were intact but had a sombre, slumbering air of dereliction. Geoff and I went in to explore the ground floor, then cautiously ventured upstairs. It was a young boy's paradise. On subsequent journeys there we explored the farm and its overgrown fields where we found the stone posts of the haystack bases, standing in rows like miniature soldiers. We knew what they were for because we had seen them on other farms.

The brook petered out as it climbed up the now shallow dale towards the moor. Wild heather and bracken had taken over the fields here. Making our way through the rough and slightly marshy ground we came to the Rowsley Bar road which formed the top of the T to Bent Lane. We must have covered around one and a half miles from Two Dales to the Rowsley Bar road. Our exploration had not yet ceased. Across the Rowsley road, through a gate almost opposite the Bent Lane junction, there was another quarry. Asking my father and mother they told me that this large abandoned quarry on the moors was called Wragg's Quarry, and the derelict farm was called White Springs but was more commonly known as Jonathan Barker's. I told Charlie about our

Jonathan Barker's hay stack stoops

amazing discoveries and he told me that Jonathan Barker was his grandad, and his mother had been born in the farmhouse. The farm was compulsorily purchased in 1904 to become the source of Darley Dale's water supply.

Geoff, Charlie and I spent many happy years exploring everywhere in the Hall Dale. On one of our expeditions we surprised a fox in the Hall Dale Quarry. It panicked and tried to escape up the steep face of the quarry, but almost at the top it slipped and fell, striking its head on a rock as it plummeted down, causing it instant death. Another time we were walking along Hall Dale road when we met a man running towards us carrying a boy aged about three. The boy's face and the man's chest were covered in blood. A few weeks later we saw the man at Hall Dale Cottage and he told us his boy had fallen and bit his tongue most seriously and he had run with him all the way to the Whitworth Hospital. Our wartime walks with the Broad Walk gang of lads often led us up the Hall Dale. We had the place to ourselves from 1939 to

1947. One of the boys found a dead man in the quarry. We also found a Derwent Valley Water Board building at the southern end of the one mile long tunnel that runs deep down under Darley Hillside from Northwood, carrying the water from the Derwent Dams to the large underground reservoir at Crich before it travels onwards towards Derby and Leicester. There used to be a badger set near the water house.

The Hall Dale quarry has been worked intermittently since the war. The railway line and the steam crane vanished just before the war, except for the rail crossing over Hall Moor road which was not removed until the 1950s. James Smith's Hall Dale nursery never recovered from the war when there were few men left to work it, finally being sold in the 1970s. It is now being re-established as a nursery but as yet is only a shadow of its former glory. My seventy years old love affair with the Hall Dale has now ended. I can no longer visit it because of ill health, but I have a lifetime of lovely memories to look back upon. They delight my inner self on the gloomiest winter's day. Alas, Geoff and Charlie have passed on. I sincerely hope that today's generation finds the joys that we did in the Hall Dale.

Fun and games

When I was around nine or ten years old I was invited to join Mrs. Eunice Muir's Concert Party called Rhyme and Rhythm. There was an accordion band section and my mother paid Marie White, who lived opposite Redlands, to teach me to play the accordion. I did not practice much so only became proficient in a few tunes which I learned by heart. I had an evening suit, complete with dickey and bow tie. I soon got over stage fright and enjoyed performing at local village halls. The Concert Party days, which lasted three years until 1939, ended any shyness I may have had and gave me confidence to perform in front of an audience.

Geoff Sellers and I had sixpence (two and a half p) a week to spend, doled out every Saturday. We also had other odd pennies in the week for running errands etc. When I was ten in 1937 Geoff and I used to go to the Old Pictures at Matlock on Saturday afternoons. Matlock had two picture houses, referred to as "Old" and "New". The Old picture house was down Dale Road, Matlock, near the railway bridge. Saturday afternoon was a time of agonising choices, since so much could be done with sixpence. The bus fare from the Grouse Inn to Matlock was threepence return or twopence one way. It cost twopence to go into the pictures and one penny would buy you either sweets or a large glass of pop. Sometimes we walked the three miles back from Matlock so that we could have both sweets and pop. We mostly walked back on the Oker side of the Derwent, exploring the south side of the valley.

As we got older and the war and the blackout came, we somehow acquired a bit more money and went to the pictures two or three times a week, at night. We had the choice of three picture houses, including Bakewell. If we went on our bikes to save money we could leave them quite safely behind the picture houses. The first time I ever rode in a car was from Darley to Matlock to see Snow White and the Seven Dwarfs, which was also the first film I ever saw in colour. I think this was early 1938. The late Mr Mick Morris had come and set up business in Darley Dale selling furniture, a business that was to keep him in work for almost sixty years. He had called at my mother's house about some furniture she was buying from him as Geoff and I were just about to go to the Saturday pictures. He was also going to Matlock and gave us a lift. Mick Morris and I were friends until he died in 1997.

Sledging was our great pastime in the winter. There were just enough cars to create flat tracks in the snow up Whitworth Road. With someone watching out for vehicles on the A6 we sledged down the hill from Stancliffe Hall drive, across the A6, down Green Lane to the Church Inn, about three quarters of a mile. Infrequent gas lamps lit the route, hissing and ticking, shedding pools of light on the snow. Nearly all the sledges were home-made and we compared all the different sorts of sledge runners, from fairly useless bed laths that slid about anywhere and were slow, to super ones about half an inch square. I remember

Charlie Thompson and I going down the allotments footpath where Crowstones Road is now. We came off the path near the bottom and ran straight down a row of Stan Willis's cabbages (Stan was a very keen gardener). The sledge's front bar knocked off all the cabbage heads, and when we stopped we were almost buried in cabbages. We were totally helpless with laughter. When I saw all the cabbage heads next morning on my way to school I was very worried in case we got found out.

On the LMS sports ground at Deeley Town, Dale Road North, Darley Dale, which became the site of the shadow steel factory evacuated from Sheffield in 1940/41, there were two old railway carriages, with all the insides stripped out, for use as changing rooms and other purposes. In the winter whist drives were held there and my mother took me with her. I would be about eleven years old. I soon learned to play whist and went off and on until the carriages were knocked down to make room for the new factory. I have since played cards all my life, playing almost every lunch time at work for the twelve years I worked for John Wm. Wildgoose & Sons. In 1956 I had a heart-stopping moment at the shadow factory, by then Firth Rixson's, whilst working on the roof.

Sometimes we used to cross the river Derwent over the old swing bridge (now demolished) which was a short cut to work for the Millclose lead miners from North Darley. This was a pedestrian suspension bridge really. We would then have a wander round the lead smelter and see the lead being run off the iron open hearth furnaces and watch the electric loco going down the drift mine under the Stanton Lees Road. We also went to the nearby old Mill Close mine, just over Cowley Knoll, and looked for minerals and explored the nearby Clough Wood where there were lots of hazel nut trees. We once found an old mine shaft with a series of ladders and landings in it. We only ventured a little way down. This was on the left hand side of the track which led to Winster. At the beginning of the war sacks and sacks of 303mm and 38mm bullets came to the smelter to be melted down. We used to take away as many as we could carry for catapult ammunition. I became reasonably proficient with a catapult and very good at making them.

Cupressus trees I found were best for the stride, the V portion. Stanley Fearn's shop at Matlock sold catapult elastic by the yard, and the missile holder was made from the tongue of a good stout boot. The string had to be first class. I took great pride in my catapults and still have one I made over sixty years ago.

Before the second war Darley Bridge became the focal point for every child in the valley in Wakes Week, mid-August. August 18th is St. Helen's Day (Darley Church is named after St. Helen). Timmy Wray came with the fair waggons and the showmens' caravans. The smaller waggons and carts were pulled by horses. All the big ones were towed by a mighty steam traction engine, showman's type, with a full length canopy over it supported by polished, twisted, brass columns. The engine was painted black and maroon, with all the copper and brass pipes and fittings polished. A large dynamo on the front supplied electricity to all the lights. This dynamo was driven by a huge belt from the flywheel of the engine. Subdued sounds came out of the traction engine as it rocked steadily; a hiss of steam, the slap of the belt joint as it hit the dynamo pulley, and a muted chuffing and clicking from the steam engine all brewed together with an unforgettable smell of hot oil, smoke, steam and grass. Timmy Wray parked the engine on the river bank, to be handy to the water. A row of electric light bulbs ran around the canopy. Looking from the south side of the river bridge at night you could see the lights shimmering in the reflections from the ripples in the Derwent.

Everyone was fascinated by the galloping-horse roundabout driven by its own small steam engine. It had a built-in fairground organ. To ride on the beautifully carved and decorated horses, which were fastened to twisted brass poles and went up and down as they went round and round, was a real thrill. A roll-a-penny stall, a darts stall, and a game of trying to make small wooden balls stay in white enamel buckets, along with a hoop-la stall, took care of your pennies. There was also a ·22 rifle range which had steel plates behind the targets. "Clang" went the bullets as they hit them. There were glitter balls on elastic, flying birds made from papier-mache with tails that spun round and made whistling sounds, plus toffee apples and some very very hard boiled sweets in fancy shapes. All the young men would try to ring a bell on top of a pole. To ring the bell one had to hit a lever with a large wooden mallet. We always called it the Wakes not the Fair. It provided an opportunity to meet all the young people who lived in the valley on neutral ground.

Before and during the second war, up to about the 1960s various circuses came to Matlock including Bertram Mills's, Sangster's and smaller, not very well-known ones. Geoff and I went to see them and look at the lions, tigers, elephants, horses and dogs. During and after the war we used to go to the Wakes/fair at Matlock, a big rumbustious effort with Noah's ark, dodgems, waltzers and lots of small amusements and game stalls. It was held on the market ground, where the Somerfield store is today. 1942 or 1943 was almost a disaster for me. I stood next to the speeding Noah's ark when someone going past pushed me. I over-balanced and fell on to the ride, hung on briefly then flew off over the guard rail and crash landed on a roll-a-penny stall. I still have a small dent near the crown of my head as a souvenir of the accident. In the 1950s a small circus came several times to Darley Dale. They erected their tent on the Tipping recreation ground. It was run by only three or four people who did everything. They had horses and dogs, and worked very hard, changing costumes and appearance like lightning. This was the last small travelling circus I ever saw. A traditional village entertainment gone for ever, killed by the advent of television. Bertram Mills's large circus came to Matlock every year, and set up on Causeway Lane football ground. I never missed a visit. It was magic, lions, tigers, elephants, trapeze artists and clowns. A visit to the circus was an exciting, thrilling time to be savoured for weeks.

School

When I first started school at Churchtown in 1932 my teacher was Mrs

Churchtown School, Old Darley

Ivy Geeson. Her husband Leonard had lived six houses away from us until he married. Leonard went to school with my brothers. Ivy and Leonard were to become my, and my wife's, friends for around fifty years. On my first day I sat with Charlie Hopkinson. I walked down Darley Hillside to school and back home again twice a day, across the A6 and the railway, around three miles a day. Charlie, Raymond Bradshaw (who lived nearby) and I used to stand on the pedestrian bridge at Church Road over the LMS main line as the trains roared underneath, wreathing us in noise, smoke and steam. I had only been at school for a few weeks when I was knocked down by a small Busy Bee biscuit van while crossing the A6. I was only bruised but it taught me a healthy respect for traffic. Nothing teaches like experiences, especially bad ones. When we moved to Redlands I missed the two daily walks home, up the hillside, across the main A6 road, in all weathers, with school friends Raymond and Charlie.

School began at 9am with assembly and prayers, and RI by the Rev Griffiths, Rector of Darley, until 9.30; 9.30 to 10.45 mental arithmetic and arithmetic; 10.45 to 11 playtime; 11 till 12 noon English; 12 to 1.30

dinner time. One or two brought sandwiches and stayed for dinner, and several who lived over a mile away left ten minutes early. Early schooldays seemed to be composed of counting shells into various heaps, copying out the alphabet, chanting tables, playtimes, dinner times and home times.

In the afternoon we studied various things, from English literature and poetry to botany. Boys also did gardening and joinery, girls learned needlework and cooking. Once a week we went swimming at the Whitworth Institute. I hardly ever went because I suffered from excema. Woodwork classes were held at the old National School in Two Dales. Charlie excelled at woodwork and I excelled at poetry and reading.

Every day at school one could have a small bottle of milk for a halfpenny or a penny, I cannot remember which. This could be either hot or cold in theory; in practice it was mostly cold. About eight or ten boys had to fetch the milk from Mr Goodwin's Abbey Farm, two hundred yards away, just before morning playtime. We ran there and hurried back so as not to miss playtime. Sport played a large part in school life. Sad to say I had very little interest in it. I played football and cricket a few times for the school, and saw other sports-mad boys get kicked, hit by cricket balls, or half drowned in the baths, which curbed my enthusiasm no end. I never learned to swim properly until I was about thirty-six years old.

Our headmaster, Mr Bartram, had been an officer in the First World War and was, I came to realise in later life, a first class man and teacher. Today I marvel at the pride he gave us both in ourselves and of being British. There was a large map of the world on the wall of the large classroom used for assembly with the British Empire and Commonwealth countries coloured red When we had geography lessons he would point out the various countries and islands in red. He sometimes asked us the name of the Jubilee class loco which pulled the Manchester to London express that we had seen that morning thundering over the level crossing. All Jubilee class locos were named after British possessions, such as Ascension Island, St. Helena, Sierra Leone, Nyasaland and Windward Islands. Mr Bartram would ask us where they were on the map. We were also taught British history over the last two thousand years.

Discipline was very strict. Strokes of the cane on the hand were an everyday happening. One of the teachers was Miss Ivy Lovell, as she was before her marriage to a Mr Bond. I well remember the day when I was about nine years old and misbehaving in class. Miss Lovell called me out to the front, suddenly pulled up my short trouser leg, and smacked my thigh hard several times. It did hurt! Ever after I held her in great respect. Much later in life, thirty or forty years after the event, Ivy and I used to joke about it. She threatened to do it again if she ever heard of me stepping out of line! Ivy taught at Churchtown and Greenaway Lane schools for many years and I remember her with great affection, as did many others. Another Churchtown teacher was Miss Slater. Fifty years later I was working in Calver, a village about eight miles north of Darley, when we met walking towards one another on the pavement. We recognised one another immediately and reminisced at length. At the age of twelve Charlie and I became probationers in the church choir and this meant turning up once a week for practice. Boys who had passed scholarships and gone on to grammar school were usually preferred as choir boys. Charlie and I also wound up the church clock every Friday after school. The slow tick of the clock in the quiet clock room high in the church tower gave an aura of peace that would be hard to match.

We had many varied and seasonal pastimes throughout the year. We played with whips and tops every spring; a stick with a leather bootlace fastened to it was used to propel the tops. There were two sorts of tops, a sedate one like a small turnip and one shaped like a mushroom which we called a window breaker. Both had a hob nail in the bottom to spin on. Marbles and yo-yos were another yearly happening and rounders, similar to baseball, was played by both boys and girls. Every winter we made slides in the school yards by carrying out cans of water and

St Helen's church clock

pouring it on the asphalt. We made some excellent slides which almost stretched the width of the playground. There was skipping, mostly for the girls, but we boys sometimes skipped with big ropes when about half a dozen boys skipped in the one rope. Boys and girls had separate playgrounds. Autumn was conker time. We tried all sorts of tricks to make them last longer; baking them in the oven was a favourite way.

There was very little bullying either in or out of school. Disputes were settled by ourselves on a piece of ground next to the railway at the bottom of Church Road, or it was settled for us. I had several fights there myself as there was never any fighting allowed at school. Four strokes of the cane was the punishment for fighting or aggressive behaviour, very painful. Practically all fights were arranged affairs conducted out of school, always viewed by a large audience of boys and girls accompanied by shouts and cheers.

The Vicar's son Eric Griffiths ran a Youth Club for young choir boys and also made films about life in Darley Dale, actual and acted. I still have copies of these films made in the 1930s. I appear twice, very briefly, on them, aged around six or seven. Some of the boys in the films served in the Forces and one or two died in the second war. My choir probation days did not last very long. One of the grammar school choir boy probationers, Ron, snatched my hat off and threw it in a puddle. A few days later he and I happened to meet near the church, and the meeting resulted in a hectic skirmish. I was promptly banned from the church choir! Before going to Church aged about eleven I had, from a small child, attended the Darley Hillside Methodist Chapel. After the choir episode I did not go to either church or chapel for years. At chapel I was a member of the Rechabites which I believe influenced my non-drinking habit.

Every Autumn Mr Walker, the Christmas pudding manufacturer who lived at Abbey House near Churchtown School used to invite the school to his orchard, and Mr Marsden his gardener shook the eating apple trees for us to pick up the apples to eat. I enjoyed my school days immensely, probably because the normal routine ended when I was twelve and war broke out. My education was then cut short.

The coming of war

In the days following the declaration of war, Darley Dale and our school were full of apprehension. It was only twenty-one years since the end of the First World War. Many children had fathers who had fought in that war and had told them about the dreadful conflict. The only thing I knew about war was what older men had told me. Bill Potter was blown up by a German mine and deafened. Mr Coe had been a machine gunner and had been gassed; he still had trouble with his lungs. Mr Holland had been an infantryman, and Mr Sellers lost a hand and an eye. All of them told me tales of the war. My mother, Mrs Pearson and Mrs Hallowes from Cherry Tree Farm and several other women worked in the Stancliffe Quarry in the First World War. They wore corduroy trouser suits to work. Armistice Days were very solemn occasions.

My pride and joy at that time was my bike which I had had for my birthday in June. I had more time to ride it at first as school had been temporarily suspended because of the war. At the end of September 1939 we returned to school, where it was bedlam, with the school also serving as a centre for distributing gas masks, ration books, and identity cards. I can still remember my identity number RBTD 185/4. RB I believe stood for Derbyshire as it was on vehicle number plates registered in Derbyshire. Babies' gas masks were huge things. The baby went in up to its waist and you had to pump air into the mask with a concertina-like contraption on the side of the mask. Every gas mask was kept in a stout cardboard box with a cord attached to hang it round your neck and shoulder. We all had to put our name and address on them and carry them at all times. Blackouts over all the windows were compulsory. My mother soon bought some that worked like ordinary blinds, and my father fitted wood down the sides of the windows for them to run in. Many bikes at that time had the lights powered by a dynamo which ran off the bicycle tyre. We made blackout shades for the bike lamps out of tin cans.

Rumours circulated of air raids with gas bombs, cities about to be evacuated, all men to be called up to serve in the Forces. Gas masks were given out, and Civil Defence volunteers marshalled. Blackouts were put in place to all windows, air raid sirens were tested. A Special Police force came into being and our headmaster, J.C. Bartram, became one of them. One of our teachers, Richard Wragg, was called up for war service. Everyone listened to the wireless all the time for news. The country was in a state of chaos.

We now shared our school with lots of girl evacuees from Lady Barnes Girls' School, Withington, Manchester. I remember the arrival of the evacuees. Each girl clutched a small suitcase with a large label attached to it and they also had another label fastened to their coats. They stood in subdued, bewildered, labelled groups under the watchful eyes of their teachers. I cannot remember seeing any parents with them. Many local children came to look, some with their parents who were to provide homes for the girls. To me it was a bit like going to the zoo. Even as a lad of twelve I could sense the apprehension and bewilderment that hung over the gathering. It was a time of great anxiety and tears were shed.

Two sisters could not find anyone to take them both in so one sister aged about twelve was taken in by the West family, who lived at Deeley Town, opposite to where Firth Rixson's steel factory is today, and her younger sister, aged about ten, went to live down Green Lane in central Darley with the Walters family. The sisters' names were Eileen and Beryl Maydon. That is perhaps not the correct spelling of their surname as I only knew it phonetically. I became friendly with them and sometimes we played together after school, either around Green Lane or three-quarters of a mile away at Deeley Town exploring the Stancliffe quarry area and Whitworth's North Park. They told me they had no mother and their father was a policeman.

Because we had to share our school with the girls from Manchester who, as far as I can remember, probably numbered fifty or sixty, making over two hundred and twenty children in a one hundred place school, education became very awkward, and it was virtually the end of mine. The evacuees were taught by their own teachers, separately from us. The school would not hold us all so we had our own lessons outdoors. Ernest Paulson, who lived in Broad Walk and had gone to Churchtown School and Ernest Bailey Grammar School, Matlock, then on to University, had now come back to Churchtown School as a student teacher. He took the top two classes on many so-called Nature Walks to keep us occupied. Ernest had a degree in history and continually told us local history as we went out, on sometimes very long walks, while the Lady Barnes girls had our classrooms. We used to walk as far as Birchover, Winster and Matlock and Darley Dale moors. I loved it. Ernest kindled a love of local history in me that has never died, and also became my friend. (He and I, and another friend John Billingham who also attended Churchtown School, formed the Darley Dale Society in the early 1970s. Ernest and I were also founder members of Darley Dale Town Council in 1980. I arranged Ernest's funeral in 1997). The winter months passed peacefully. By spring most of the girls returned home to Manchester where the air raids never materialised. The two sisters also went home in the spring of 1940.

Still grieving the loss of one son, mother and father became even more distressed when my brother Jim was called up into the Army in May 1940. I can still remember his number, 1564408, and where he went – Oswestry. The next two months were very gloomy times, the fall of France, the Dunkirk evacuation, and threats of invasion looming. My brother Clifford, who lived at Matlock, joined the LDV (Local Defence Volunteers), which was soon renamed the Home Guard. He was told to report to the rifle range on Cavendish Road, Matlock on Sunday morning. I arranged to meet him there to see if there was anything I could do.

I was thirteen years and two months old and was found a job target marking in the butts. This was pretty hair-raising to start with. The targets were fixed to a steel frame which alternated the targets in the up and down positions, from a deep trench in the ground. Bullets whistled over your head. When the target was up you had to show where the bullets had hit, by placing a disc attached to a long lath over the bullet hole. Meanwhile your partner stuck paper over the bullet holes in the target, which was in the down position. They said I was too young to join the Home Guard but in return for marking at the butts I was taught how to fire a .303 Lee Enfield rifle. The man who was with me in the butts told me LDV stood for Look, Duck and Vanish. The memory of that year, the sudden change from a child's carefree life to wondering what is going to happen next, made me truly aware of life and the sudden surprises, some good, some bad, which happen on one's journey through life. Incidentally Jim, despite fighting in many battles including Caen and the Rhine crossing, survived the war.

All street lamps were turned off, not a glimmer of light to be seen in the valley except for the railway sidings. In the midst of all this black-out Rowsley Sidings stayed lit. It was far too dangerous and time consuming to try and assemble goods trains in the dark. They only put the lights out when the siren went and an air raid was imminent. We had many air-raid warnings and for years after the war the sound of an air-raid siren made you feel apprehensive and gave you a sinking sensation in your stomach. The wireless, which most people had only acquired in the previous eight or nine years, became very, very important. We had our first wireless just after we moved to Redlands, about 1934, a Mac Michael, which ran from an accumulator in the cabinet underneath. There was also a dry battery. To me it was a miracle. The wet battery, the accumulator, was charged up at the Stancliffe Works every now and then. Our second wireless, purchased in 1937, was a Pye seven-valve, electrically operated, very powerful, with a long aerial from the chimney to a scaffold pole in the garden. Mother bought it from a man called Harry Brooks. I still have it over sixty years later and it still works.

In late July 1940 our headmaster, Mr Bartram, the ex-First World War officer, called everyone in the school together and told us that an invasion and severe bombing raids were expected. Always carry your gas mask, he said, and wear it if an air-raid siren sounds. If the church bells ring it is the signal that the invasion has commenced. Go home immediately and stay there, and listen to the radio for instructions on what to do. Everyone was most apprehensive.

In June 1940 some tired bedraggled soldiers arrived at the Whitworth Institute following the evacuation from Dunkirk. I lent my precious bicycle to one so that he could visit someone he knew who lived in a nearby village. At the beginning of the war Mrs Muir's Rhyme and Rhythm Concert Party used to provide entertainment in blacked-out village halls. We gave a concert for the soldiers who had come to the Whitworth Institute. The soldiers soon organised their own concerts and the dozen or so young lads who went about together in Darley were always invited.

The 1940s Battle of Britain, in which I was most interested, gave way to the bombing raids of 1940/41 on surrounding cities. I well remember going up the Hillside on my bike to watch the flashes and gunfire from the air-raids on Derby and Sheffield. 1940 saw us settled into an unreal existence, with the blackout strictly enforced. National Service was made compulsory and boys a few years older than me started to be called up. Railway workers were mostly exempt from call-up. In early 1940 nothing had happened regarding the war, and some evacuees drifted back to Manchester. Special Police and Air Raid Wardens were appointed. Dozens of stirrup pumps were handed out (ours is still in existence). Buckets of sand were provided ready to put on incendiary bombs, and a few air-raid shelters were built. Everyone was lulled into a state of false security. All basic foods and sweets were rationed. Father built a small air-raid shelter at Redlands out of concrete blocks and I demolished it in 2000. It would have had a job to protect us from a strong wind!

With the Whitworth Institute now an RASC Driver Training School life became hectic in Darley, the village of the quick and the dead. You had to be quick because of all the learner drivers, and lorries in convoys with practically no lights. The back axle centre was painted white and a light shone on it from underneath so that the vehicle behind could follow it. They were always knocking down walls and practising three point turns. Soldiers were becoming plentiful everywhere. Then a bitter blow fell. Public transport was restricted. The last bus left Matlock for Darley at 9pm but fortunately a passenger train to Darley left at about 10.10. Women appeared on the stations, the railways and the buses, in the factories, and in all manner of jobs which had previously been the domain of men. Many wore overalls and boiler suits. Clothes were rationed. Bananas, oranges and grapes became non-existent. The wireless held the country together, providing information on the various battles in the air and on the sea. Britain and the Commonwealth standing alone against what seemed an unstoppable Germany.

To my delight our valley was selected as a low flying area in 1940 and is still one today. I have seen almost every type of plane you could mention. I collected aircraft spotters' manuals and studied them. Our

Pye radio was great and we could listen to programmes from Germany with Lord Haw-Haw. I think his proper name was William Joyce. Near to and at the end of the war in Europe I used to listen to the AFN. The announcer used to say "This is American Forces Network, a branch of the Troop Information Education Bureau of the United States in Europe." This was usually followed by the name of the city they were broadcasting from. I fell in love with the Americans, their Army vehicles, and everything to do with them – music, flamboyance and weapons. I admire them even more today, their high standard of living is no accident. I believe it stems from being a country full of get-up-and-go people, who did just that to get there, so forming the national character.

In 1940 neither I nor any of the other lads in the gang could actually join the Home Guard – we were just that bit too young. 1943/4 saw a few of the older boys called up to the Forces, and the deaths of some who were older still but whom I knew from school. Mr Donelan had an allotment behind Redlands and helped me to keep my bike in tip-top order. One day he called to me and told me that his son Peter, an air-crew member, was missing. It was confirmed later that he had been killed.

Chapter 4: Work, bikes and romance

Paton's and Baldwin's

My brother Clifford, who had been working at Smedley's Hydro, was drafted to Paton's and Baldwin's wool factory on Smedley Street, Matlock when the Hydro was requisitioned by the army. He told me that there was a job for me there too if I wanted it. This led to me leaving school at thirteen years of age on 31st May 1941 and starting work.

The factory was about to be taken over by a tap and die company called Lehman, Archer and Lane from London. They were evacuated to Matlock because of the heavy air raids that London was enduring. Taps and dies are used for manufacturing nuts and bolts respectively, and were essential to the war effort. I worked from 7.45am to 5.45pm and finished work on Saturdays at 12 noon. Many of the other workers worked Saturday afternoon and Sunday. I spent a year at Patons and Baldwins, a year which convinced me that factory life was not for me,

Paton and Baldwin 1959.
Andrew 3, Beryl 7 and Lesley 5

and left after a spell in hospital having my appendix removed.

THE CO-OP

At that time I lived at Redlands opposite Darley Dale's Co-op. Mr A. Shimwell from Youlgrave was the manager, and Miss M. Wall managed the Ladies' department. In August 1942, after my convalescence from the appendix operation I drifted into employment there as errand boy, sweeper up, cleaner, packager of various goods, and boiler stoker and apprentice counter hand. In the first year I discovered the miracles of how to bone a side of bacon and name all the different parts, break open the barrels containing two half-hundredweight cheeses made in various Commonwealth countries, and cut it up with cheese wire, and weigh rice, sugar and flour in bags of various weights for stock, all on brass balance scales which had to be cleaned and polished daily.

Most goods came loose, from yeast in seven pound bags to sugar in two-hundredweight sacks, all types of dried fruit in boxes and sacks, flour in ten-stone sacks, animal and poultry feed in one-hundredweight sacks. Coffee beans came in fifty-six pound sacks to be ground by hand and packed in quarter pounds. Sacks of soap flakes were a nightmare. If we were short of bags it was a work of art to parcel them up in a sheet of wrapping paper. The packing had to be perfect, so that the soap flakes did not contaminate the rest of the groceries. It still only takes me a moment to make a bag out of a plain sheet of A4 paper which will hold water. Twist tobacco came in a roll, shag tobacco in tins, all to be weighed out in ounces.

When you had learned to pack all grocery items you were turned loose on the provisions counter. Butter, lard and margarine mostly came in half-hundredweight boxes, usually made of wood lined with grease-proof paper. We had wooden butter pats which were kept in a clean jar of water. The fats were cut and shaped into half and quarter pounds. If I remember correctly the weekly food ration of 1942/43 was eight ounces of sugar, two ounces of butter, two ounces of lard, four ounces

The bakehouse Smedley Street, now being converted to apartments 2006

of margarine, four ounces of bacon and two ounces of tea. Tea mostly came in quarter pound packets, occasionally in twenty-eight pound foil lined plywood boxes, to be weighed into whatever quantity was required. Dried eggs, dried milk and IXL jams from overseas all came in tins. Cheese was also rationed with heavy manual workers allowed an extra amount. For old age pensioners the ration for one was barely enough to keep them alive, but green grocery was never in short supply in the country districts. In those days Co-op shops had no refrigerators, and all fresh meat and bacon etc had to be kept covered with muslin, sprinkled with pepper to keep the flies away.

After a year's apprenticeship Mr Owen, the chief executive of the Derwent Valley Co-operative Society, asked me if I would be a relief worker at other Co-ops when people were off. Out came my trusty bike and away I went on a voyage of discovery around various village Co-op shops from Bonsall to Youlgrave and also in the warehouse under Tom Cassells, as well as in the bakehouse. Smedley Street Co-op, Matlock, was a very hard working assignment – we put up and delivered orders to a large area every day.

I sometimes worked with Mr Ottewell who was the baker at Wellington Street, Matlock. We used to put clean yeast bags on our hands and knock the hot freshly baked loaves out of the tins and put them on trays. A large hot plate was used for baking oatcakes. Armed with a large cup and a bucket of oatmeal gruel, at just the right consistency, you lightly oiled the large hot plate and poured the gruel on, a cup at a time. By the time you had poured out about twenty the first to be poured were ready to be taken up and put in a basket and the cycle was repeated. Except for the washing-up and continuous cleaning I loved working in the bakehouse with the chirruping crickets. Everyone at the Co-op wore a white coat and a white apron, except the van drivers who wore a long buff coat, all of which had to be self-provided. Occasionally I went out on the bread van as a runner. We delivered from Tansley to Bonsall, Ible, Middleton by Youlgrave, Elton, Winster and Via Gellia. The van drivers were Fred Hawley, Vic Toft and Ted Dakin. Johnny Mellor from Hartington, Jim Barnes from Matlock and Charles Hollis from Youlgreave drove the coal delivery lorries which, after a wash, became the grocery order lorries.

My cousin Betty and I worked together at Birchover Co-op. Fred Haslam from Tansley managed Bonsall Co-op and incidentally it was at Bonsall Co-op that I first met a coloured person, a Mrs Koffe Nelson. Ernest Belfield was the manager of Winster Co-op, Mr Hardaker at Matlock, and Norman Walker managed the Two Dales shop. Rowsley and Birchover had various managers as staff kept getting called up into the Services. Albert Shimwell from Youlgrave who managed Darley Dale Co-op was a distant relative of mine.

My favourite Co-op to work in was Youlgrave, partly because my grandfather George Toft helped to found it, built it and lived next door to it at Fountain Cottage where my mother was born in 1887. Youlgrave Co-op commenced trading in grandfather George Toft's Fountain Cottage joiner's shop, evenings only, in 1870. Mr Joseph Shimwell from Old Hall Farm, Tom Birds of Hall Farm, and a Joseph Smith were the founders. In 1874 Eli Toft was Secretary and my grandfather was Treasurer. Youlgrave Co-op closed, as did all the other local Co-ops, in 1968 when the Derwent Valley Co-operative Society ceased trading.

Youlgrave Co-op was an old fashioned shop in the early 1940s. Just to arrive there was a momentous occasion. It was such an imposing building. We entered by the rear basement door into a large storeroom full of everything, a complete all-round rural store needed to sustain village life. Lit by several naked electric light bulbs, and a few north-west facing high windows, it was a dingy area. Three parts of the length of the basement away was a broad set of wooden stairs leading up to the shop. The shop area before the window blinds were rolled up was a scene to behold, polished brass scales and weights glinting gold, mahogany counters burnished to a rich brown, the glass-topped biscuit tins and the chrome fittings of the provisions counter all reflecting the glow of the bare light bulbs hanging from the ceiling.

Best of all was the wonderful exquisite aroma (to call it a smell would be an injustice) of fresh ground coffee, dried fruits, newly cut cheeses, bacon and ham, and a myriad other items all blending together to permeate the shop area with a richness rarely found today. In the early 1940s people still purchased paraffin lamp glasses, soft soap, mouse traps, washing lines and brushes alongside their rations, and flour and yeast. Biscuits always came in tin boxes, vinegar in a barrel, and rough salt in very large blocks for salting down beans. It was an Aladdin's cave. Everything was stocked from babies' feeding bottles to paraffin, Bile Beans, Carter's Little Liver Pills, Castor Oil, Syrup of Figs, Andrews' Liver Salts, brands of cigarettes unheard of today, Pelaw shoe polishes, Brasso, Zebo Black Lead, and washing blues. A ladies' shop upstairs also sold a very wide range of goods, from reels of cotton to lingerie and hats.

Just to work there was an education. Some of my workmates included Doug Doxey, Edith Rose, David Wragg, and Eunice Birds who worked upstairs in the Ladies' Department. It is lovely to close my eyes to think and visualise in my mind that familiar scene from long ago. I also remember the comforting all-embracing feel of well-being and belonging that went with Youlgrave and the other Co-ops. To compare it with modern, soulless regimented superstore is like comparing a spring walk through Lathkill Dale with a journey on a London underground train. 8.30am pull up the blinds, unlock the door and greet the first customer by name. Come 6 o'clock in the evening you had acquired knowledge of everything that was happening around the village, and passed on useful information as part of village life. Pull down the blinds, lock the door, clear and tidy up while the person in charge endeavours to balance the ledgers. Tom Cassells, who was in charge of the Co-op warehouse at Matlock lived behind the Youlgrave Co-op. All branches opened at 8.30am and shut at 6 except for Friday which was 7 or 7.30pm with Thursday half day closing at 12.30.

The wartime government of the 1940s introduced double summer time so that it remained light longer in the evening. This of course ensured that it took one hour longer to come light in the morning. To get to work at Youlgrave Co-op in 1943/4 I cycled there, as I did to all the other Co-ops. One truly dark winter's morning cycling along the A6 about 150 yards south of Rowsley railway station, I heard the Manchester to London express belting its way down the gradient towards Rowsley station making a sound like rolling thunder. In a split second the sound altered as it came out of Rowsley station. The throttle closed and steam stopped spurting out of the loco chimney. A shrill metallic screeching split the air. The loco and carriage wheels became gleaming circles of fire as a ring of sparks outlined each wheel. The train slid down the rails as it hurtled towards the branch line that led into the sidings area. I gazed at the scene with awe and apprehension. It was a long train with many carriages, all their wheels throwing off circles of sparks. Just when I thought a catastrophe was about to occur the circles of sparks vanished along with the metallic screech. Steam spurted out of the chimney as the driver opened the throttle again. A rapid rythmic chuffing with a background of muted thunder died away. as the train sped off alongside the A6 road towards Darley Dale. The whole episode only took a few seconds from first hearing the train crossing the railway bridge over the A6, just before Rowsley station, to its disappearing out of sight. I can only think the express must have been slightly late that morning and the engine driver, in trying to gain a few seconds, had had

Rail track to and from old railway yard to Rowsley siding. Express Dairy water cooler on left

Express Dairy lorries – the site of today's Peak Village at Rowsley

Jubilee loco

Darley Station

to reduce speed sharply. As I rode along the A6 in the quiet dark, peaceful morning, the sudden shattering of the peace by the sight and sound of that express train stayed in my inner vision for years. I saw the express going down the track many more times but never like that morning. It is a sight and sound that has long vanished from our valley, together with the craftsmen of steam who drove and maintained those almost living monsters of yesteryear that dominated our valley for one hundred and twenty years.

I graduated to travelling for orders to outlying farms and houses, and when I was seventeen acquired a 1927 Ariel 500 motor bike and a petrol ration. This made travelling a great joy. Driving tests were suspended during the war so I sometimes drove the bread van, as did seventeen years old Margaret Seymour, also from Darley. All Co-op members had a number; my mother's was 925. I think they reached around five thousand. Purchases were put down in your Co-op book in indelible pencil and paid for on pay day. Tills and ledgers had to be balanced every night (no adding machines or computers then). We also carried out Co-operative Society Bank transactions for the members. At one house I visited for orders were a retired couple who always had the table laid and a pot of tea on the go, kept warm with a tea cosy supplemented by a large black cat who was always wrapped around the teapot fast asleep in the middle of the table. Another dear old lady, poorly sighted, used to ask us to do bits of jobs around her house. We also delivered messages. The butcher, the baker, the milk and paper men, the postmen and the Co-op men who came for orders and delivered them, formed an invaluable contact in the wartime for isolated lonely elderly people. I felt so sorry for elderly people who lived alone in the wartime. The rations were so small and if they lived any distance from the shops it was difficult for them to get there. I do not know how the elderly and infirm survived these hard times, especially the hard winters as coal was in short supply.

Lots of girls and women took over as the men were called up into the forces. Joan Woolley managed Darley Co-op for a time after her husband Horace was called up, and Elsie Parks took her brother Reg's place at Darley when he too was called up. One problem family in an outlying village, who lived very near to a Co-op, were in and out every hour for something or other. One day the mother asked the manager if he had anything for her daughter's spots. Quick as a flash he produced a scrubbing brush, a bar of carbolic soap and a bucket to put hot water in, after which her husband came round to interview the manager. He was only placated by a visit to the public house across the road, where they reached an amicable settlement over a few pints while I held the fort!

I eventually left the Co-op because I refused to work any more unpaid overtime. We were always short-handed and after the shop was shut you were expected to mop the floor and clean up, restock the shelves, make sure that orders to be delivered the next day were put up, and the till balanced. My Co-op days came to an end one Friday night at Two Dales Co-op early in 1946. I had been sent there in my job as relief worker. Norman Walker was the manager and at 7.30pm, after a hectic Friday, he said we would have to put up the grocery orders which were to be delivered in the morning. We would still have had to clean and re-stock the shop after we had finished the orders. I told him that I had had enough unpaid overtime to last a lifetime, and that I was going home. Next morning the chief executive of the Derwent Valley Co-operative Society, Mr. Owen, appeared and after a less than amiable discussion about loyalty, overtime and commitment it was decided that I would finish the following Saturday. I knew that the men who had worked at the Co-op before being called up for war service were being demobbed, and were entitled to have their jobs back. So ended another term in the University of Life. I had learned to do accounts, meet people, accept responsibility and also learned to love a wandering, diverse life, albeit fairly local.

My first year at Paton's and Baldwin's, followed by working at the Co-op for about three years, where again everyone was part of a large happy family, was marvellous. Everyone pulled together in those difficult times of war. Dealing with innumerable different types of customers gave me a good insight into people's attitudes to others. Looking back, I think, in fact, that I had acquired my first degree in the University of Life from the Co-op.

THE LADS

Reg Parks was one of the dozen or so boys who made up our gang, and Reg and I are still friends and went out together exploring villages in the summers of 1986 to 2002. Two years older than me he was called up, along with Tom Helliwell, in 1943. Both were in the RAF and survived the war. Some of my friends in the gang, Geoff Sellers, David Holmes, Billy Goodwin, Brian Allwood and David Brown all went to work for Lehane, Mackenzie & Shand, civil engineers, repairing huge excavators and bulldozers.

The blackout came to be taken for granted, as did food on ration, no sweets, oranges or bananas, and only limited transport. Sunday was the gang's big day in the 1941/45 time. Every Sunday afternoon we all met around 2pm and went for a walk exploring for miles around. We had fairly organised battles with one another at night, including the use of airguns, catapults etc. Our most mischievous happenings were to do with home-made bombs and guns. Remember this was wartime and people were nervous. We used to go into someone's shed and make gun-

Tom Helliwell

powder. Fuse was readily available from the surrounding quarries. Bomb making started around 1942. Charcoal we made ourselves. Saltpetre and sulphur were obtainable from the chemist at Broad Walk by the pound. In the experimental stage we had some remarkable episodes trying to perfect the mix. Cigarettes were used to ignite the mixture. I once remember foolishly trying a sample on the corner of the mixing board. A spark leapt from it and set off the rest. Luckily it wasn't too good a mix. Balls of red-hot gunpowder ran madly all over the place. Enormous quantities of smoke were generated, then the shed floor caught fire. We managed to put it out using our own natural material!

Tommy Helliwell and I became dab hands at making gunpowder and bombs. Because of the blackout you could only test indoors at night. One night Tom went into their outdoor wc where he lived on Broad Walk with a jam jar full of gunpowder. The idea was, you took a pinch of gunpowder, applied the cigarette and could tell by the size of the flare-up and the composition of the residue if the mix was any good. Tom disappeared into the outside wc to test it. The next minute an enormous blaze of light came from under the door, followed by billowing smoke and shouts for help. The door opened inwards. I pushed it open. Tom was standing on the lavatory seat, his overcoat over his head, gasping and choking. All the wall was black and the jam jar had melted. We never seemed to learn that sparks sometimes flew quite a distance from our trial samples. To make bombs that made a loud bang we used short lengths of steel pipe with one end bent over, a hand full of gunpowder, well rammed with paper then clay and the end bent over again, being careful not to damage the fuse. At first we used to light the fuse, which was quite short, and throw the pipe. This turned out to be very dangerous because when the remains of the pipe flew off it was a matter of luck where it went. We soon learned to be careful and either have a tree or a wall between the bomb and us. The effect on the surrounding population was amazing, especially at night. When we exploded some really good sized ones people used to think an air raid was occurring, and the next day they would be looking for craters and damage. I am ashamed now of how thoughtless we were and the anxiety we must have caused.

Tom was called up in 1943 and went into the RAF, and of all things became an armourer. He came on leave with some aircraft cannon ammunition. We took the powder out of the cartridges, mixed it with gunpowder and decided to make a small gun out of strong two-inch seamless pipe. A friend who worked at the new steel shadow factory in Darley heated the pipe and stamped one end up, then drilled a hole to take the fuse a couple of inches up from the closed end. After much deliberation we decided to fire a small shell from the gun. This was made out of a cannon shell cartridge with a fuse about four inches long. The gun fuse was about three inches long. Several boys set off up Darley Hillside in order to spot where the shell landed. The gun was firmly wedged in some big rocks, where Darley Council's recreation area is today alongside the Broad Walk estate. When the other lads, who were to do the spotting, were halfway up the Hillside we decided to fire the gun to give them a thrill. Tom and I lit both fuses together. I dropped the shell down the barrel and we took cover with the other lads who had stayed at our end behind some nearby rocks. The bang was beyond our wildest dreams. Retrieving the gun we saw the end of the barrel was flared out, resembling a dying wind-blown tulip. We never knew where the shell landed or if it exploded. The noise of the explosion reverberated around the valley, so we all cleared off at top speed. People reported the explosion to the authorities who investigated, and our friendly policeman told us we had got to stop. That was almost the end of the bomb making, except for a few home-made hand grenades which we used to try to kill or stun fish to help boost the food rations. Fishing with bombs is not to be recommended. We were astonished to see a huge ball of fire under the water followed by the remains of the bomb case hurtling out of the river, somehow nearly always in our direction. Bomb making passed into oblivion. It was far too dangerous a pastime and is not to be recommended.

Geoff and I, and sometimes Charlie, used to go exploring on our bikes at night, often in the dark. I really mean dark, since there was not a light to be seen anywhere in the wartime blackout. One night in 1944 when I was working at the Bonsall Co-op Geoff and I had gone to Bonsall, about six miles away, on our bikes for a mooch round. On the way home when we stopped at the bottom of the hill opposite the Viyella Rag Mill on the Via Gellia road we heard the sound of glass cracking. As was normal in wartime all the windows in the mill had been painted black because of the blackout. Parking our bikes we went round the back of this three or four storey substantially sized mill, tried a few doors and found one open. The place was on fire. Geoff ran to the Pig of Lead pub to tell them and I stopped a passing army dispatch rider who went off to Cromford to phone for help. Geoff and I went into the blazing mill, picking up fire extinguishers and squirting them on the burning textiles to stop the fire spreading. The men from the pub came, including the night watchman who was having his supper there. With the bell ringing the fire engine tore up the drive and soon put out the fire. Geoff and I were absolutely covered in fluff – we looked like two large mad chickens. The mill owners sent us a letter of thanks and a postal order for one pound five shillings (£1.25p) each, a substantial amount in those days.

In 1944 I was roaming about Derbyshire on Sunday mornings on milk lorries, perhaps once a fortnight, collecting milk in ten gallon churns. Some nights we went to Ashbourne or Sheffield. Ashbourne was home to Nestle's Dairy and they had their own small churns. Sheffield was the exciting night run, all blacked out, no lights anywhere, people milling about. The streets seemed to be thronged. Trams in the middle of the road, bomb sites everywhere, no road signs to anywhere. I also went to Nottingham which was very similar. Reg Parks's brother Ron, who was a bit older than me, learned to drive and got a job with the Express Dairy Company based at Rowsley collecting milk from farms in the Peak District. He let me drive the three ton Bedford petrol-engined lorry sometimes. Ron's first shift was early in the morning when he collected around seven hundred gallons of milk from Peakland farms, all in churns. Each churn weighed about one hundredweight (approximately 50 kilos). After processing the milk had to be delivered, after tea, to Sheffield, Ashbourne or Nottingham for bottling, for next morning's milk delivery. I went many times to Sheffield with Ron after tea to the Wharf Dairies.

In the autumn and winter of 1944 the Germans sent occasional bombers over on nuisance raids, dropping bombs and machine gunning places. Matlock and Darley suffered one such raid. After the major blitzes of 1941 and 1942 Sheffield people were understandably very nervous. I am again ashamed to say that sometimes when Ron and I were driving our way across Sheffield through the blacked out streets we would turn off the ignition switch then when the unburnt petrol had filled the exhaust system turn the switch back on. This would result in a loud explosion followed by panic, with people looking to the sky and scurrying frantically about under the illusion that an air raid was taking place. It was very difficult and downright dangerous driving a lorry through the city then over the high moors on wet or foggy nights with practically no light because of the headlight visors which only had a few shielded slots in them. To me, a country boy, Sheffield in wartime was a place of excitement and mystery, traffic and people. The excitement came from driving through the blacked-out city centre, passing bomb sites, dodging in and out of trams and buses, army lorries and people on bikes, all this to me very heavy traffic, which had practically no lights. When it was moonless foggy or overcast night driving became very difficult. Sheffield in wartime, as everywhere else in Britain, was devoid of signposts and directional signs. One wrong turn took you into a mysterious maze of dark back streets. The only good thing was that there was hardly any traffic in the back streets.

There were Air Raid Wardens, dressed in dark blue uniforms and steel helmets, with white armbands, and ARP posts on almost every street were manned by men and women who had probably worked a long hard day already. Moonlight nights were a blessing while crossing the bleak lonely heather and bracken-clad moors. It was hard to believe that not long ago bombs had rained down on and around Sheffield, killing people at random. Scars of the blitz were everywhere in the Sheffield area. We were so lucky to live in tranquil Darley Dale.

Before I went on the milk lorries on Sundays I used to help Jack and Charlie Hallowes from Cherry Tree Farm on Hall Moor Road, Darley Dale, with their milk round. Seven-thirty a.m. at Stancliffe was the start. Most people left their milk jug out, covered with a cloth or saucer. We carried the milk in a pail which held about two gallons and had two measures inside, a pint and a half pint. I became so proficient that I could pour milk from the measure into a pop bottle without spilling any. Around 9.30am we went to the farm on Hallmoor Road for breakfast, and to record in the book the amounts of milk we had delivered. Wartime breakfasts at Cherry Tree Farm, built in the 1600s and now demolished, were an experience to wonder at. Before Jack and Charlie left home to milk the cows and get ready for the milk round, breakfast was prepared. A large, and I mean LARGE, cast iron pan had a knob of home-made pork dripping placed in the bottom, a couple of slices of bread then several slices of home cured ham about half an inch thick lined the base. Six eggs were broken on top of the ham, then several more slices of home baked bread, about half an inch thick, were carefully cut and placed to seal the contents. More dripping went on top. The old black range was lit, the fire banked up and the flue to the oven opened a little. The pan was placed in the oven and the door shut.

Three hours later when we came back to the farm the wonderful smell that greeted us as we entered made all thoughts of food rationing and hard times vanish. We all sat round the table and had a wedge each. The bread on top was really crisp, the underneath bread was suffused with cooked egg yolk and the eggs and ham were so delicious that the fat round the ham slices melted in the mouth. A pint mug of tea, with two depth charges (saccharins) completed the meal. I can close my eyes and see and savour those breakfasts now over sixty years later. I only went round with the milk for Hallows on two Christmas Days. Every customer offered you an alcoholic drink. I didn't drink, and never have, but Jack and Charlie more than made up for me. One of the brothers had to be taken home incapable of carrying on, the other just sat in a daze in the passenger seat while I finished the milk round then drove him and the van to the farm. I was still under driving age the first Christmas.

The war became extremely interesting to me and I followed its progress, increasing by leaps and bounds my knowledge of the world, already quite good because of our headmaster Mr Bartram and the Jubilee class locos. A lad who lived across the road from me and who I worked with at Paton's and Baldwin's was killed in action, along with several other men and boys I knew. Food was getting scarce. My father, a born poacher, kept us well supplied with rabbits and pheasants, mostly from the Duke of Rutland's Haddon Estate. Father occasionally borrowed a ferret and some nets, and these were red letter days. We netted all the holes leading to the burrows. Father then put the ferret down a hole into the burrow and a few moments later the poor rabbits would come rocketing out of the hole into the nets. Father, who had very strong hands, would grasp a rabbit by its neck which he then broke. The rabbit died instantly. We carried the rabbits home in a sack, the ferret travelling in father's pocket.

Thursday was half day closing at the Derwent Valley Co-ops. My friend, Bill Allison, one of the gang, also worked at the Co-op. He lived, and still lives, nearby, and we sometimes spent Thursday afternoon poaching fish. The Hall Dale and Ladygrove brooks joined together in Two Dales behind the Blacksmiths Arms, then continued on their journey to the river Derwent, passing underneath the railway and the Old Road bridges near where the DFS now stands. This is where the trout used to congregate. The area between the two bridges was fairly sheltered. Bill used to strip off then holding a stout carrier bag with his teeth gently lowered himself into the usually icy cold water and disappear under the bridges while I kept watch. A few moments later a very wet, shivering Bill would emerge with a bag full of fish.

Tom Helliwell, then in the RAF, had acquired a Canadian Ross ·300 calibre rifle and sometimes when he came on leave he brought it with him. We used to shoot a few pheasants on the moors over towards Chatsworth and I remember them as very messy and bloody occasions. The rifle was equipped with a device called a Morris tube which effectively converted it to a ·22 calibre and made much less noise. I don't think I have ever known anything more stupid than pheasants. They would sit on the wall while the bullets flew past them, bobbing their heads, wondering what sort of insects were flying by. Fish, pheasants and rabbits made a welcome addition to the meagre rations of wartime. We never got caught because there was no one left to catch us – everyone was very busy working or in the Forces.

I always took my catapult along, having become very proficient with it. Steel three-eighths Whitworth nuts proved to be excellent for rabbit hunting. Silent and deadly one could almost feel sorry for the rabbit, busy nibbling grass near the mouth of its burrow, as it was struck down. After the rabbit was retrieved you cut its belly open from stem to stern and dropped out its insides. On arriving home I would cut off its head, tail and paws with a hatchet, insert my hands between the skin and the rabbit's back then pull them sharply apart. This left you with the complete rabbit fur in one hand and the skinned rabbit in the other. This operation took only a few seconds. Plucking pheasants took ages. I found the best way was to tie the birds legs together then hang the pheasant upside down at a convenient height from a tree branch. One could use both hands to pluck it and there were no feathers to clear up and dispose of.

As the war carried on the low flying in our valley increased and early 1944 saw a steady stream of all types of aircraft whizzing up and down. One day fifty B17 Flying Fortresses flew over Darley Dale in formation, a noisy majestic sight frightening in its power. Lancaster bombers flew very low up the valley on training flights towards the Bamford Dams and the Hope Valley areas. American P38 Lightning fighters buzzed about the valley like gigantic wasps, as did Spitfires, Hurricanes and all types of bombers. For the first time I saw

Darley Bridge

condensation trails left by high-flying aircraft. A Miles Master training plane crashed at Bridge Farm, Darley Bridge, also a Wellington bomber near the cross roads above Gladwins Mark Farm. The plane knocked the tops off a line of trees before doing a belly landing in a ploughed field. The bomber was very battered. I found the ten-gallon aluminium antifreeze tank near the trees which I took home for a souvenir. One day while I was working as relief on the bread van, delivering bread to the Co-ops at Darley, Winster and Youlgrave, on our way from Winster to Youlgrave we delivered to several farms around the small hamlets of Gratton, Smerrill and Middleton. The farmer's wife at Smerrill told us there had been a fearsome crash of a heavy bomber nearby in the night. The plane had completely disintegrated and all the crew were killed. There is now a memorial to them at Middleton by Youlgrave. Reg Parkes became an RAF flight controller, based at a May-Day airfield which specialised in landing damaged planes. He said it was both shocking and exciting to talk a damaged plane down and watch it attempt to make a safe landing.

One night in 1944 a lone German aircraft fired its cannon into the centre of Matlock. There are still marks on the Tansley side of the former Cinema House. Around 1948 George Twigg and I pointed the shop adjacent to Matlock's road bridge (Dakins Newsagents) and I noticed a broken slate on the roof. When I took it off to replace it I found a cannon shell embedded in the roof purlin. The enemy plane also fired at the lead smelter in Darley, and half a dozen small bombs were dropped alongside the railway sidings, just on the Stanton side of the river opposite the bottom of Northwood Lane. That and the couple of plane crashes, and the soldiers at the Whitworth Institute, were about all the excitement we had in Darley Dale, thank goodness.

We were out by the river Derwent one day when we discovered the makings of an adventurous afternoon. Our eyes lit up at the sight of a large flat-bottomed boat belonging to the River Authority, securely chained and padlocked to a tree. Eight or ten lads all heaved at once on the chain, and the staple came out of the tree. Collecting a few tree branches to use as extra poles we all piled in the barge and set off, somewhat inexplicably, up the river. It was a large craft, used for felling and clearing trees. We made poor progress up the Derwent. Coming back down was great, once we got it up to speed. We only had to fend it off the river bank when it got too close.

We were just arriving back to the mooring place, with the intention of chaining it back to the tree and going home, when a large, irritated water bailiff rushed down the bank. We had all disembarked except Edward Moorby, aged about fifteen. Not wishing to cause trouble we all ran off, except poor Edward. Looking back I saw Edward and the man in the river. The barge was floating away and Edward was being very voluble. They both climbed out of the river, very wet indeed. Edward had turned into a maniac, shouting at us for leaving him, shouting at the bailiff for pushing him in the river, and passers by for staring. We walked a little way up the road to the Hide and Skin

Company shed above the cricket ground, Edward leaving a watery trail behind him. He then took off all his clothes and we wrung them out for him. That was on Sunday afternoon. On Monday morning the barge was stuck on the weir at Artist's Corner, Matlock Bath. We all denied all knowledge of the episode to our policeman friend, PC Thorpe. He asked if Edward had caught a cold after his immersion in the river.

Another night fourteen of us got on the bus and went to Bakewell pictures, purchased ninepenny tickets and at the interval moved into the one shilling and threepenny seats. A very nice lady usherette asked to see our tickets and we told her that the lad at the opposite end of the row (Geoff Sellers) had them. While she was making her way across to the other side we all dispersed all over the cinema. Geoff was caught by the usherette and when asked if he had the tickets he strangely and foolishly replied "No, but my brother is in the French Navy and wears clogs." Shortly afterwards the film stopped, the lights came on and the usherettes examined everyone's tickets in the dearer seats. Needless to say we were all back in the ninepenny seats, except Geoff who was expelled from the pictures.

Motor-bike days

June 6th 1944 was my seventeenth birthday and D-Day. I at last obtained my driving licence. There was no driving test in the wartime and I still have not taken one for a car after driving for over sixty years. I did, however, take a Class 1 HGV test in 1974 and passed first time. I had been driving lorries on and off since 1944 on my wartime licence. While out travelling for the Co-op in 1944 I noticed an old motor bike leaning up to a Mr Lee's wooden house on Darley Hillside. His son Eric was the owner. The bike, a 1927 Ariel 550 side valve, had been slightly bent in a crash and he sold it to me for two pounds ten shillings (fifty pence). I free-wheeled it down home from Darley Hillside, and David Holmes and Geoff helped me to sort it out and get it going. I enjoyed about two years very happy motor cycling with the Ariel. It suffered from a lack of lights so I fixed a bicycle dynamo to run off the back tyre. This proved to be a bit unnerving at night, tearing along twisting rural roads on a powerful motor bike with hardly any light. It is not to be recommended. Noise was also a slight problem as the Ariel had no silencer, only a fish-tail. My mates could hear me coming ages before I arrived. My friend Geoff rode pillion.

Charlie acquired a Cotton Sports 500cc JAP engined motor bike, David Holmes a 350cc Triumph, Tom Helliwell a 600cc Panther. Several of the other lads also owned either old motor bikes or very old cars. In late 1945 I bought my first car for twenty pounds with a loan from my dad. It was a 1929 Top Hat Austin 7. My Austin had about as much go in it as a three-legged tortoise.

Alan Gutteridge and the author, aged 18, on a 1927 Ariel at Redlands. The Derwent Valley Co-op (now CostCutters) is in the background

Where once we went on walking expeditions we now went on motor bikes, up the footpaths of the Derbyshire Dales, Dove Dale, Lathkill Dale, Bradford Dale, and all over the moors. We all dressed in dreadful old ragged clothes, mostly remnants of Service uniforms, as clothes were still rationed. People very rarely took us to task for disturbing the peace of their village and countryside. We also had some very funny moments. We made friends with other local motor cyclists, one in particular from Cromford, Philip Gregory, and his friend also called

David Holmes. Philip had a 1,000cc Brough Superior, a mighty machine which almost proved my undoing.

We were at the Black Rocks at Cromford one Sunday afternoon. Being very clever, and gormless at the same time, I decided to show off and ride the Ariel up the steep Black Rocks footpath. When I successfully carried out this dangerous and absolutely pointless deed I casually remarked to Philip Gregory that I was so good a motor cyclist I could ride the monstrous Brough Superior up the path. This path was about two in one and very rough. Philip called my bluff and gave me permission to try. I managed to ride it up to the top where the path became almost vertical, with steps. I lost it, went backwards, swung the bike round and laid it down, knocking off one of its silencers in the process. I leapt back on and slid untidily back down the path on this fearsomely heavy bike.

When Tommy purchased his 1930s Panther 600cc motor bike he had never ridden a motor bike so he asked me if I would take him for a ride on it, and we went to Bakewell. Tommy kept chanting "Go slow and be careful." Coming back through Stanton Lees, for reasons still unknown, I left the road on a bend, went through a hedge and down a steep field at a good rate of knots. I slid up the petrol tank and my knees became firmly wedged under the handlebars. Tommy was now sitting in my seat, chanting louder than ever. I missed several trees then managed to slow it down and we eventually stopped, just before hitting a substantial stone wall. I rode the bike back up the field and through a gate back on to the road. After even more chanting and a lot of persuasion from me Tommy got back on and we returned home.

Another of our expeditions was when we decided to take our motor bikes on the footpath from Conksbury Bridge, near Youlgrave, through Lathkill Dale to Monyash. Charlie Hopkinson was on his B.S.A.350, David Holmes on his Rudge Ulster 500cc and me on my Ariel 550cc, with my friend Geoff Sellers riding pillion. All went well till we got near Monyash when, because of rocks, the path became impassable so we did a detour through several fields. One field gate entrance was extremely muddy, a veritable bog. David Holmes's motor bike got bogged down. A wild looking shire horse galloped up to investigate then turned round and lashed out with his dustbin-lid like hind feet. David was keeping the bike between him and the horse. We managed to pacify the horse and shoo it away, then covered in mud and exhausted with pushing and pulling David's bike through the muddy gate we escaped from the mad horse, who by now had come back again to have another go at us. A large shire horse kicking out at you while you are trying to hold a motor bike upright in a bog can be quite a daunting experience.

We had a few fairly mild accidents with the cars and bikes, till tragically one of the gang, Tommy Hibbert, was killed on a motor bike near Matlock Gas Works, and Mervyn Needham's father died in roughly the same place whilst riding Mervyn's motor bike. David Brown, another member of the gang, was driving a digger for Shand's when it touched the overhead electric cable and he died. Yet another member, Ron Waller, caught pneumonia and died. Despite all the hazards that go with motor bikes I enjoyed a wonderful time. After the Ariel I had acquired a 1933 Douglas Twin. The adventures we had with cars and motor bikes could fill a book on their own.

Harry Keyworth lived in one of the villas on the A6 between Broad Walk shops and the present telephone exchange. The villa had a large garage which for a time became the gang's headquarters. Tommy Helliwell acquired an old Lanchester car which we kept in there. Geoff Sellers and David Holmes had become proficient in mechanical skills at Lehane, Mackenzie & Shand. They got the Lanchester going and we did a few furtive trips up and down the road. Tommy was then given a 1935/6 Morris 8 Tourer which had caught fire somewhere up Broad Walk. The fire had started under the dash-board and consequently burnt the steering wheel and the front seats. Mr Johnson at the Grouse Inn rented us a garage and it was decided to move the Morris to there. Slight problems – no foot brake, no steering wheel, only slight hand brake. David Holmes and Tom Helliwell set off from the eighth row up

Broadwalk and the hand brake proved to be quite useless. The spanner which was taking the place of the steering wheel did not live up to expectations. Luckily there was no traffic about when they attempted to turn on to the A6. The car hit the wall on the A6 a glancing blow. Because the front seats had been burned in the fire Tom and David were sitting on boxes. One of the lads went over the wall. We quickly pushed the car on to the Grouse Inn; it was looking decidedly the worse for wear now. The reason we pushed it quickly was because the police house was opposite. A few days later Constable Thorpe, called at the Grouse garage to let us know he knew all about our escapade. PC Thorpe missed very little in Darley Dale, and was in my opinion a splendid policeman, keeping us on the straight and narrow.

(A knock came on the door in 2000 and there stood my old friend and accomplice in many an escapade, Tom Helliwell. He had returned from New Zealand and Australia and now lived in Lincolnshire. We reminisced for hours and Tom said he was hoping to come and live in Darley Dale. It was great to see him again as we had not met for over twenty-five years. We never did meet again as Tom died a year later, never having returned to Darley Dale).

Our practical jokes sometimes went wrong. One of the gang lifted our house gate off its hinges and leaned it up in place to catch me when I went out. Unfortunately my mother chose that moment to come home and fell headlong over it. Another time we leaned a hefty plank against another of the gang's house door, knocked on the door and ran down the path. Instead of the lad his father came to the door. The plank knocked him down. He was not amused.

One night, behind Matlock Cinema House, I was seeking to impress people, my future wife Barbara Quinlan in particular. Revving the bike's engine high I dropped the clutch; the bike flew off and a split second later I was firmly embedded in the wooden palings of the fence which ran between the Cinema and Steep Turnpike.

LONG WALKS HOME:
NOCTURNAL ADVENTURES WITH YOUNG LADIES

These wartime adventures are not about great escapes from prisoner of war camps or fighting one's way across Europe. True they are wartime tales and true ones at that. All relate to young ladies. It is hard to imagine today the complete austerity of the Second World War especially in 1944/5. On Sunday no cinemas or shops were open and transport ceased at 9pm. Only public houses were open and drinking laws were very strict; no one under eighteen was allowed in. In my mid teens Matlock, after dark, was just that, dark, sometimes very dark. Matlock, like the rest of Britain, was blacked out with not a glimmer of light to be seen. Vehicles were the only exceptions, casting a dim glow from their masked lights on to the roads. A few pedestrians had heavily masked flash lights looking for the edge of the kerb or steps. After a year or two the blackout became an accepted way of life. Because public houses were no-go places to young people under the age of eighteen, and the cinemas stayed firmly shut on Sundays, teenagers' recreation on Sunday usually consisted of having a lie-in after six days at work, going for a walk in the afternoon, or visiting friends and relations. Sunday nights were spent, weather permitting, walking around Matlock. Over the A6 river bridge, down Dale Road, turn left over the pedestrian river bridge into the Hall Leys Park or vice versa. Lots of seats were scattered about the park and these were great places to sit and talk to other young people mostly in small groups.

A great snag to Sunday nights out was wartime public transport. The last buses to nearby villages left Matlock between nine and nine-thirty. There were not many buses and they were always thronged. However with the seating arranged round the perimeter of the bus the large space left in the centre held a huge number of standing people. No one was left behind. There must have been at times almost one hundred people on some of these buses. The conductress (the men had gone to war) had a small battery powered masked light fastened to the money bag strap, shining down on to the money and ticket dispensing machine. This was the only light on the bus besides another dim, masked light illuminating the entrance steps.

Missing the last bus was not the crisis and trauma it would be today. The world of sixty years ago was a world where walking was considered normal. Not the namby-pamby world of today where children are ferried a few hundred yards to school in an immense private vehicle, sometimes the size of a small lorry. Some newcomers to our valley have lived in it for years and are still only familiar with the small area adjacent to their dwelling. Teenagers of the early 1940s were more phlegmatic in their outlook on walking. Another drawback of the blackout was that a moonless, overcast night meant you could not properly see who you were talking to and making a date to meet again, perhaps for a visit to the pictures. Come the light of day there were more than a few surprises. Don't forget all clothes and shoes were rationed and more soap and water was used on faces than make-up.

Then, as always, it was nice to meet unknown young ladies from the surrounding district. There were just a few young ladies who were old beyond their years. They mostly went out with members of the armed forces. After meeting a young lady you invariably took her to the cinema because there was nowhere else to go. Seats were reasonably priced at ninepence (3p) or, to really impress her, you bought one shilling and threepenny tickets (6p). After the film it was then customary to escort the young lady to the bus stop or walk her home. In the summer time, of which we had a double ration in the war, i.e. clocks put forward two hours instead of one, it was a delight to meander one's way to her home, say cheerio, give her a discreet hug or kiss and run back to catch the bus home at 9.30.

The winter time was a different story altogether. The weather in those days seemed to be more frosty and snowy than today. Nights were very dark. I always asked my date if I could walk her home if she lived in the Matlock area. One winter Sunday night, walking round Matlock, I became acquainted with a girl from Matlock Bath and we made a date to go to the cinema together. The first time I saw her properly was when the lights went up at the end of the first house film. One could go into the cinema at any time and stay until it closed. She was a nice looking girl and after we came out of the picture house I asked if I could walk her home. I thought it was not far to Matlock Bath where she lived. I might be able to get a bus back to Matlock in order to catch the last bus home to Darley Dale at 9.30. I remember it was a dark moonless overcast night. Just going into Matlock Bath we turned right up a steep hill called Holme Road. Eventually after climbing a hill like a miniature Mount Everest we left the houses behind us. I asked where she was taking me and she told me to her home which was just along the lane which led to a hamlet called Upperwood. Upper is the right name. Once you arrived there the only way to go was down hill. Eventually puffing and blowing, we arrived at this lonely cottage. I said goodnight and tried to give her a quick kiss. It was not to be. I had not got enough breath left! She said that if I went a little further along the lane there was a footpath that was a short cut down to Matlock Bath.

Half an hour later I was still stumbling down this perilous path in the pitch dark, eventually coming to an even steeper narrow stone paved lane. Feeling my way by the roadside wall I arrived on the A6 just in time to miss the last bus. As I hurried homeward towards Matlock I rejoiced in the fact that I might be able to catch the last train home. It was not to be my night. When I arrived at Matlock station, exhausted with hurrying, the porter was locking up. He told me the train had gone. I limped off up the A6 and eventually arrived home. Mother was waiting up for me and gave me a telling off. I was sixteen years old and I said to myself never, never again. It was the premature end of our relationship. I could not bear the thought of that steep mountain track.

Shortly after the Upperwood episode I was with the Darley gang one Sunday night, doing the monkey run as we called it. We met up with a gang of local Matlock girls who we vaguely knew. It was still winter time. I spent quite a bit of time talking to one of them and made a date to take her to the pictures next night. When we left the pictures I asked if I could walk her home. One of my friends had told me she lived up

Riber hillside

Starkholmes way. Hurrah, I thought, not too far. Off we set, arm in arm, across the river bridge and into the Hall Leys Park. We sat on a park seat and kissed and kissed and I became very excited. We then set off up the hill towards Starkholmes. Passing Matlock's St. Giles Church she then led me up a footpath near the Duke William pub which I knew led up the fields towards Riber. My heart began to pound; it was pounding even more when we had walked about half a mile up the staircase-like path to Riber. "Let's stop here", I said. She said "No, told my mother I would not be late" and went off up the almost vertical path. I asked her where she was going and she replied "To Riber village, that is where I live." "Goodbye" I replied and dashed off at a long striding rate down the steep path to catch the last bus. Losing my footing in the pitch dark I tumbled down the field. No harm was done to me, only to my clothes. I ran into Matlock, missed the last bus again and decided to walk home to Darley. It was our first and last date. I met the young lady several times in later life when we had a laugh and reminisced of times past. She said living at Riber village in wartime put quite a damper on one's recreational life so she shied away from telling young men exactly where she lived.

It is said things come in threes. I asked the next girl I dated where she lived before I took her out. She said Chesterfield Road and I thought that's not so bad. She was a lovely fair-haired girl with amazing blue eyes, and exceptionally nice. We met outside the cinema on Causeway Lane, Matlock, sat in the double seats at the back and held hands. Leaving the cinema, we set off up Steep Turnpike which, as its name implies, is not the flattest hill in Matlock. We lurched over the top of Steep Turnpike on to the slightly less steep Chesterfield Road. Continuing our way up we passed Smedley Street. The night was moonless but not exceptionally dark because it was slightly frosty and very clear and thousands of stars lined the sky. Looking back I could see the top of Masson Hill, approximately one thousand feet (300m) high above us across the dale outlined against the sky. A quarter of an hour later, and way past the Duke of Wellington public house, I looked across at Masson again. We seemed to be almost level with it. Wearily I asked whereabouts on Chesterfield Road she lived. "Not far now" she replied "it's just off Chesterfield Road."

We then started to go downhill which cheered me up no end. We walked past Lumsdale Road junction and a hundred yards later she said this was where she lived. We kissed and kissed again and then she said, "Let's go and sit in the bus shelter for a while." My heart leapt then and putting our arms around one another we set off up the hill towards Chesterfield. The bus shelter was way up the hill near the Matlock Golf Club. It was a lovely night, no traffic on the road, stars shining, we had the world to ourselves. We kissed again and again. Looking back, even though we were both sixteen we were as naive as it was possible to be. No sex education classes in those days, no simulated or otherwise sex on television, no lurid sex magazines for young people on how to do this and that with one's various bits and pieces. After a short time I made a very tentative move towards her. Putting her mouth to my ear she whispered "I know where there is a place we can do this." I nearly had a fit. "Where, where?" I asked. "At home in bed when you are married" she said. I took her home and asked for another date but she refused, thanked me for the night out and we said goodnight.

I knew I had missed the bus again and set off to walk home, making my way towards Hackney Lane. I was light hearted as most of the way home was down hill on very good roads. The young lady married an acquaintance of mine about the same age as me and in later years I worked with her father. They were both very lucky to have the love and company of such a good, lovely woman. My last episode was on a glorious spring evening. I was going on the bus to Bakewell when a young lady got on at Rowsley and sat next to me. We talked and I was taken with her. She had only just come to live in Rowsley. Her family had moved there from a big city. She was a bit older than me, very sophisticated, well made up and very trim.. We went to the pictures a couple of times at Bakewell, which was not my usual area. She invited me to her home for tea. I took her a bunch of flowers. To tell the truth I was fascinated and scared by her at the same time.

After tea we went for a walk. I took her up the river Derwent on a footpath that leads from Church Lane, Rowsley, to Chatsworth Park. The young lady was dressed up and had on a pair of shoes more suitable for dancing than walking on a rough path. Out of nowhere it started to spot with rain. I think she was not thrilled to bits with me. At the side of the footpath somewhere opposite Beeley stood a large high open hay barn (it is still there), tightly packed almost to the roof with hay. Cows were in the field and they had eaten the loose hay from the side of the stack as high as they could reach. This left the sides smooth. The farmer had cut the hay from one side of the top of the stack with a hay knife, leaving a ledge about eight feet off the ground. The only place to shelter was on this ledge. A ladder was lying at the base of the stack so I reared it up and we took shelter. It was very uncomfortable standing on the shelf of cut hay so I suggested I move the ladder so that we could sit on top of the stack, be more comfortable and under cover of the tin roof.

No sooner had we got on top of the stack, snuggled down in the hay, put our arms around one another, than we heard a voice. It was a farm worker talking to a horse. He scrambled up the side of the stack on to the ledge and started cutting hay then threw it down on to the cart to which the horse was harnessed. He was talking gently to the horse whilst he was doing this. We kept very quiet and still. By the time the rain stopped the young man had loaded the hay he had cut out of the stack. He then moved the ladder, climbed down it then placed it on the ground and led the horse and dray away down the track. The top of the stack was about fourteen feet high, much too far to jump. It was about seven feet down to the cut area. The young lady became upset, thinking we were stranded on top of a haystack. What had set off as a peaceful country walk had become an adventure and we were marooned on top of the haystack.

I wanted to stay a while but the young lady became anxious about her clothes. Going to the end of the stack above the cut hay I slid down the seven feet or so on to the cut area, then another seven feet or so to the floor, reared up the ladder and helped the young lady down. She was wearing a flowing skirt, a blouse top and stockings that seemed to go on for ever. She was a lovely sight. Both our clothes were full of hay. I suffer from hay fever and could hardly stand up for sneezing. Where the rain had dripped off the roof it had turned the area where the cows took shelter around the stack into a miniature bog. The young lady promptly lost a shoe and put her lovely stockinged foot into the smelly, squelchy bog. Her precious silk stockings, unobtainable in wartime, were splattered with mud. I could tell on the long walk back to her home in Rowsley that she had lost her sense of humour. I thought it was a hilarious episode. Shortly afterwards I was given an ultimatum which I did not accept, so we parted company. Our paths crossed several times in later life in unexpected places. I don't think I was ever forgiven.

I first met my wife-to-be Barbara when I was seventeen and she was fourteen. When we started dating about a year later I asked her where she lived before I offered to walk her home and she said at the top of Bank Road, just below Smedley's Hydro boiler house. I thought to myself I can live with that. After one date I stayed talking too long, resulting in a headlong run down Bank Road. I was again just in time to see the last bus disappearing up Bakewell Road en route to Darley Dale. I was working in Matlock at the time and had what I thought was a good idea. I would ask to borrow her bike to get me home and return it in the morning. I staggered back up Bank Road, knocked with some trepidation on the door and luckily Barbara answered it. I told her of my predicament and she said she would be pleased to do so, except that it had no lights on it. I said I would go home over Hackney so I would be all right as it was not too dark.

This was optimistic. When I got pedalling along Smedley Street in the blackout I could only see the outline of the buildings against the sky. On reaching the end of Smedley Street I turned up Farley Hill towards Hackney Road. As I passed the Laburnum Inn a commanding voice shouted "Stop, Police". My immediate response was to pedal off as fast as I could. Moments later I looked back and I could see the dim glimmer of a masked bicycle lamp following me. I pedalled madly, pursued by cries of "Stop!" I knew of a dangerous short cut down a precipitous footpath to Johnson's Mill at Ladygrove, Two Dales. The footpath was at the end of Holt Lane which led off Hackney Road. We must have raced about a mile before I turned on to narrow Holt Lane. Still the policeman came after me, almost catching up with me before I turned down the steep tree-shrouded footpath. The policeman stopped at the top, no doubt waiting for sounds of an almighty crash.

It was a terrifying ride down the footpath in the pitch dark. My relief on reaching the bottom in one piece was immense, nothing short of a miracle. I still had to make my way home from Ladygrove to Crowstones Road where I lived. I pedalled on, crossing the A6, going down to Darley Station then on the footpath alongside the railway line to home. I knew that if I had attempted to ride along the A6 one of

Darley Dale's beat policemen would probably be lurking about somewhere with his bicycle. The policemen were very good to the lads and I wanted to keep the right side of them. Whenever I go near the Holt Lane to Ladygrove footpath I look at it and marvel. I would not even ride down it in broad daylight, never mind in the dark on a bike with no lights.

PIG DAYS

I believe it was in 1948 that father said Enthovens, the lead smelters, were ceasing to keep livestock on their farm. Everyone in Darley Dale knew that the land around the lead smelter was poisoned, and all livestock, from cows to birds, suffered from lead poisoning, not to mention some of the men who worked there. This was in the days long before health and safety at work was a big issue. Father and I talked it over and decided to go and have a look. We arrived at Bridge Farm where there were a few cattle and some pigs and the farmer told us he had an in-pig sow for sale which was in a sty round the back. Peering over the sty wall my gaze was met by a pair of twinkling grey eyes with lovely long blonde eyelashes that any woman would have died for, the eyes partially shaded by two huge ears. An enormous long wet snout stuck out in front. I had never been so close to such a large pig before. My only other experience of pigs was when I was asked to hold some very young ones while they were being ringed. Ringing consists of inserting a metal ring into the bridge of its nostrils. The ring inflicts pain in a pig when it roots, thereby stopping it from rooting up the fields when running free. Father and I discussed whether we should have the pig and decided yes. I made a tow bar and bolted it on to the old Rover then went to Tor Farm and borrowed Mr Dakin's small sheep trailer.

Father and I arrived at Bridge Farm and let down the high rear door to the trailer. The door then became a ramp. Once more I saw those bright grey eyes weighing me up. The farmer said her name was Lizzie and that she would follow me to the ends of the earth if I had a bucket of pig food. When Lizzie came out of the sty my heart sank; she was colossal, about sixteen stone of pregnant lop-eared Large White pig. We put the bucket of food at the back of the trailer and Lizzie scrambled in. Up with the ramp door and away we went home to Highlands.

We had cleared out the old apple store shed for her. Lizzie disembarked from the trailer, which was quite a job as there was no room for her to turn round. I went down to Matlock Library and found all the books I could about pigs. Pig food was still on ration in 1948 so father registered Highlands as a smallholding and we were supplied with a ration book and a record book. We had become registered smallholders, and had the nucleus of a pig farm. Mr Wilson from Burley Fields farm, just up Bent Lane from us, provided us with hay and straw for bedding. I installed a farrowing rail in the old apple store, ready for when Lizzie farrowed. A farrowing rail is made from a stout piece of wood; mine was an old wooden scaffold pole. The rail is fixed about fifteen inches from the floor and about eighteen inches from the rear wall. This is so the young piglets can shelter there when the sow is going to lie down or is thrashing about when she gets up.

A week or two later Lizzie collected all the hay and straw together into a heap and lay down on it. She was very clean, as most pigs are, rarely soiling their bed. My future wife Barbara and I decided that Lizzie was about to farrow. Milk was leaking from her teats and she was doing a lot of grunting. We fixed ourselves up with a pair of scissors and a paraffin storm lantern. Barbara was about to become a pig's midwife. Sitting in a pig-sty with a farrowing sow is not many seventeen-years old girl's idea of a night out. I felt closer than ever to her. A pig has a gestation time of three months, three weeks and two or three days and we knew her time was nigh. The night was cold and dark. We were absolutely amazed as Lizzie had her piglets very quickly. The apple store was quite cool and the newborn piglets steamed. We were totally astounded by their ability to walk about within a few minutes of being born. Father came up to see how things were going. While he stood with the door open one piglet popped through the gap and wobbled off down the drive, making little squeaking sounds. When all was finished Lizzie had eight young ones. They were soon all suckling as Lizzie lay on her bed grunting contentedly.

We hung the paraffin lamp from a beam and went home. I had read that sows could become very protective and ferocious when they had very young ones. Lizzie, I am pleased to say, was not. After a few days we let them out into the orchard for a little run round. I found that pigs are very intelligent though not as sensitive as dogs. They will come when called and will always let you know when it is near mealtime. Father was not as confident with pigs as I was. One of my farmer friends told me the way to handle an obstreperous pig which is intent on biting you is to hold it firmly by its tail and an ear. This works well while you have the pig in your grasp. The tricky moment is when you let go. This can prove to be a very exciting moment when hasty movements are paramount and athletic agility a necessity.

Lizzie and I gradually established a relationship. Once or twice she tried to bite me, such as when I made her return to her sty when she did not want to go. Other times she would come to me, greet me with a grunt or two and wait for me to give her back a good scratch. Seven of her young ones I took to Bakewell market and sold. The eighth piglet, a sow, we kept and christened Phyllis. When she was ready to mate I borrowed the trailer and took her to the boar at Mr Pugh's who ran Smedley's Hydro Farm at Farley. Phyllis grew up to be even more intelligent than her mother. I built three more pig sties and bought and sold pigs at Bakewell market where I became friendly with a Mr Andrews from Bakewell who kept pedigree Large Whites. He had the largest pig in the 1949 Bakewell Show. He taught me how to geld boar piglets. I purchased an in-pig gilt from him. Gilts are female pigs that have had no offspring. We called her Big Lizzie and that is what she became, a truly gigantic pig. Big Lizzie duly farrowed. She was not a good mother and because of her size she literally squashed several of her offspring as she lay down to suckle them, in spite of the farrowing

Left: *Barbara feeding pigs*
Right: *Big Lizzie and Beryl*

rail being there to protect them.

We kept the offspring of all three sows and reared them, then took them to Bakewell market, always keeping my record book up to date. Sometimes I purchased litters of piglets at the market, usually about eight weeks old. In the late 1940s there were many different breeds of pigs which are now rare. Soon I could recognise and name around seven or eight different breeds. At one time or another we kept them all, Lincolnshire Curly Coats, Black and White Essex and Wessex, Ginger Tamworths, Black Berkshires, Gloucester Old Spot, straight eared and lop eared Middle and Large Whites and also mixed breeds.

Using my expertise as a builder I built a tandem copper boiler. In 1949 large metal clothes boilers, similar to the one we had at Vineyard Terrace, were still available to buy. If I remember rightly these coppers were made of cast iron, around two feet to two feet six inches across and deep. The shape was like a globe cut in half with a four inches rim around the outside which sat on the brickwork. We bought potatoes by the ton at a cheap rate. These were dyed blue to stop them from being used for human consumption. On each side of the brick structure which held the coppers I made a wooden bin about four feet square with a lid and a drop-down front.

In those days I worked from 7.45am till 5.45pm. Most days I went to work in the old Rover car so I was back home again about 6pm when I would feed the pigs, clean them out if necessary, then have my evening meal. Every third night I would fire up the coppers and load them up with potatoes. After they had boiled for a short time I ladled them out and placed them in the wooden bins with two or three shovels of pig meal mixed with them. This operation usually occupied a couple of hours. In very cold weather the mixture would keep warm for a couple of days. All the pigs loved it. Charlie Hopkinson worked for Mr Wilson at Burley Fields Farm. He lent Charlie his paraffin-engined Fordson tractor with a plough and ridger. Charlie ploughed and ridged about an acre of ground at Highlands. We then set fodder beet seed. Because the pigs were free range the fodder beet had to be fenced off with pig netting.

Tom Goodwin of Abbey Farm, Churchtown, who I went to school with, sold me a circular saw bench. I modified the petrol feed to the old lorry to take an extra fuel pipe which I had wrapped around the exhaust pipe. Utilising the glycol tank from the plane crash near Gladwin's Mark as a paraffin tank I started the lorry engine on petrol then when it became warm switched it over to paraffin. A canvas belt running from the jacked up rear wheel of the lorry drove the pulley on the circular saw bench. This arrangement enabled me to cut all the posts we needed for the pig fence out of various trees which we had felled around Highlands. When we harvested the fodder beet we found it was too large for the pigs to eat so had to chop them up with a hatchet. The pigs ate the fodder beet raw.

Though Old Lizzie with her twinkling grey eyes and long blonde eyelashes was my favourite pig her daughter, the breeding sow Phyllis, was by far the most intelligent. She answered to her name and found that by rubbing against fruit trees, fruit would fall off, almost in to her waiting jaws. I found that pigs could swim when she rooted the lid off the large underground water tank one day and fell in. The tank was roofed over with large stone slabs. The water level was about one foot below the slabs. Feeding the pigs at teatime I missed Phyllis, no sign of her, no hole in the fence, very perplexing. Then my attention was caught by the lid lying on the ground at the side of the tank. On investigation Phyllis's head bobbed into view, eyes looking up at me saying "get me out". I don't know who was most pleased to see the other, Phyllis or me. When I went off to fetch a rope Phyllis made a series of loud grunts – a plea for help. When I arrived back with the rope Phyllis was nowhere to be seen. I called her name anxiously and she calmly swam back into view. Putting the rope around her neck I heaved her up out of the water far enough for her to get her front legs out. With our combined efforts, me pulling, Phyllis scrabbling with her legs, she eventually managed to get out of the water tank. She had probably been in the tank for hours but came to no harm, even though she was pregnant.

All the sows got to know when I backed the pig trailer up to the enclosure gate when they were in season that they were going to spend a day or two with the boar. Sometimes I took them to Mr Statham's boar at Mount Pleasant Farm, Farley, or Mr Pugh's which was about six hundred yards further up the road. Both their boars were Large Whites. Mr Statham's boar seemed to me to have a dirty disreputable air about him. He was always very eager and I am sure looked forward to our sows' visits. Pigs are very tiring creatures to look after, as indeed are all farm animals. Pigs let you know in no uncertain terms when feeding time is due, squealing, grunting and battering at the gate. To add to all this mayhem we had half a dozen geese who lived with the pigs. Honking away, the geese pecked the pigs unmercifully at feeding times. This was because they shared the pigs' food, eating out of the same trough. Father also kept poultry and guinea-fowls nearby. If a pig escaped a bucket of food waved in front of it ensured it would follow you back in.

To be a farmer one must love the work, the lifestyle and try to keep sentiment at bay, always being prepared for unfortunate happenings beyond one's control, bad weather, disease and death, and above all try to be ever-present, to watch over everything night and day while accepting hard work and long hours as the norm. I enjoyed going to Bakewell market and the camaraderie of other farmers and small-holders. Keeping pigs gave me a feeling of pride, achievement and independence, combined with the knowledge that only experience can give. A farmer's life is full of daily decisions that are absolutely vital to the success of his business. On balancing the books I could see that if I had spent the hours I put into the pig farm doing building work I would probably be better off financially, have freedom to please myself about working or not working, and less worries. Reluctantly I decided to pack up pig farming. I felt awful disposing of the three sows who had played such a large part in my life for around three years. I took my last day off work to help the cattle truck driver to load up all the pigs and gave the three sows a final farewell pat. Old Lizzie gave me a last inquisitive look as if to say what is this all about, as she went up the ramp into the truck, and out of my life for ever. I had not the heart to go to Bakewell market to see them sold. I did not want to know who bought them or what happened to them. I hoped that only good things were in store for their future. Fifty odd years later I remember them all and the pleasure they gave me. They imbued a more caring attitude in me by my being responsible for their lives and welfare. There would be no more sitting in the farrowing sty, delivering piglets by the flickering light from the paraffin lamp, no more stoking of the potato boilers on a still cold frosty night with clouds of steam around one. Pigs are clean, intelligent animals. I could never have a modern pig-rearing farm with each animal imprisoned for life in a small steel cage. To me it is cruel.

Marriage

I remember as if it was yesterday the first time I met and talked to my wife-to-be Barbara Quinlan. At seventeen I was fairly naive as far as girls were concerned. I was on the opposite side of the road, walking along with Geoffrey Sellers. I looked across and she looked at me. Geoff said her name was Barbara so I went across the road and made her acquaintance. She was wearing a green coat, orangey brown boots and a head scarf, with nice length hair peeping out from it. The more Barbara and I talked, the more I took to her. She told me she was fourteen and that she was working at Heny and Loveday Solicitors, Matlock, and was training to be a shorthand typist. We became friends, seeing one another round and about Matlock. I became fond of her and admired her. When I was around nineteen, even though I had taken a

Left: *Barbara aged 14*
Right: *Barbara at Highlands Cottage*

Our wedding day, Saturday 31st March 1951

few girls out I knew that she was the girl for me and Barbara and I became a pair. She was everything I had ever dreamed about, full of love, understanding, patient and tolerant, with her feet firmly on the ground. We took one another home to meet our parents and relations. Barbara and I were absolutely suited for each other, and have had a wonderful life together thanks to her patience, tolerance and thoughtfulness.

Early on the morning of our wedding day, Saturday 31st March 1951 I went up to Highlands Cottage which we had so lovingly prepared for our home. Highlands Cottage was in existence one hundred years before the Highlands Estate came into being as Sir Joseph Whitworth's private and kitchen gardens. Originally it was a one up and one down cottage with a small barn attached. Sir Joseph extended and converted it into a four-bedroom (two of them very small) cottage for the under gardener Ben Bradshaw, whose grandson Raymond and I went to school together.

Because it seemed very cold and damp I set fires with sticks and coal in the living room and the bedroom. I did not want us to be cold on our first time together. I was over the moon with joy and contentment. Father gave me five pounds, equal to a week's wage and Barbara's father had given her forty pounds. We were rich, we had a home and a few pieces of furniture. Colin Evans who had married my Co-op workmate Elsie Parks, sister to Ron and Reg, took me in my old Rover to the Bank Road Chapel (now closed) opposite Smedley's Hydro boiler house. He then took Barbara from her home (now demolished), just below the boiler house, to the Chapel the long way round, via Smedley Street and Henry Avenue.

It was a very wild and windy day. Charlie Hopkinson was my best man and Barbara's cousin Margaret was the bridesmaid. While I was in church waiting for Barbara, Lubin Wildgoose played "Moonlight and Roses" on the organ. During the wedding it thundered and lightened, and there was a flurry of snow. Miraculously when we went out after the wedding the sun shone in time for the photographs. We then walked up Bank Road to the reception held upstairs over the cafe on the corner of Rutland Street and Smedley Street, now part of the County Offices.

After the reception we went home to our cottage. What a magical word, Home. I lit the fires again, piled on more coal and we spent our first night together by the light of the flickering fire. We were so happy and contented it was like a dream, absolutely wonderful. Our week's honeymoon was mostly spent at home with a few trips out. We decided to go to Buxton swimming baths one day and came away again as there was no mixed bathing allowed.

Barbara and I redecorated the cottage, scrubbed the stone flagged floor, laid lino on roofing felt and polished the brass door knobs till they twinkled in the light. The cottage had only the one old immense brass tap over the shallow stone sink, gas lighting and a huge cast iron range with oven and hot water boiler. Because the hot water boiler was constructed of cast iron the water became tinged with rust. It had no tap and water had to be ladled in and out. The toilet was about seventy-five feet (twenty-three metres) away from the cottage, up ten steps, and alongside the nine feet (2.7 metres) high boundary wall. Adjacent to and shrouding the toilet was an old yew tree. The toilet consisted of a wooden bench with a hole in it and a large galvanised pail underneath. The door had a four-inch (100 mm) gap top and bottom. In the winter the snow blew in and in autumn one was ankle deep in leaves. Insects of all types abounded. On our wedding night Barbara, armed with a flashlight, went up to the toilet, and after some time, when she had not returned, I went to look for her. A branch of the yew tree had been gently scratching the roof slates in the breeze and had frightened her. Our earth toilet could be a very scary place. The Matlock Urban District Council emptied it once a week – not the world's best job being a night-soil man, the old historic name for the job.

We had a gas point in the small kitchen which served a double gas ring and a gas clothes boiler. The gas boiler also heated the water for the tin bath. We had a lovely surprise. One of my workmates, Sam Green, made us a small table and dresser as a wedding present. My mother gave us a few pegged rugs and we purchased a sideboard. In wartime and just afterwards furniture was known as Utility furniture and was stamped with a Utility mark, and was very scarce. Highlands Cottage, with its absence of central heating, bathroom and indoor toilet, provided little privacy, comfort and warmth. The early morning and after work wash was carried out in the kitchen in a round white enamel washing up bowl. Hot water came from the kettle, cold water from the large brass tap fed straight from the main by an ugly lead pipe. The sink was stone with sides about three inches (75mm) high and had no plug to the crude lead waste pipe. Early in the morning the kitchen became a hive of chaotic industry – washing ourselves in the bowl on the sink, Barbara cooking breakfast on the gas ring which also heated water for washing and breakfast drinks, Barbara making sandwiches for my packed lunch, all carried out with one eye on the clock because I usually had a van or lorry to catch to take me to wherever I was working. This entailed a half-mile run down the steep hill.

Bathing was a luxury to be savoured, preparations had to be made well in advance. As I have stated the living room was dominated by the black cast iron range, 1880s vintage, with an oven and a boiler which had a lift-up lid. Flue dampers at the back of the range controlled the oven and boiler. The first jobs were to stoke up the fire, fill up the gas boiler and light it, then bring in the tin bath from the shed and clean it. Pull the peg rug back from the front of the fire and put the bath in place. When the water in the gas copper was boiling we ran a couple of buckets off and poured them into the bath followed by a couple of buckets of cold water and a Radox bath cube. Next strip off and into the bath, the gas and firelight casting a lovely warm glow and the heat from the fire warming you, Barbara washing my back or me washing her back. The only downside to bath night was emptying the bath with the bucket until it was light enough to carry out and empty down the drain from the sink. This was our bath ritual for the eight years we lived at Highlands Cottage.

I was a building trade worker by then and as such received an extra ration of cheese in 1951 when some foods were still rationed. Money and petrol was scarce so when it was fine and I was working nearby I went to work on my bike. Whoever came home first lit the fire in the old cast iron cooking range, put the kettle on ready for tea and a wash. I was so lucky that Barbara was a wonderful cook and cake maker. While Barbara saw to things in the house I worked in the garden. We missed having the luxury of electricity in the first few months at the cottage. Overhead electric power lines ran adjacent to the cottage and I persuaded father to have electricity installed by Harry Brookes, a Darley Dale electrical contractor. George Allwood and Michael Strange, Harry's workmen duly appeared. After we had electricity life immediately became much better. We bought a small electric cooker (happily named The Jackson Giant), an electric fire, a wireless and an old second hand record player. The stone sink was replaced by a pot sink which I acquired from work, out of a house we were modernising, and my friend and workmate Brian Horobin helped me to install it.

Life was marvellous. We had also purchased a small new table wringer from Hall & Co where Barbara was now working. We thought we had all life's necessities within a few months of getting married. Our first year together, which culminated in the birth of our daughter Beryl, was one of ecstatic happiness. We had our first three children whilst living at the cottage, Beryl, Lesley and Andrew, two years between each child. Barbara had all our four children in Darley Hall maternity hospital where I had worked on its conversion in 1946. She usually stayed about two weeks, and after our first child her mother and mine looked after the other children. When our fourth child, Russell, was born Beryl was eleven, Lesley nine and Andrew seven. I had a couple of weeks off work to help look after them. Beryl caught pneumonia when she was five and spent time in Derby City Hospital followed by a spell convalescing in Bretby Hospital. Andrew has never been in hospital and Lesley only to have her two children. Russell has been in hospital twice, both occasions due to his wandering. He spent three months in Africa and caught malaria while he was there. During a six months stay in India he, not unexpectedly, contracted a bowel disease.

Joe Ashton the baker, a Youlgrave butcher, and the International Stores from Matlock, all delivered to Highlands Cottage together with the milkmen the Hallowes brothers. In later years Beryl married and lived at the cottage with her soldier husband Chris and their two children, Mark and Sara. Because Chris spent a lot of time away with the Army Mark and I became close. I taught him to drive the tractor when he was ten or eleven. Mark also became very mechanically minded because of helping me with my constant mechanical tinkering. Mark and I are still at our happiest wrestling with vehicles. In the summer to earn some extra money I used to go out to work at night quite a bit, building for people.

Winter nights were spent at home playing cards, darts and dominoes with Charlie, Geoff and various other friends. I smoked about seventy cigarettes a week and ran the car, a 1933 Rover 14, with money for the tax and insurance put by in an old cocoa tin every week. In 1953 or 1954 a back wheel came off the car as I was going down Park Lane, Two Dales. The car was distorted and never the same again so I sold it and eventually purchased an old Series E Post Office van for £27.50. Barbara and I and the children went everywhere in the van, with holidays in Wales and on the East Coast. The van went very well because a friend of mine, Sam Stevenson (who worked for Shand's and lived just up the road from us), put a fairly new Morris engine and gearbox in it, out of a wrecked car. I maintained its appearance as a Post Office van and everyone mistook it for one. We could park it anywhere, any time. We had two or three old Post Office vans which cost between twenty-five pounds and thirty pounds each.

I got to know a Mr Hardy, a scrap vehicle merchant from Dunston, Chesterfield, and used to ferry a few scrap cars for him. He sold me a scrap 1927 Morris 2 ton lorry with a failed clutch which I towed home with the old Rover with Tommy Helliwell at the wheel of the Morris. It was a nerve-wracking job as the lorry brakes were quite useless and the hills between Highlands and Chesterfield were very steep. I took out the gearbox and found that the failed clutch was made of dozens of corks which ran in oil. I put new corks in the clutch and new linings on the rear brakes, making the total cost of the lorry £22.50. I taught Barbara to drive on this lorry. I taught her how to double-declutch, an essential when driving a lorry with a gate change and no syncromesh in the gearbox. We

*Barbara with the
1927 Morris lorry*

Named after the submarine, Osiris, Barbara and I built this in 1959

never drove it on the public highway, only on the hard drives around the Highlands.

Our three children, Beryl aged 7, Lesley 5, and Andrew 3 when we left eventually Highlands Cottage, were also bathed in front of the fire unless it was a hot summer day when they sometimes had their bath on the lawn. If you have never had a nice hot bath on a cold winter's night in front of a blazing fire, having your back washed while listening to the wireless and drinking tea, you have missed a treat. When we moved to Osiris, the new bungalow we built together on Moor Lane, Darley Dale, we had a lovely bathroom with washbasin, wc and radiator, very convenient but lacking in ambience. The downside of living in any old cottage in 1951, with no mod cons is the early morning organisation of getting ready for the day.

CHAPTER 5: THE BUILDING TRADE

CROSSLAND'S

My brother Jim, who had worked for a time in Stancliffe Nurseries in the 1930s, was demobbed in early 1946. Derbyshire County Council had purchased Darley Hall in order to turn it into a maternity hospital and Jim started work there as gardener/caretaker. In the week after I had finished at the Co-op I paid him a visit at the hall and he showed me round the house and gardens. In a front downstairs room seated at a small table full of plans and papers was a small bespectacled trilby-hatted man. He introduced himself as Fred Crossland of Crossland Brothers, Matlock, who had obtained the contract to convert the Hall. He offered me a job as an improver because I was too old to be an apprentice. I accepted there and then. I believe it to be one of the best decisions I have ever made. When I walked up the drive to Darley Hall I had no thoughts of a job in the construction industry. I had failed my medical test for the Forces, being assigned as grade 3, and my future prospects seemed to be limited. I had left school at thirteen with no qualifications whatsoever but I was determined never to do factory or shop work again.

The following Monday morning at 7.45am I walked along the A6 from Redlands as far as where the telephone exchange and Parkway are today, climbed over the wall and walked across the fields to Darley Hall. On the way over the fields I passed two huge shire horses from the Fearns' Hall Farm. In the days to come I used to stop and have a few words and I became friendly with them, on most days taking them a bite to eat. One day however, during the bad snow of January to March 1947, I did not take anything. I had forgotten but the shires had not. One of them opened his enormous teeth-filled mouth and grasped me by the shoulder, then shook me. I was completely taken by surprise. We were eyeball to eyeball. He then let go of me. Instead of being angry and afraid I felt sorry for him marooned in a world of snow and ice when he should have been in a nice warm stable.

My first two terms in the University of Life had been excellent. Engineering work and factory work, followed by shop work. I was now commencing the building work term. Little did I know how long this term was to last. In 1946 the building trade was absolutely traditional. Our only mechanical aid was the petrol-engined concrete mixer. Digging the lime pit was the first job. Myself, Ben Haynes from Wensley (ex-Millclose Mine worker), Bill Salt and Edward (Ted) Bispham, both from Darley Dale, dug a hole about six feet by ten feet by two feet deep which was filled with water. Smith's Builders Merchants (run by brothers Ted and Lewis) from Darley Station delivered a load of burnt limestone which we carefully placed in the water filled pit. To my amazement the burnt limestone made this vast quantity of water boil. Next morning the pit was full of lime the constituency of toothpaste. Mixed with sand and a little cement this was the traditional mortar mix for building prior to the second war.

All drain pipes were earthenware, with named bends, ie barren bends, slow bends and channel bends. Tarred gasket was used to fill the collar to stop the one-to-one sand and cement jointing mix protruding into the pipes' interior. I found that bricks had indents called frogs. Stones had beds, timber had shakes. Roof drainage had downspouts, offsets, stop ends and hopper heads. Slates were named after nobility, ie Duchess and Countess. In those days scaffolding was constructed from long wooden poles and short 7 x 2$^{1}/_{2}$ inch timbers called putlogs. The poles were sorted into two types, rangers for horizontal use and uprights for vertical use. Sometimes we let them in the ground about two feet. Everyone had to learn to tie a scaffold knot; either a wire lashing or hemp rope was used. Men's lives depended on these ties. Another Ted, Edward Lane, also of Darley, was the foreman joiner. At the outbreak of war Ted enquired which branch of the Army would be the best for him, signed up with them, and rose to become a Regimental Sergeant Major. The other joiner was Basil Mount from Elton. Reminiscing, they found they had both sheltered from the Japanese in some railway tunnel at the Indian border with Burma at roughly the same time. Ted later became my boss when I worked for Shand's in 1962. Bill Salt and Ted Bispham were very experienced construction workers.

In 1946 all bricklayers had a plumb rule – a piece of wood about four and a half feet (1350mm) long by four inches (100mm) wide, with a lead weight on a thin string. When held upright if the line matched a small groove down the centre of the wood the work was plumb. Putting a square up to it also ensured the work was level. Some plumb rules had gauge marks on them to keep the work to the right height. Five simple tools, a trowel, brick hammer, lump hammer, chisel and a plumb rule/level are all that are needed to build anything from a small cart shed to a cathedral or a castle – plus the necessary skills.

Joiners required many more specialised tools, plus a tie and brown shoes or boots, and a superior attitude to all other building workers. At that time most construction workers wore remnants of army surplus clothing. By knock-off time on my first day at Darley Hall I knew the construction industry was the life for me, interesting and exhilarating, a chance to play a tangible part in creating the landscape.

The Bland brothers, Ernest and Arnold from Darley, carried out all the plastering on the Darley Hall conversion. Ernest's father and my grandfather refurbished Haddon Hall together in 1899/1906. The Blands used wooden laths and plaster made with putty lime. I was fascinated to see them beating cow hair with two sticks to separate it before putting it in the mix to bind the plaster backing coat together. Cow hair came in sacks, and a type of cement called Keenes was used to form external corners as it set very hard.

The plumbers used sheets of lead to make all the soil pipe bends and wc connections. Red lead, hemp and putty made joints water-tight. Sometimes I gave them a hand, bobbin knocking. Three boxwood bobbins were threaded on to a length of window cord; the large four-inch centre bobbin was left loose, while the two smaller outside bobbins were fastened to the cord and were pulled backwards and forwards to knock the centre bobbin through the pipe they had made from sheet lead. Great skill was needed to make bends. Men were judged on their knowledge and skills, not by the way they spoke and dressed. Hall & Co from Matlock carried out the heating contract. Derbyshire County Council's electricians, overseen by a Mr Fearn from Matlock Bath, completely rewired the Hall. Every man on the job had a terrific pride in his work and the job in general. Crossland's transport was an ex-American Army Chevrolet, left-hand drive, one ton truck and sometimes I drove it collecting materials.

Going to work early one morning, crossing the fields from Broad Walk to Darley Hall, I noticed clouds of smoke coming out of one of the chimneys. I thought that Ben Haynes had lit a good fire in the first floor room we used for our meals and keeping tools in. Ted Lane was

Darley Hall

running to the Hall in front of me and as I got close I saw Ben standing on the upstairs window cill, his clothes on fire, flames and smoke belching past him. Ted reared up a nearby ladder and carried him down, shouting to me to run to the telephone and get help. The telephone in those days was answered by an operator and I told her to send lots of help quickly as the Hall was on fire and at least one man was badly burnt. Ted sat Ben in a chair, his overcoat and cap burnt. He was in a bad way. Hall & Co's plumber Jack Johnson and I foolishly decided to rescue some tools and fittings from the ground floor room under the first floor room which was by now blazing nicely. When we opened the door the room went bang, the ceiling fell in and a huge sheet of flame seemed to fill the room. Never had a door been shut more quickly. (Incidentally Jack Johnson's son Bernard, who is also a plumber and heating engineer, and I worked on a contract together in 2002, fifty-five years later. Bland's plasterer apprentice, Philip Taylor, also worked with us on a 2002 contract).

DAVID SHELDON'S

The fire put the Crossland brothers, Jack and Fred, out of business and put me out of a job. I then went to work for David Sheldon, a subsidiary of Hall & Co, run by Mr Heath, architect, and Francis Wildgoose. David Sheldon was a splendid man. He was one of Henry Boot's first foremen before the war and the best boss I ever had, in spite of his sacking me three times, mostly because I had a slightly distorted sense of humour when things went a bit wrong, like the time I accidentally poured a bucket of sloppy plaster all over him which promptly set. His trilby hat, face and coat were smothered in plaster. I was helpless with laughter. We were putting a new kitchen ceiling up at a Dr Dobson's house on Imperial Road, Matlock. Dr Dobson was a very religious person. I just hope he could not interpret David Sheldon's building language finishing with "You are sacked". When I started to leave he screamed "you are not **** sacked until you have cleaned all the **** mess up."

I loved building and still do, and in my years in the building trade I have worked with lots of wonderful characters in many different places. Every day the building trade throws up a challenge of one sort or another. Another slight catastrophe occurred up Starkholmes, just above and across the road from the old Starkholmes Primary School. I had been sent to take down a tall chimney which served a kitchen extension at the rear of a house. Charlie Hurley was my mate at the time. To speed things up I decided to drop the chimney stones down the chimney to save carrying them down the roof and the ladder. Charlie fetched them out of the kitchen. Not much soot came down as the chimney had been swept. Things were going well, the chimney was half way down and there was almost no mess in the kitchen. All of a sudden the chimney started to shake, then slid down out of sight into the house. As I looked in horror down the hole in the roof where the chimney had been a second earlier a huge cloud of dust erupted out of the hole, accompanied by loud bangs and crashing noises. Going down the ladder I looked through what remained of the kitchen window. A scene of destruction met my eyes. Bits of ceiling, kitchen furniture, ceiling joists, and tons of rubble from what had been the chimney and chimney breast filled the kitchen.

I went to the phone box and left a message for David Sheldon to come as I had a problem and about an hour later he came. I explained that we had had a bit of a set-back and that it was not my fault as the chimney breast had not been tied back into the existing house wall. After leaping up and down he told me, once again in builders language, to go away as I was sacked. As I was leaving he shouted me to come back and try to do something about this woman's kitchen before she came back, and explain to her that we would soon put it right!

In 1948 David Sheldon's was building a house for a Mr Bowlzer, buyer for Hall & Co, about one hundred yards past the Duke of Wellington, near the entrance to Gritstone Road at Matlock. The house was practically finished. The heating was on and I was tiling the kitchen. When I finished I was very hot and sweaty so I decided to have a quick bath. As soon as I was in the bath the people who were having the house built came to the house with some friends to have a look round. I was just getting out of the bath in a big hurry when two ladies came into the bathroom – they were very surprised! My future wife Barbara, whom I was by then courting very seriously, was working for Hall & Co as Mr Bowlzer's secretary, and heard all about it next morning.

George Twigg, one of the men who I worked with at David Sheldon's had been well trained in roof work and from time to time George and I would strip and replace roofs, including natural stone slate roofs. Great skill is needed, plus detailed preparation and concentration. I divide roof covering into various categories with stone at the top. With seasoned oak pegs they last up to 250 years. Stone slate roofs usually have very heavy hardwood timbers to take the weight. The roofs are usually constructed of hardwood timber, mostly oak, with riven oak laths from which to hang the stone slates. Preparation consists of sorting the stone slates into lengths, then the lengths into thicknesses. The thickest slates go on the verge (gable end) and are bedded on with mortar. The longest slates go on the eaves (bottom of roof). Stone slates vary in width but joints must be put as near the centre of the one underneath as possible. Never put a thick slate in the centre of a roof or on top of another thick slate, except at the verge. Verge slates are bedded in between with mortar as well as underneath. Ridge tiles are solidly bedded with plenty of mortar.

Westmorland green slates are next to stone slates for durability. Fixed similarly to stone slates with copper nails they have a life expectancy of 150 years. Welsh slates vary in quality with 60 to 120 years of life. Staffordshire Blue clay tiles will last as long as the roof timbers – unlimited life. Red Staffordshire clay tiles last only 60 or 70 years. Concrete tiles last 40 to 60 years, but large flat concrete tiles only last about 45 years. A built up felt roof has a life of 15 to 20 years, depending on the amount of sunshine it gets. Lead roof covering has a life of 50 to 200 years, depending on size, thickness, and pitch. Thatch I have no experience of and know nothing about it. A general rule is the steeper the pitch of the roof, the longer it will last. Any roof whose ridge runs north to south is less prone to moss and frost damage. In my opinion the roof structure is the most important part of a dwelling.

I was once sent to work with Harry Spencer at a public house called the Horse and Jockey at Wessington, a small village near Alfreton. Harry Spencer lived on a smallholding on the Darley Moors called Grouse Cottage. We were constructing a new beer cellar under the existing building We dug a large hole adjacent to the gable to form an access. We then broke through to under the floor below the gable, propping up the gable and fixing a concrete lintel to hold it up. In the following days we excavated under the concrete pub floor a small room about six to seven feet wide, perhaps ten feet long, propping and concreting as we went. While we took every precaution it was a downright dangerous job. The sides kept falling in. We had to constantly prop up the rough concrete floor that was above our heads.

Harry was a capable man, always cheerful, filled full of confidence that he could overcome any difficulties we encountered. This particular morning in late 1947 Harry and I started work in the cellar. Morning break time was 9.45. As we sat quietly in our small site shed, drinking our tea. I had a sudden feeling of apprehension. I said to Harry that I had a very strong feeling that a disaster was about to happen to us. When we returned to the cellar the feeling of dread persisted. These feelings of impending doom gradually got worse. Lunchtime came and I was so pleased to be away from the cellar.

We usually ate our lunch with the shed door open, watching people and traffic go by. Harry said "Look Lew, there is a police car coming down the road in a big hurry." As we gazed at the car it braked sharply and drew into the pub yard. The driver leapt out, came to the shed and asked if there was a Harry Spencer working here. Harry replied yes and the policeman told him to go with him now. Harry told me to look after things, climbed into the police car which accelerated out of the car park and up the road. The feeling of apprehension left me. Harry returned to work a few days later and told me his wife had fallen down the stone steps which led to the hay storage loft in the barn over the cattle below. She had lain there on this cold winter's day until the delivery man called. He raised the alarm, which included finding and taking Harry to the hospital where his wife had been taken. I had never had such a premonition before, and have never had one since.

After the Horse and Jockey episode I was sent with Charlie Hurley to work on a new house on Hackney Road, Darley Dale, now named Millfield. Charlie and I were helping Jack Johnson of Hall & Co to fix the heating pipes and the lead flashings around the chimney. Millfield had been built in a large field and the portion where the house stood was fenced off with wooden stakes and two or three strands of barbed wire. In the field were a few cows and what we thought was a very placid bull. The farmer then turned some sheep and a ram with big horns into the field. The bull went to investigate the new arrivals, and after an inspection he wandered off back to his cows. The ram followed the bull, eyeing him up and down. The bull ignored the ram. Moments later the ram trotted back about fifty or sixty feet, again eyed the bull, which was broadside on to him, and then started to run towards the unsuspecting bull at full speed, leaving the ground a few feet before striking him a mighty blow with his head and horns in the ribs. The bull turned from a placid animal to a raging beast in an instant. They charged one another again, head on but this time the ram met his match. He scrambled to his feet and ran off with the fearsome bull charging after him.

We had all lined up at the makeshift fence, having a grandstand view of this one-sided battle. All of a sudden the bull noticed us, turned and charged at us. He knocked down the fence, skipped over its remains, and flew after us as we raced to the half-completed house, and leaped in through the open doorway. The house had no windows or doors in at that stage. The bull was too massive to get through the doorway, thank goodness. He put his head through the window opening, snorting and bellowing. He then carried on around the outside of the house searching for a way in. He tossed anything he came across – Jack Johnson's plumber's bench, the wheel barrow and the mixer, and tried to get through the doorway again, still clearly very upset with life. Jack and I decided that discretion was the better part of valour and climbed through the first floor joists into the bedroom area, telling the others to scare him away. This was the equivalent of telling a man on a bike to frighten off a Tiger tank! When the bull eventually wandered off we put the fence back up but we had lost all faith in its ability to protect us. A quarrelsome ram and a bull do not make good neighbours.

HALL & CO.

In the early 1900s Robert Hall started a business in Dale Road, Matlock called Crown Hardware, in a shop close to the Olde English Hotel. Around 1932, after considerable expansion and diversification, the name was changed to Hall & Co Ltd. Frank Wildgoose, a plumber who had worked with Robert Hall for many years, had become a partner in the firm. In the late 1940s Hall & Co employed about one hundred highly skilled tradesmen, and I had the great pleasure of working alongside many of them. Most of them had served a seven-years apprenticeship with the firm. There were also shop and office staff, altogether a large happy family of workers. The shops and workshops could supply almost anything, from a ball of wool, pots and pans, to an industrial Robin Hood boiler. They could paint you a sign, or your house, and supply and fix things as diverse as a bathroom suite or a car windscreen. Hall & Co also had a travelling hardware shop. The tradesmen covered most trades. The plumbing foreman was George Bridge, painting and decorating was run by Bert Farnsworth, glazing by Bob Wragg and Graham Spencer, tinsmithing by George Gallimore, sign-writing by Bill Hodgson, Noel Walton and Norman Ash, and the electrical jobs by Eric Morton. In the shops were Miss B. Slater, Fred Pursglove, Charlie Gale and Ted Morton among others. Office staff were Ted Rogers and

Don Slater, and the heating wholesale side was run by Mr Bowlzer. My wife-to-be Barbara was his secretary. At her former employers, Heny and Loveday, the chief clerk was our friend and neighbour Leonard Geeson. Leonard sent us both a Valentine Card for a joke. He never told us for a very long time and Barbara and I each thought we had someone else fancying us!

On site all the painters wore white overalls and aprons, the joiners wore a white apron, other tradesmen dressed in blue overalls. Foremen usually wore brown shoes and a tie, and most of them wore a hat – anything from an ex-army beret to a trilby. A quick glance around a large construction site in those days told fellow workers who was who. The wonderful organisation of Hall & Co under Francis Wildgoose could, with its subsidiary David Sheldon, supply and fix almost anything in the construction industry. Sadly Hall & Co and David Sheldon ceased trading in the early 1960s. They were among the last of the old traditional and completely self-contained construction firms in this area. They had an excellent well earned reputation for craftmanship, service and satisfaction, from fixing a pane of glass to heating, plumbing, glazing and decorating a large school or hospital. Times have altered in the construction industry. Large firms now employ hosts of sub-contractors who are not always known to one another. Apprenticeships have now been replaced by relatively short-term training schemes such as NVQs.

WILDGOOSE'S

I eventually left David Sheldon and went to work for John Wm. Wildgoose & Sons in 1950, another excellent decision. The name Wildgoose has been associated with the construction industry in the Matlock area for at least one hundred and fifty years. In 1862 John and Lawrence Wildgoose were recorded as masons. By 1895 John was recorded as a stone merchant and quarry owner, and Lawrence T. as a builder and contractor. On 19th August 1896 John Wm.Wildgoose Ltd.

commenced business. Today, over one hundred years later, the firm is still prospering. Three generations of the family have led the firm, John William, his son Horace, and grandson John who is in charge today. The Wildgoose company have always maintained excellent relations with their workforce, some of whom are the third generation to be employed by them. In 2000 they had about eighty employees, twenty-two of whom were site managers, thirty office-based, and a team of fully experienced site workers.

When I worked for them in the 1950s they were a self-contained firm, strong on the stone side, with their own quarry on Matlock Moor run by Arnold Wagstaff. The blacksmith's shop was situated in their yard and works on Industrial Road, off Rutland Street, Matlock. The blacksmith, Jack Seedhouse, sharpened all the quarry tools and the workmen's tools, besides manufacturing railings, and helping to repair all things metal. They had a large joiners' shop, staffed by some of the best tradesmen to be found, run by foreman Harry Morris.

Horace Wildgoose

I owe a lot of my comparative success in life to Mr Horace Wildgoose and his marvellous band of construction workers. The older ones, some thirty or more years older than myself, were all first class tradesmen. Looking back I can see that we were like the travelling bands of builders of the 1300s and 1400s. Each and everyone had great pride in his particular job, from the lorry drivers to general foremen. Every day was an education. A lot of the men had been in the Forces and taken part in battles all over the world. Older men had been drafted to construct air fields and one man, Sam Oldfield, had even worked on the Mulbury Harbour – immense hollow concrete structures used in the invasion of France in 1944. I was becoming quite proficient at building.

The lorry picked us up in the morning at the Whitworth Institute at 7am. Most mornings I ran the mile from Highlands Cottage to the Whitworth Institute, not always in time for the transport, so I became a useful hitch hiker. In the winter we went to work and came home in the dark. I did not see much of our children. We always worked Saturday afternoons, returning to Darley Dale about 5 o'clock.

My first job with Wildgoose & Sons in 1950 was helping to build a large factory for the production of rock asphalt at Cawdor Quarry, Matlock, for the Ragusa Ashphalt Company, to which I was later to return several times. When we finished at Cawdor we moved to Greenaway Lane, Darley Dale, to build a new school. My mate at work, Harold Allen, and Brian Horobin, apprentice bricklayer, went with me. Brian had put the apex brick (top) on one side of the seventy feet high asphalt factory tower, and I did the same on the other side. Brian and I dug the first sods off to commence building the new school. The first job, as usual, was to build a snap (food) cabin. Excavating machinery arrived to strip the site. George Eaton drove the 10RB excavator and Sam Green drove the lorry. We had only been there for a few days when I heard a bang, looked over to the snap cabin and saw flames pouring out of the door. Bill, the disabled mashing man, had poured petrol on the sticks and coal in the stove to make it light and foolishly lit it whereupon, to his great surprise, it exploded. Brian and I charged in to the snap cabin and dragged him out, perhaps a bit more than slightly singed. He had the shakes so much he was almost vibrating. We boiled the kettle on the still burning wood plank seats and made him a cup of tea. He soon recovered.

We had a cold, wet winter on that job. Ernest Farnsworth was the general foreman and Harry Woodhouse was the foreman builder. Harry had served his time with Twyford's Builders, Darley Dale who ceased trading around 1936 while building the Eversleigh Rise houses at South Darley. Harry was a real master craftsman and an excellent man in every way. He taught me the finer points of building including Pythagoras's Theorem which enables one to be absolutely sure the building is square. Harry was a perfectionist – every detail of the building had to be exact and he also ensured that everyone else's work was.

After working on the Greenaway Lane School at Darley Dale Harold Allen and I found ourselves in the vanguard of yet another new school, the Charles White School at Starkholmes Road, Matlock. After we had erected the cabins the Ruston-Bucyrus RB10 tracked excavator arrived with its long-serving driver George Eaton. George and I had worked together several times before. He was around sixty years old, a flat cap and pipe man, a seasoned campaigner who had seen it all, a consistently hard and careful worker and one of the nicest men I knew. Driving the Ruston-Bucyrus was a very demanding job which required great skill and care. George expected the same level of skill from the men he worked with, refusing to work with men who were irresponsible about safety. When working in close proximity to a large excavator one has to be very alert.

George dug out the access road and all Wildgoose's lorry drivers worked on the job carting hardcore in and moving spoil around the site. These were Frank Hubbard, Harold Burnett, Sam Green, Alec Wood, and Harry Gebbie and Harry Evans when not working on other jobs. Wildgoose's lorry drivers were in a class of their own. Sam Green was small of stature, large of heart, sharp eyed, rarely seen without his trilby hat, and a cigarette dangling from his mouth. When Sam was a bit upset, when things weren't going well, he would put his head on one side, look up at me and tell me in no uncertain manner what should or could be done to put things right. Harry Evans had a straight-forward attitude towards work and his fellow workers, and always pulled his weight at work. Harry actually spent more time working with the builders than lorry driving – always willing, never moaning. Rugged featured, tall and well-built, Harry was not a man to be taken advantage of. Frank Hubbard was a placid, thoughtful man. I never saw him upset, always willing to help, another flat cap and pipe man. Comfortable springs to mind. Alec Wood was mostly on the road, carting sand and stone to various jobs, or working with the digger. Alec was self-assured, perky, with plenty to say. At lunch-time, with a little encouragement, he would tell us of his life's great adventure – driving his beloved army lorry from Egypt to Austria via the western desert, Sicily and Italy. Alec was inclined to be a bit belligerent when aroused, especially if his driving ability was questioned. Harold Burnett drove an ex-Army lorry, an Austin six-wheeler. He was a quiet man, and he too wore a flat cap. He rarely worked with the builders; he was always on the road fetching bricks, limestone and sand for the big jobs. Harry Gebbie drove a light lorry. Both the Harrys' lorries had a light metal and wood portable shelter which the men sat in on the back of the lorry on their way to and from work, which could be up to thirty miles away. Some of their time would be spent fetching material to the job, or working with the men. Harry Gebbie was a nice quietly spoken man, a steady driver, not always thrilled with the rough and tumble of the building trade. Another lorry driver was Fred Hayes. He rarely left his lorry to actually work with the workmen on various jobs. Fred mostly worked with the excavator or transporting materials to the sites. He was a quiet, dependable, unassuming person who got on with the job in hand. The two Harries, Gebbie and Evans, worked as a rule with the wandering stone gangs. Harry Evans could always be relied on to be, shall we say, resourceful when it came to acquiring equipment when needed. Fred Hayes, Alec Wood, Sam Green and Frank Hubbard provided the link between Wildgoose's various hands of builders – who was working where, new jobs, gossip etc. Wildgoose & Sons had well over a hundred men scattered on sites around Derbyshire.

As at Ragusa and Greenaway Lane Ernest Farnsworth was the site boss. He was busy setting out the large school. Harold and I worked with George Eaton on excavating the foundations to level, using lines, profiles and boning rods. Profiles mark the exact position and dimensions of the building to be. Boning rods are three identically-sized pieces of wood with a T piece on the top. In practice a rod at each end is set to a given level. The third rod is the traveller. When the top of the traveller lines in with the other two the ground under its base lines in exactly with each end.

On one particularly warm day we were working at the bottom of the site near to a public footpath to Riber from the Duke William pub. After lunch Harold, George and I wandered back down to where we were excavating. We had noticed a number of what looked like very large wasps, grey and yellow, darting about. George told us to look out as they were hornets. One settled on the boning rod – it looked like a miniature Lancaster bomber with a tail gun stuck out behind. The day was getting hotter and my shirt was open. The hornet suddenly took off, hit my chest and dropped down inside my shirt to the waist band of my trousers. I tried not to panic. Peering down my shirt I saw this horror-on-wings peering back up at me. It then set off crawling along my waist line. Still trying not to panic I felt it making its way towards my back. I decided it was now or never, so I carefully undid my belt and the two top buttons of my trousers. Grasping my shirt with both hands I suddenly ripped it out of my trousers and under pants. My mates were astonished at my actions. Leaping up and down I took my shirt off and shouted "A b***** hornet has gone down my shirt." At that moment I felt a stabbing burning pain, just as if someone had stuck a red hot poker in my hip. I was in an absolute panic when I was stung again in my groin. Throwing all caution aside I pummelled the area vigorously with my fists, then pulled my trousers and pants down. Still shouting swear words I searched my under-pants for the hornet. It was nowhere to be found. While I was standing there with my trousers and pants down a lady came walking down the footpath, took one look and immediately turned round and walked back up the path. Needless to say George and Harold were beside themselves with laughter. I made absolutely certain the hornet was nowhere to be seen before I dressed again. I don't think

I had ever seen a hornet before, and I certainly did not ever want to see one again. When we had built the school up to the floor level Harold and I and most of the gang that had been assembled left the job. The school was a Clasp Build type, similar to a giant meccano set. The Charles White school and the one at Greenaway Lane were designed to last for around thirty-five years. They are both still standing some fifty years later.

Hurst Farm

1950/51 saw me working on the new Hurst Farm Estate at Matlock where we were to build around sixty houses. The foreman was a fearsome character called Dick, an old-fashioned type, a tall, well built, square shouldered man with a ginger moustache and an uncompromising attitude. He was singularly devoid of any humour, as I suspected a man who had sixty houses to build and forty or so men to look after would be. The only machinery we had comprised one large and one small concrete mixer. There was no demarcation on the job. He ordered, we obeyed, and on occasion the bricklayers had to help the labourers to excavate foundations and drain trenches etc.

One morning a new bricklayer appeared and reported to Dick who told him to leave his tools in the cabin and collect a pick and shovel, and join the gang digging out the foundations for a pair of houses. There were perhaps ten men, including myself and four other bricklayers, digging steadily on this particularly cold drizzly morning. The new man announced to us that he was a bricklayer and felt he should not be digging. We told him that Wildgoose's bricklayers had never been known to have to dig and incited him to go and put the foreman straight. We held our breath as he went into Dick's cabin. A second later the cabin door flew open and out came the new bricklayer, closely followed by Dick, waving his arms, pointing at us and informing him in no uncertain terms "that we too were bricklayers and the faster he *** dug the sooner he would be *** bricklaying." The new man was a good sport and took the joke we played on him in good part.

If we had severe rain Dick would blow the whistle and we would adjourn to the cabin, usually about thirty of us on this quite large job. The stove would be stoked up, sometimes a kettle placed on it for a brew, wet clothes put to dry, and makeshift tables and seats set out for card schools. This was usually solo whist with moderate stakes. Other men talked and reminisced. Probably about one third of the men had been in the Forces. Some of them talked of the places they had been to, world-wide battles and experiences they had taken part in on land and sea. One man had been in the Parachute Regiment and told us he had been dropped into action twice, once in Africa and again in France. Another had been in the Far East, jungle fighting. Another man talked about life on board a warship in the Mediterranean convoys. None of them was shooting a line. One man kept us enthralled with humorous tales of his adventures in Cairo and the western desert, and the various ladies he encountered in the Middle East.

The ex-parachutist took command of the conversation, quizzing men as to where they had been and what they had done, also regaling us with his very interesting adventures in the paras. I was playing cards and my mate at that time, Dennis, sat quietly watching us and listening to the conversations. The para asked me what I had done in the war, and I told him nothing as I was only seventeen when the European war ended. I had failed my medical for the army. Turning to my mate Dennis, who had taken no part in the conversation, he asked "What did you do in the war"? Dennis remained silent for a few moments before he said "Nothing great like you! I was just a prisoner of war of the Japanese for three years, eight months and so many days. Beaten, starved and almost worked to death, praying every day to be spared, while my mates were dying around me." He bowed his head, obviously very upset. The cabin suddenly went quiet and still. Dennis had never previously mentioned to any of us that he had been a Japanese prisoner of war. All the men treated Dennis with great respect after his disclosure.

Later on, when Dennis and I were working alone, he told me of the totally unnecessary cruelty he and his fellow prisoners of war had suffered. They had worked on the docks about twenty miles away from Nagasaki unloading ships, and one day a bag of dried fruit burst. A fellow prisoner of war, who was literally starving to death, picked some up and ate it. He was seen and reported, and subsequently was beaten to death with bamboo sticks as a warning to the others. Poor Dennis wept as he told me. I could scarcely comprehend the pain and anguish which had been inflicted on Dennis and his comrades. He then told me it was the happiest and most satisfying day of his life when they dropped the atom bomb on Nagasaki. I have never forgotten Dennis's revelation.

Around this time I suffered from severe pains in my chest which some ten years later were almost to be the end of me. I went to work when I felt really too ill to go. One such day I was feeling particularly ill with these mysterious pains so I asked the foreman if he could find me a light job that day. He replied in builders' language that I could either work or **** off as there was no place for sick people on his jobs. I bore him no ill will, he had his job to do.

Mr Horace Wildgoose, the owner and managing director of John Wm. Wildgoose & Sons, was a truly excellent man. His company found employment for several handicapped people. They cleaned the snap cabin, boiled the water, kept the stoves going and in the winter dried your clothes and ran a few errands. One of the mashing shed cleaning men on the Hurst Farm job had very bad eyesight, and as a consequence wore spectacles with lenses like jam-jar bottoms. He was old, miserable, short and squat. The men had only a fifteen minutes break for breakfast so every moment was precious. When the whistle blew the men immediately formed a queue outside the mashing shed, where the water was boiled in an open cast iron coal fired clothes boiler. An arm holding a small pan of boiling water used to emerge from out of the steam from the mashing shed and pour the water out. You endeavoured to hold your mashing can in the right place to catch the boiling water without being scalded. When your can was sufficiently full you smartly took the can away and stood clear of the torrent of boiling water. Matters were not helped by the steaming up of the mashing man's thick glasses. Throughout each episode this mashing man groaned and grumbled as he tipped the pan towards your can or mug, pouring boiling water over hands and feet. This led to the men becoming very wary of him.

At Christmas time the men had a collection for him, which only raised seven shillings. At dinner time we presented him with the money and a chicken that one of the men had brought for his mate. We told him how wonderfully he looked after us, and what a nice man he was. Someone gave him the tip that if he plunged the chicken into a bucket of boiling water it would pluck very easily. The mashing man then made a very moving speech in which he mentioned that he had always thought we were rubbish and the scum of the earth and did not care about him but had now changed his mind about us. He then plucked and dressed the chicken and wrapped it in newspaper, and tied it up with string ready to take home. When he turned his back we stole the chicken and returned it to its rightful owner. The mashing man went mad when he found out and told us exactly what we were and got quite carried away with rage. He never saw the funny side of anything!

Another Christmas someone from Wildgoose's office came on to the job with our Christmas boxes in envelopes, which he gave to the foreman George White to distribute. We decided to play a joke on one builder who was slightly volatile. We steamed open his envelope, extracted the one pound note which was everyone's Christmas box, and put a ten shilling note in and re-sealed it. George then handed them out. The builder's face was a picture when he found he had only ten shillings. He was so upset that with our encouragement he got on his motorbike and went to see Horace Wildgoose. He angrily stormed into the office and gave Horace his ten shillings back. Horace said that only pound notes had been put in the envelopes and perhaps he ought to go back and have words with us. When he came back we all fell about laughing as he himself had a reputation as a practical joker.

The volatile builder of the ten shillings joke had us in fits of laughter when he told us quite seriously of his experience when he took his test for a motor cycle licence. He had an hour off work to go to Chesterfield to take the test. He was not familiar with the back streets of Chesterfield. He left us at 1.30pm and failed to return that day. Next day when we asked him how he had gone on he told us the sorry story of his test examination. He said the examiner had told him to proceed down the road and take the first turn left, then the second turn left, then the first turn left. He then told him that somewhere along the way he would step out into the road, holding his book in the air, when he should do an emergency stop. The builder took the second left instead of the first left, then the first left, then carried straight on. After a mile or so and seeing no-one he retraced his route, only to turn left at the wrong road, and become lost. He eventually found his way back to where he had started and the examiner, who by this time was conducting the next test, told him to go home, apply again, and listen to his instructions next time.

Also on the Hurst Farm job two of the men made blowpipes out of copper tube and fired lumps of putty at unsuspecting men. I became their target for a couple of days. They were a bit too rough and tough for me to handle so on the third day I took my trusty catapult. When the first lump of putty hit me I took out my catapult and fired a granite pebble back. The pebble burst on the brickwork alongside the putty shooter, severely marking the brickwork. I fired another which did the same, and I had no more trouble.

Toilets on building sites before today's health and safety rules were very primitive. In 1947, when I was working for David Sheldon, George Twigg and I had carried out repairs to a cottage alongside the River Derwent at Wenslees near Darley Bridge. The toilet to this dwelling was a wooden structure protruding precariously about eight feet (2·4m) over the river. One very cold winter's morning I had occasion to use this toilet, which was constructed similarly to an earth closet. A bench seat with a hole in the centre stretched from side to side with a plank front and a wooden floor. Looking down through the hole I could see the river down below. The door had a gap underneath and over the top. This particular morning it was not only freezing but an icy wind was blowing down the valley. It was so draughty in that toilet that the wind kept blowing my shirt up. I must still hold the record for the shortest time spent in a loo.

On large jobs we constructed an earth toilet by digging a large hole about four feet (1·2m) cube then planking it over leaving a hole about two feet (600mm) square in the centre. We then fixed the thunder box with the hole under the bench-type seat. Next to the thunder box we constructed a urinal out of timber and zinc sheets with a drain pipe leading to the pit. On the Hurst Farm job a collie dog came to visit us most snap times, hoping for a few scraps He was a very inquisitive dog and this curiosity led literally to his downfall. While waiting for lunch time the dog decided to investigate the toilet and somehow managed to drop in the pit. We could hear him whimpering and trying to get out and after removing a plank or two and digging one side in a bit the long haired collie dog made it out. He was a nightmare sight. All of a sudden he shook himself. I have never seen men move so fast. Someone threw a bucket of water over him. The poor dog had had enough and he went trotting off back home, surrounded by a multitude of flies and a dreadful smell. I only hope they had all the doors shut when he arrived home.

Using the thunder box could be hazardous if the men on the job decided to play a joke on the occupant. The commonest one was to pass a rope around the toilet box and then tie it tightly. The door always opened outwards so the occupant was a prisoner. The box would then be rocked from side to side. The most hazardous for users were chemical toilets which had a pipe from underneath the rear of the seat to the outside for ventilation. After a few minutes of occupation by some innocent unsuspecting person a piece of newspaper wrapped around a thin piece of wood was lit, and when well alight it was smartly inserted into the pipe. This had a miraculous effect on the occupant who suddenly found himself sitting on a fire. If the door had been roped shut the outcome could be dramatic. I have seen the most placid, peaceful man one could ever meet turn into a raging maniac. It certainly tested one's sense of humour to the limit.

Sometimes several of us were drafted to another gang led by Harry Woodhouse. 1951 was the year of the Festival of Britain and Harry had the great honour of being picked to build all the stone walls and fix the masonry at the Festival site in London. I was so proud to work alongside such a great craftsman and teacher. To make life even better he was a truly nice man.

Harry Woodhouse, Harold Allen, Harry Gebbie and I were sent from the Hurst Farm job to build a hall on to the Methodist Church at Hathersage, a village some thirteen miles north of Darley. On this job we had nowhere to put the pump which kept the foundation trench free of water on this very wet site, so we put it in the allotment garden next to the site. Next morning we found a large notice fastened to the pump. It read "Whoever put this pump on my allotment has got a bloody cheek. You have ruined my raspberry canes and flooded my plot." Arthur Hayes, who was also working on the job, stopped off and acquired some wild raspberry plants about 5 feet (1·5m) high. He dug out the bedraggled old plants and planted the new ones, covering the roots with soil. He then concreted the plants in, topping them off with a few inches of soil. We then removed the pump. Next morning a new notice read "Thank you."

1952 was the year of the birth of our daughter Beryl. I was quietly working on the Hathersage job when, on 4th April 1952, the local post office manager came up the drive, asked for me and told me he had received a telephone call to pass on to me. The message was that Barbara had had twins. I was staggered. About an hour later the men told me that Barbara had given birth to one child, a daughter. They had previously been to the post-office across the road and asked the manager to help them with their joke.

Another joyless job we were posted to was the Ogston Reservoir.

Harold and I built the brick manholes to the drains on the new main road. Again we had no facilities, only an old decrepit barn to share with about thirty other workmen One of the men I met there was a shot firer called Jack from Ashover. He was clearing the bed of the reservoir-to-be of large trees. He accomplished this by drilling a two inch diameter hole down through the base of the tree to underneath it, putting a stick or two of gelignite down the hole and firing it. This produced a spectacular happening. With a loud bang the tree, complete with its root, leapt into the air then fell with an almighty crash to the ground. Jack and I were to meet again years later on another job.

THE STONE GANG

After the birth of our second daughter Lesley in 1954 I asked Horace Wildgoose for more money. He said he could not pay me more per hour, but I could go on the stone fixing gang who worked up to thirty-six miles away so you got more time in, an extra hour per day. We were only paid travelling time one way. The lorry left the Whitworth Institute at 7am sharp and returned to the Whitworth at 6.45. I was still living at Highlands Cottage, Bent Lane, Darley Hillside at that time.

When I became an outside worker on big jobs in local towns and cities, fixing masonry stone for Wildgoose, my confidence grew in leaps and bounds. We worked these outside jobs in gangs of four to ten men. Looking back we were a fairly wild bunch, always commandeering the best place in the snap cabin, always endeavouring to outclass and out-work the other firm's men in every way. We were arrogant and proud of our skills, and all-round abilities. We all looked after one another, and all of us knew that Wildgoose's would look after us. Harold Allen, Charlie Hopkinson, George White, Vic Shimwell, Jack Carter, myself and Harry Evans our lorry driver/labourer were the nucleus of our gang of travelling masonry fixers. George White, the gang foreman, taught me how to work and build masonry. I took up masoning, practising at home to improve my skills. For several years I did nothing else. I also worked for a very short time in Wildgoose's Lumsdale Quarry. We were all also competent drain layers, bricklayers, concreters and scaffolders. I thoroughly enjoyed every day right through the 1950s. We were an excellent gang of men who all got on with one another. We had such fun and adventures at work. The escapades we got into were unbelievable

Nineteenth century mason fixers who built the railway bridges and abutment walls, also huge stone dam walls, were I believe the best stone craftsmen the world has ever seen. I am sure they could have built the pyramids with no trouble, probably better and more quickly than the original builders. The immense stone clad walls similar to the Derwent and Howden dam walls in the Peak District of Derbyshire are a work of art, sneck walling at its best. With the correct number of "through" stones sneck walling is the strongest. A through stone is one that goes through the wall, tying it together in depth. No two sections of wall are exactly the same. Building it is similar to playing chess, weighing up in your mind the possible results of your present action. When several men are working together on a length of sneck walling, which was our speciality, concentration and co-ordination whilst carrying out the construction is paramount for a good job.

Harry Woodhouse and I built three Methodist Church Halls together in the early 1950s, two at Darley Dale. Harry had been a keen footballer, as a goalkeeper. I believe he played for around thirty years. His friend was Eddie Shimwell from Birchover who won an FA Cup Final medal with Blackpool in 1953 and later kept the Plough Inn in Two Dales. Harry told me about Eddie Shimwell's final while we were building Darley Dale's Dale Road Methodist Hall. Harry must have been disappointed in me. I was no football fanatic. Harry described in detail to me almost every kick in the game at break times. Harry and I, Harold Allen and Lew Farnsworth from Starkholmes, who was Harry's mate, also worked together on the extension to the Darley Hillside Methodist Church. When passing by some of the buildings I worked on over a wide area I visualise them through their various stages of construction from first going on to the site, a vacant plot, to the final completion. I remember the men, some of whom were real characters and had spent their lives moving from one construction site to another, leaving behind lasting monuments to their skill and way of life. Those who became addicted to it were a very hardy breed of men.

Our stone gang, led by George White, repaired or rebuilt about a dozen chimneys on Worksop Manor, a huge building like Chatsworth House. It was seventy feet to the chimney tops from the ground, and the chimneys were in a very dangerous condition, but Harold and I had no worries as we always did our own scaffolding and had complete trust in our scaffolding ability. Worksop Manor was the home of the Farr family who owned the Home Brewery and at that time, the mid-fifties, also owned about sixty race horses including the world famous Shining Light. To repair the chimneys, which were built of stone with overhanging caps, we scaffolded up to the lead flat about two feet wide which served to run the roof water off. The lead flat was on top of a corbelled cornice which protruded about two feet from the building, about fifty feet from the ground. We used a roof ladder to help us fix the scaffold up to the ridge. The roof ladder had a hook at the top which hooked over the roof ridge to stop it sliding down. When we had finished scaffolding we put the roof ladder further along the roof out of harm's way.

Captain Farr's son climbed up the ladders fastened to the scaffold from the ground to the lead flat to inspect the work to the chimney. We did not pay much attention to him. He then walked along the lead flat over the corbel and had climbed halfway up the roof ladder, which had been lodged temporarily on the roof upside down, with the hook away from the ridge. He was halfway up when we noticed him. All went very quiet. A couple of the men then went on the lead flat and held the roof ladder. Why ever it did not slide off the roof, with Farr on it, is a mystery.

We worked there for about four months, and towards the end of the job it was Christmas. Captain Farr's land agent/estate manager said that the Captain would like us to line up at dinner-time on Christmas Eve with the rest of his estate workers. We were full of anticipation, which palled a bit when we saw the estate workers appearing with small parcels containing scarfs, gloves and woollen hats. My turn came and I was called into the Estate Office by the agent, who looked to me like Captain Farr's ex-Army Sergeant-Major. The Captain sat at his massive desk laden with parcels. He thanked me for the work we had carried out on the chimneys, then reached down behind the desk, picked up a rabbit and gave it to me. The estate was alive with rabbits at that time, and we considered them pests. Harry Evans the lorry driver then sloped off into the woodland pheasant pens adjacent to the Manor and came back with several pheasants, then we all went home.

On another job were given a very steady labourer who was very adept at not working. He had the habit of stopping work half an hour before knock-off to wash his wellingtons in a hole he had made, about six inches deep and eighteen inches square. Sending him out of the way we dug it two feet deep and filled it with muddy water. When, as usual, he stepped in the water he fell in over his wellington tops – result, cured of welly-washing and time wasting.

Around the mid 1950s Harold and I were sent with Harry Woodhouse and his mate Henry Waterfall to Bakewell cattle market to built an extension, in stone, to the pedigree cattle shed. I was used to the market because of going there with my pigs. The cattle market was not only a market, it was a gathering of farmers, large and small. Tractors towing trailers loaded with all manner of farm stock and produce were scattered around the market area. Men endeavouring, with the aid of sheep dogs and walking sticks, to unload their trailers and put the bewildered stock into the sale pens. In summer time towny-type tourists could be seen anxiously eyeing up the cattle that were occasionally walked from their transport to the pens, cooing over the young lambs and piglets. Some livestock was still walked to market. One could buy almost anything there, from a load of hay or straw to a clutch of young chicks. There was a hustle and bustle about the market, the shouts of the auctioneers, the lowing of the cattle, pigs grunting, sheep bleating, cocks crowing and dogs barking. There was cow muck, loose straw, and an all-pervading smell of the farmyard.

We were working there when they held what must have been one of the last horse fairs at the Bakewell market ground. Men and horses of all types and sizes appeared all morning, young boys ran and rode them up and down the market road. Teeth and feet were thoroughly scrutinised, legs and necks felt, eyes looked into. Men stood in small serious-looking groups discussing various points. These men were dressed differently from the usual farmers who mostly wore leather leggings, cord trousers, a battered and weather-stained hat, and a buff coloured smock. The horse traders wore, to my practised eye, a more civilian-type dress, with shoes instead of mucky boots, and jackets and trousers. I surmised a number of them to be gypsies who were noted horse traders. It was the end of an era that had lasted thousands of years, the finale of the working horse, man's faithful workmate redundant, now in 2006 just a relic of a bygone age. When I was a boy horses were commonplace, a necessity on a farm. Today they are a liability. When you think of the first world war you think of the suffering of men but thousands of horses also suffered dreadful deaths there. Today's Bakewell livestock markets, compared with the ones I knew fifty or sixty years ago, are about as lively and interesting as a dead sheep. In those days it was common to see several horse and traps waiting patiently for their owners, animals of all shapes and sizes milling about. Excitement and expectation flowed through the market area. I have been very fortunate to have worked and taken part in that age-old institution, Bakewell market.

We worked on several churches and George White and I altered All Saints Church at Matlock, taking down the gable and extending the church with a new entrance. The previous gable had a large stone cross on top of the west gable end. (Any embellishment on top of a gable end is called a finial.) The Minister asked for the cross to be saved. We put a treble extension ladder up the roof from the ground resting on the

Left: *Crich Church*
Above: *Harry Evans*
Below left: *New entrance to All Saints, Smedley Street, Matlock*
Below right: *Finial cross on gable*

slates but it only reached two-thirds of the way up the steep pitched roof. We then hung a wooden roof crawler ladder from the ridge and securely tied it to the ladder. Harold and I went up and stood on the ridge, then lifted the one hundredweight cross out of its socket and lowered it down on a rope. There is a magnificent view of Matlock from the top of All Saints Church roof. I sometimes look at the new entrance and marvel how we built it with no crane, and very little equipment.

We replaced the gargoyle on Crich church tower and made it as a caricature of Harry Evans, the lorry driver, who had rather a big nose. Harry has now passed away but our tribute to him will be there for centuries. After the Crich church job we went to Conjoint Lane at Tideswell to build a semi-bungalow for Mr Shaw, a cattle dealer. Mr Shaw's wife was secretary to L. du Guard Peach, the playwright. Mr Peach visited the job often and I enjoyed talking with him about Derbyshire. He signed and gave me one of his books. Harold and I and our boxer dog Mandy used to go hare chasing at dinner-time over Tideswell Moor. I worked on the stone extension to Queen Elizabeth's School at Ashbourne. This included a tall chimney which narrowed the higher it became. We built the extension out of rough rubble stone which we dressed ourselves under a tarpaulin sheet shelter, mostly when it rained.

We did a lot of work around Nottingham and Worksop. Once, while we were working at Nottingham, one of the gang had his tea mashed by a very comely lady who lived nearby and exchanged conversation with him when she passed by the building site. After a while he stayed at her house for dinner, and became very friendly with her. We were all busy at work on the stone boundary wall to this public building when a furious man appeared. "Which of you has been with my wife?" he shouted, and pulled out a wicked looking knife. If he was trying to intimidate us he had no chance. All seven of us immediately armed ourselves with picks and shovels, hammers etc. The foreman told him that if he set foot on the job we would "have him." We were all in our prime and could be, when necessary, even more intimidating than him. "I know which one of you it is" he said "and I am going to get him." Just then a passing bus slowed down in the traffic on the road next to the site. As it speeded up the person he referred to leapt on it and vanished. We told the man to clear off (or the builders' equivalent) and the builder in question never went back to that job at Nottingham.

Our gang worked around Nottingham for several years. We worked on the Teachers' Training College at Clifton, now part of Nottingham University, the Queen Charlotte Pub at Carlton, the Hemlock Stone at Wollaton, the Magpie at Stapleford, the Fire Station at Ruddington, a block of flats at Stapenhill near Burton. Our stone building gang usually consisted of six or seven men. George and Harry travelled in the cab of the lorry. The rest of the gang travelled in a tin shelter on the back of the three-ton Bedford lorry. Solo whist was played all the way to work as well as at lunch time and on our way home if it was not too dark in winter time.

At Clifton the site ran adjacent to a main road and around forty men in total worked there. On the second day a shout went round the site. "Line up, show some respect." Some of the main contractor's men went to the edge of the pavement, took off their hats and bowed their heads, all looking very solemn. They beckoned us to join them, to pay our respects, which we did, as did several people who were passing the site. I could see no sign of a funeral cortege as we all stood silently with the passers-by. All of a sudden the men cheered and waved their caps in the air as a brewery lorry went past. We played this joke two or three times a week, and embarrassed many who joined us in showing our respects.

In the winter we would troop into the snap shed early on our first day of a new job and sit on the seats near the usually glowing stove. This inevitably led to friction with the men who usually sat there. We were all united.in our stance, and an unknown quantity to the resident workers. With having a rough appearance, and all of us well built, this ploy usually worked. I became used to arriving on a construction site, weighing up the men and the job as they too were at the same time assessing our characters and skills. Each job had a hierarchy of men with great skills and character. Many of them had more practical common sense than most people. They had an initiative test every other day. When people look at a completed building they always assume that when it was built conditions were excellent. In reality it was probably raining, freezing or going dark, the scaffolding was not the right height, and the materials not as satisfactory as they could be. The tradesman is either too cold or too hot, or cannot easily reach the work, and there is no time left to remedy the situation. Skill, persistence, experience and loads of common sense, combined with fortitude, are essential for construction workers. We travel to some empty space, set up a factory of sorts, and produce a product which could be anything from a wc to a cathedral. Our carefully manufactured product, probably unique, is expected to last for many years trouble-free. We then move off, complete with the factory of sorts, to another empty space and repeated the process. By the very nature of the job it consists of a life of moving on to pastures new, and rarely making the same product twice.

When we arrived on one fairly large job in Nottingham the general foreman on the job was called Derek. I thought I had seen them all, but I had not worked with anyone who was such a character as him. At dinner break he came in and collected the money for the daily sweepstake. Every one received a raffle ticket which was then drawn out of a bucket. The winner received half the money and Derek took the other half. He had the joiners making small garden sheds which he sold to local residents. His crowning achievement was getting the men to build a garage for someone in the next street. If you worked on one of Derek's private enterprises he paid you a bonus out of the sweepstake money. He wanted us to build a stone boundary wall on one of his private enterprises and could not understand how we could forego earning some extra money on the side. In spite of his sidelines Derek ran the job extremely well, setting out and inspecting everyone's work thoroughly.

Horace Wildgoose called me into the office and told me I was going to be sent to build a railway bridge facade on the new A1(M) part of the Doncaster bypass scheme. There would only be four men on the job, and would I transport them in my ex-post office van. I said yes and two or three days later Harold, Jack, Vernon and I embarked on our journey at 7am from Darley Dale. It was summer time. We knew our way to Worksop having worked on Worksop Manor, and from there went on the B6045 to Blyth, then on to the partially constructed motorway to the site of the railway bridge. The bridge had already been constructed out of concrete and all we had to do was to build a stone facing to it. Two of Wildgoose's lorries duly arrived with loads of stone all cut to size and shape. The wooden shuttering to form the arch was already in place.

Studying the plans I decided to check the measurements before we started. It was just as well I did as I found the opening was approximately eighty millimetres (three and one eighth inches) too wide. I went off in the van to interview the general foreman and the result was a full-scale meeting headed by the engineer in charge, a Mr. Gordon Race. It was agreed by all that it was much better for the opening to be a little wider than too small, which would have been a catastrophe. I told Gordon Race I had the answer. I would make the keystone eighty millimetres wider so there was no need to make a fuss. The job went exceedingly well. Very few trains ran on the branch line. When building the parapet wall which was above the arch, I found that it was cambered and so became a relieving arch, taking weight off the bridge. I have since noticed this on many bridges. It must have been one of the last rail bridge facades to be built of stone. Gordon Race and I were to meet again a few years later.

Our largest bricklaying job was building the west gables to Firth Rixson's factory at Darley Dale. Hundreds of thousands of bricks were all delivered by rail to Rowsley railway sidings, then were shunted through the factory by Firth Rixson's own standard gauge loco. We unloaded them by hand. The only mechanical aids we had were one mixer and a barrow hoist. George White was the foreman and many different bricklayers worked on the job, including sixty-nine years old Tom Ainscoe. The gable was about fifty feet high.

Shortly after building the gable at Firth Rixson's we were sent there again to take down two old furnace chimneys from the fifty feet high asbestos-sheeted main roof area. These chimneys were made of steel and were about fifteen feet high. Our difficulties began with access. Neither Harold nor I had any fear of either heights or depths, and had had no trouble removing the finial from the high gable of All Saints' Church. This job presented us with the same problem – there were no ladders long enough for the job. Harold and I spliced two long pole ladders together so we could reach the gutter which was about forty feet from the ground. We climbed up into the gutter and firmly secured the ladder with rope to a gutter stay, as we had always been taught to do. Health and safety in those days was a common sense attitude to dangers to yourself and others around you. Once established on the roof we pulled up planks and scaffold tubes, ropes etc. to do the job. About 4pm I went down the ladder to tie some equipment on to the rope for Harold to pull up, which he did while standing in the twelve inch (300mm) wide cast iron gutter.

I went back up the ladder, perhaps in too much of a hurry. The ladders were swaying in and out from the building a bit. My head was

Firth Rixon

about five feet below the gutter, when with a bang the top ladder broke in half under my feet, and the rung fell out. Luckily, or through "know how," my hands were positioned exactly right for me to take hold of the sides of the ladder. When I worked for David Sheldon with George Twigg I was taught never to take my hands off the sides of a ladder. After hanging on for a few moments to the remains of the ladder, which was dangling by the fastening rope some thirty feet above the concrete yard, I managed to scramble up and, helped by Harold, get into the twelve inches wide gutter. It took us almost an hour to gain someone's attention, and another hour before another long treble extension ladder could be obtained to enable us to get down. They say that anything that makes your heart beat does you good. I must have been set up for life as I hung from the ladder.

When working on the rectory at Morton, near Clay Cross, we had occasion to strip off part of the roof. When George White's gang arrived next morning we found a small river flowing down the stairs and out from under the front door. A strong wind had ripped the tarpaulin sheet off the roof in the stormy night. The Rector, Canon Cross, and his wife and daughter had to go and live in a caravan in the garden. The rectory was having a complete renovation, plumbing, heating, electrics etc., which entailed taking up sections of floorboard upstairs. We were working in a passage-way on the ground floor, concreting, when suddenly a leg came through the ceiling, bringing down a shower of plaster on to us. It was an old ceiling constructed of wood laths nailed to the underside of the floor joists, with plaster pushed up between the gaps in the laths to form a key to hold up the plaster ceiling. The laths which had broken formed a ring, sticking into the leg which now protruded through the ceiling to the top of the thigh. It was an early 1800s vicarage with high ceilings. We had to get a step ladder to break free the laths which had formed a vice-like grip around the leg when the owner of the leg tried to withdraw it. Blood was running down his leg when we managed to free him. The Rector's wife, alerted by his shouts and screams, placed a chair in the garden for him and administered first aid to his wounds with some disinfectant, which produced more screams and moans. The reason for the waving leg through the ceiling was the result of someone putting a piece of hardboard over the hole where the floorboards had been taken up, to save the ceiling underneath.

Canon Cross and his wife were very, very nice people; we found it a joy to work for them. George White and I were taking out a bedroom window and in the gap between the window and the wooden window bottom we saw a ticket, about 75 x 40mm. It was a ticket to the opening of the Stockton Thirsk Railway in the 1830s. Can you imagine how they must have searched for it. George took the ticket home. This must have been around 1956. On the same job Harold found a silver coin from Henry VIII's time. A week or two later, working on the roof of the vicarage on a hot cloudless day I became ill with sunstroke. Canon Cross took me home in his car, for which I was most grateful. Otherwise I would have had to stay until knocking-off time, then walk the last mile up to my home on Darley Hillside.

The following year I found a gentleman's sword hidden behind a beam in an old empty stone-slated hall roof. I still have it. I took it to an Antiques Road Show at Chatsworth and they said it was made in the 1700-1750 period. The strangest find I ever saw was when we were digging a deep trench under the railway at Darley Dale station. We found this massive tree trunk at about 2·7 metres deep. It was solid oak and as black as the ace of spades. It had large smooth pebbles all around it and only the first few centimetres were rotten. The trunk must have been thousands of years old.

In the mid 1950s in order to earn a bit of extra money Harold Allen and I took on the job of looking after large Lancashire and Cornish boilers that heated places like Rockside Hydro, Smedley's Hydro (now Derbyshire County Council headquarters), St Elphin's School and Miss White's School at Wellington Street, Matlock. After the boilers had cooled down for two or three days Harold and I used to completely strip, put on old overalls and very very old coats and disappear down the flue, fetching out the soot and bagging it up. When the flues were clean we repaired the firebrick work in the flues and made sure that the flue dampers worked properly. After we had finished for the day we bathed together and scrubbed one another's back.

At St. Elphin's we bathed in the laundry in a large bath with wheels on. St Elphin's was at that time a religious girls' school and the staff seemed to be chosen for their piety. We gave them some tidy shocks. One day a man polled up from the school to assist us. I told him to watch his language, no *** and blinding as they were mostly religious people here. He replied "Don't worry about me, I am a parson doing voluntary work for the school." Rockside Hydro had been converted to a teacher-training college. I examined the boiler flue which went a long way underground to the chimney. When I came out my skin had turned pink and my overalls fell to pieces. Acid had condensed out into the flue, and my boots also disintegrated shortly afterwards. When we had finished in the flues for the day both we and our clothes were absolutely jet black so we went into the domestic coal shed, took off our clothes and gave them a vigorous shaking, then came out naked and went for a bath. The coal shed was very full so it would only hold one of us at a time. Harold had gone in to undress and shake his clothes when a young lady came into the boiler room and asked me if I had the key to a nearby room. I thought it would be fun to tell her that the man who had the key was working in the coal house and she must knock on the door to get his attention. This she did. The door opened and there stood Harold in all his black naked glory, his eyes and teeth gleaming white. The young lady forgot all about the key and ran off up the stairs.

Harold and I helped to install a new Lancashire boiler at Smedley's Hydro boiler house. We worked continually for about twenty hours changing the boiler over. The soot was so ingrained in our skin with sweat that Smedley's let us use their Turkish baths to try and get us clean. Talk about Victorian boy chimney sweeps! We got paid about one shilling extra per hour for this work, which is why we undertook this very demanding job on. I still had the occasional pains in my chest.

At Stapenhill, near Burton, we built the stone front to a block of flats that were being built in the grounds of a very large, empty brick Hall. The Hall had been securely locked and boarded up. We had our dinner in the nearby horticultural out-building. The overgrown garden contained many rose borders and every day I used to pick and take home a lovely bunch of roses for Barbara or my mother. We found a small cellar in the outbuilding which had a narrow dark passage leading off it. This passage led to another cellar under the Hall which was full of junk from yesteryear, almost impassable. Making our way through and over the junk we ascended some steps and found ourselves in the Hall. The Hall interior from kitchens to attic was clean and empty. Imagine our surprise when on the first floor we opened a door and found ourselves in a ballroom, complete with a large built-in organ and a small stage. It was a lovely Hall. I have never been back to see what became of it.

Of all the places I worked in Nottingham impressed me most, the teeming streets and especially the thronged square in front of the Town Hall. Occasionally we would pile into the lorry at lunch time and have our dinner in the square haranguing the ever present speakers. Our favourite tactic was to call out "It's all lies; that's another lie; he's talking rubbish," and so on. One or two of the speakers used to lose their cool but with six or seven working men interrupting them and shouting abuse, who wouldn't. No matter what their subject was we vehemently opposed it. Onlookers cheered and clapped us. Public speaking in the square was a great pastime and entertainment for everyone.

Our stone gang and George Eaton with the 10RB excavator were sent to build an immense ten to fifteen feet high retaining wall for Brocklehurst Motors of Chesterfield. The site was a disused quarry on the old A61 Sheffield Road, which Brocklehurst's had been using since the end of the war and which is now occupied by Iceland and other shops. A civil engineering firm called Mullan's levelled off the area and extracted several hundred tons of gritstone to be used to build the huge retaining wall. My experience of cutting up large stones came in very handy; some of the pieces weighed up to twenty tons. Large stones are comparatively easy to cut up. First find the bed of the stone. These are the layers mostly visible in the stone, similar to pages in a book. Place the stone so that the beds are in a vertical plane and cut a narrow groove about two inches deep, with a quarry pick, against the bed, ie at right angles to it. Knock steel stone-edges in the groove with a small hammer. When tight hit them in rotation with a sledge hammer. If possible the groove should be in the centre of the stone. If the stone is very deep it pays to knock a pointed steel punch in each side, about two thirds of the way down. With the 10RB George moved the cut stones, several weighing over one ton, and lifted them into place on the wall. The wall was constructed without any scaffolding. We actually stood on the four feet (1·2m) thick wall to build it. I have been back many times to look at this monumental piece of work.

We had a four-tool compressor on the job, powered by a weary Ruston-Bucyrus diesel engine. The apprentice on the job was told to check the oil level on the engine at dinner-time. After dinner we started the diesel engine with the starting handle. It ran for a few moments then the speed of the engine increased. Huge clouds of smoke came out of the exhaust and one of the men pulled the engine stop. It made no difference, the engine was now running faster than ever. Because it was a still day the dense engine smoke was assuming the dimensions of a small atom bomb. We knew the engine was about to explode. George picked up a hammer, calmly walked up to the engine and knocked the fuel pipe off, but instead of stopping the engine, if anything it went even faster. We all took cover and I had visions of the engine disintegrating and showering us with shrapnel. The engine was now literally humming. Motioning onlookers to clear off we waited for the engine to explode. Miraculously it held together and after a good while missed a beat or two and gradually slowed down then stopped. George asked the apprentice what he had done to the engine. "Nothing" he replied "I only filled it up with oil." George asked if he had checked the dipstick. The apprentice hung his head and asked what a dipstick was. "I filled it up to the top of the oil filler with oil." Because the engine was old and worn it had been running on the oil splashed up from the sump. It says a lot for the quality of the engine that after draining out some oil and refixing the fuel pipe it ran normally. The apprentice learned a lesson he would never forget, and he wasn't the only one. The amenities on this site were atrocious. There was no glass in the cabin window, no stove, no toilet, lots of mud and large puddles. Wellington boots were a necessity. It was very hard work and we were glad to get away from this joyless job.

At the time of the dreadful east coast floods in the early 1950s all Wildgoose's heavy lorries were sent there carrying loads of limestone from Matlock to help plug the gaps in the sea defences. Only one man lost his way. Needless to say it was Alec, the lorry driver who was always telling us how he navigated his way from Cairo to Austria. Alec always denied he had been lost but never lived it down.

For a short time in 1958, between stone fixing jobs, our usual gang was sent to Hurd's Hollow at Matlock to work on a stone built bungalow with a shop attached. About 11am one morning I was building away on the scaffold when a police car stopped on the road outside. The policeman got out, walked on to the site and asked for Lewis Jackson. I could tell by the look on his fact that it was something serious. I was about to suffer another of life's jolts. "Bad news" he said. "I have just been to your mother-in-law's house to tell her that her husband has been killed, and she has sent me to ask you to break the news to your wife." I went home to to Highlands Cottage and broke the bad news to Barbara as gently as I could and took her to her mother's house at Matlock. Barbara's father had served seventeen and a half years in the RAF including war service in the western desert and the middle east. He was a sergeant armourer and had not long to go before the end of his service. He had been killed in an accident on the Great North Road while riding his motor cycle back to his RAF base. I promised Barbara I would never ride a motor bike again. I was reminded of the dreadful day in September 1939 when mother and I had to break the news to her daughter-in-law Bertha that her husband John had been killed.

I was moved away from the stone gang in 1959 to work with Fred Walker on an extension to the Tor Hosiery on Dimple Road, Matlock. Fred was the brother of Norman Walker who I had worked with at Two Dales Co-op. I was then posted to Bakewell to work on a large single storey building being constructed on the site of what was Taylor's Garage on Matlock Street, which we first had to demolish. We found the building had once been an old sawmill. We uncovered a pit with the carriage bits and pieces in it. The general foreman was called Smith. I knew most of the men on the site.

Wildgoose & Sons had also been awarded the contract to demolish the Wheatsheaf Inn on Bridge Street at Bakewell and build a new one on the same site, keeping at least one room open for the public – an almost impossible task! Bob Ainscough, brother of Tom, and I were moved from the Taylor's Garage job to build the large single storey dining room extension to the Wheatsheaf. While Bob and I were

1962 The dining extension to The Wheatsheaf Inn, Bakewell

working there the men working on the actual pub, excavating the foundations, uncovered an old well. My thoughts turned to buried treasure. Who knows what valuables may be lurking at the bottom of this old well. Unfortunately it was ten feet deep and three parts full of water. I knew there was a good water pump on the Taylor's Garage site so I borrowed it and pumped out the water, put a short ladder down, and delved about in the mud at the bottom. The only thing I found was a smallish bowl-like object made of stone with a small lug on each side. I took it home and placed it in the garden. Years later, when visiting Bakewell church, I noticed the old font appeared to be a much larger version of my stone bowl. I subsequently found that before the Reformation (1530s) holy water was carried in these miniature fonts and sprinkled onto the congregation by the priest. I knew it was part of Bakewell's heritage so I gave it to the Old House Museum where, so far as I know, it still is.

Building our Bungalow

Highlands Cottage was very old, damp and cold, and when our daughter Beryl was five years old she had pneumonia and was taken to Derby City Hospital. From there she was sent to Bretby, near Burton-on-Trent to convalesce. I was at that time working on the Firth Rixson wall job. I finished work at 5.45pm which gave just enough time for Barbara and me to take our two younger children to one of their grandmothers, then visit Beryl at Derby. Bretby was too far away to visit after tea. I mentioned this at work and a workmate from Wirksworth, Les, who was the proud owner of a 500cc Triumph Twin motor Cycle, offered to take me from Wirksworth to Bretby on his Triumph. Les and I must hold the record for the journey. The men at work asked after Beryl every day and when she returned home a lovely surprise awaited her and me. One of Wildgoose's men, Ben Edge, from Oker, had made her a rocking horse which gave many hours of pleasure to Beryl and our other children over many years.

Having three young children we decided that if possible we should utilise my skills and build ourselves a bungalow. A Mr Cook had purchased Hallowes's Cherry Tree Farm, the farm of the never-to-be-forgotten wartime breakfasts, which included land at the junction of Moor Lane and Whitworth Road on Darley Hillside. This area of land had sentimental memories for me as it was where my father had kept his poultry, and where, as a young boy, I had hitched rides on Stancliffe's steam locos up to the Hall Dale Quarry. Mr Cook asked two hundred pounds for the building plot and, borrowing a little money off our parents, we scraped the money together, about thirty weeks wages. We were on our way to a bright future. The plans I had drawn up were for a three bedroom bungalow. Why a bungalow? Because I had no scaffold and knew that four forty-gallon oil drums and half a dozen planks would be all I required to build it.

Barbara copied out six plans, in pen and ink, four for the Local Authority and two for on site. I made a small shed out of second hand asbestos roofing sheets, purchased an old concrete mixer and a wheelbarrow with a pump-up tyre, and in March 1958 started work on digging out the drive and foundations by hand. Mr Bert Woodley, who lived at the house "Strathallan" next to our plot, owned the adjacent field which included part of an old Stancliffe Stone tip. Bert very kindly allowed me to cut up and remove stone to help build the bungalow. I resolved that I would go straight to the site every evening after work to speed up the job. For the next year Barbara, who had three small children to look after, Beryl, Lesley and Andrew, took my tea down to the site.

She and I mixed all the concrete for the foundations, and the stone filling for under the floor came out of the tip. Barbara and I then concreted the floors. I always had Friday and Saturday nights off to spend time at home with the children. On Sundays I worked from dawn till dusk and by the end of June I had built the bungalow up to the damp-proof course. We then took out a mortgage using the site and foundations as deposit. With some of the money we bought nine thousand London bricks. My friends and workmates Harold Allen and Charlie gave up their holiday week to assist me, Bert Woodley's son Jim, aged fifteen, who was on holiday from school, laboured for us with a little help from Barbara. Another quarryman workmate, Harold Pearson, helped me to cut up and dress stone out of the tip. Harold would not take any money for his work. We dressed enough stone to build the front of the bungalow and it took less than one month to build the bungalow from damp-proof course to square ready for the roof timbers.

Once at the square we had another stage payment from the Building Society to pay for the roof timber, tiles and the windows. I knew how to put all the woodwork on ready for the tiles. Barbara and I then tiled the roof with good quality ten-inch by six inch Staffordshire tiles. By October it was roofed and glazed. Michael Strange from Harry Brookes wired it. Jack Johnson plumbed and installed the central heating from a Dunsley high output back boiler. Another of my workmates, joiner Duncan Frost, hung all the doors for me and Joe Wood, one of Wildgoose's plasterers, plastered it for me in his spare time. Most of the

Osiris, at the junction of Whitworth Road and Moor Lane

stone gang appeared from time to time with advice and help. Barbara decorated the bungalow inside and out.

We moved in on 31st March 1959, our eighth wedding anniversary, and a landmark day in our life. We were over the moon with our lovely new bungalow, with its nice warm bathroom with flushing loo, hot water on tap, central heating, airing cupboard and fully fitted kitchen with a ceramic tiled floor. Mere words cannot describe the pride, joy and comfort we had in our new home and the children loved it. We decided to call the bungalow Osiris after the submarine that brother John served on in China. I was just about exhausted with the sheer effort and persistence required to build the bungalow in twelve months from start to finish in my spare time. Mandy our boxer dog was soon at home because she had spent many hours there with me when we were working on it.

Civil engineering

Because of losing six hours a week travelling time, and now having a mortgate to pay off as soon as possible, I was not ecstatic about working at Wildgoose's Bakewell site. The Building Society manager had told me that every pound I paid off the mortgage in the first two or three years was worth double. A knock came on Osiris front door one night and there stood my old Darley Hall workmate Ted Lane. He explained he now worked for Lehane, Mackenzie & Shand, who he had worked for before the war, on the concrete road viaducts to the Ladybower Dam project. Around this time I had built for Lehane, Mackenzie & Shand in my spare time, and had met Ken Dabell who was then a trainee plant manager, and was eventually to become managing director of the Shand empire.

Shand's had been awarded the contract for the Darley Dale new sewerage scheme, a mammoth job stretching from Beeley Road at Rowsley almost to Matlock, with an upgrade of the sewer main in Matlock Dale and Matlock Bath. Ted said Shand's would pay me twice the wage I was now getting but I would have to work longer hours and take more responsibility. He was to be the general foreman, and would work with me. He told me he had also asked Brian Horobin to join him and he had said yes. I talked it over with Barbara and my friend and workmate Harold Allen and we made the momentous decision to leave Wildgoose & Sons and join the civil engineering industry. Another term in the University of Life. I had no illusions about the job and knew it would be hard, rough and tough and short term. I was now thirty-three years old, full of confidence, and fit, or so I thought.

Brian, Harold and I reported to the site base on Old Road, Darley Dale in 1961. I knew many of the men in the workshop and management at Lehane, Mackenzie & Shand headquarters at Rowsley. These included several of the Broad Walk gang of lads including my life-long friends Geoff Sellers, David Holmes, Brian Allwood, Bill Goodwin, also the managing director Ken Dabell. I was acquainted with few men on the site. Our gang of three had a welcome addition of a local man, Pat Pritty; we could not have had a better person to join us. Pat had been a professional soldier before and through the second war. We had all worked before on many different construction sites but the lack of facilities on this job was an eye opener. Because of the nature of the job, continuously moving around, we usually had no cabin or toilet.

What we did have was a small van to ferry ourselves and our tools etc. about. It proved to be an invaluable asset. We built all the brick manholes, laid pipes, concreted, made good to roads and kerbs. Three or four gangs of professional, mostly Irish, navvies armed with JCBs, lorries, dumpers and compressors carried out the excavation side of the job. A small portion of the job at South Darley was carried out by a Chesterfield civil engineering firm called Harry Camm. We built a few manholes for the firm. The foreman was called Eric Bennett.

Working in deep trenches five to nine feet deep in a busy main road is a somewhat daunting experience, and we had to make sure the trench sides were firmly propped to prevent a cave-in caused by heavy goods vehicles running alongside the trench. We also had to deal with the

Darley Bridge

water pumps, fix up the traffic lights and signs, set out the red paraffin lamps at night, and place guards around the excavations. Some of the manholes were of the storm overflow type. These can deal with excessive water flows by taking the surplus sewage and storm water to the nearest stream or river. Where it enters the water-course the pipe has an automatic one-way valve known as a penstock. Ted said the Derwent was reasonably low and we had got to cross it with a steel rising main from a pump station at Darley Bridge to another pump station at Four Lane Ends on the B5057 Station Road.

The foreman of one of the Irish gangs was experienced in this type of work. I watched enthralled as they very quickly barricaded half the river off with steel shuttering, then lined it with polythene. It was strange to work on the river bed with the Derwent flowing by at waist height. They then did the same with the other side. I had spent many happy hours walking and playing alongside the river but I had never seen fresh water crayfish until we crossed the Derwent at Darley Bridge. While we were on this job a pipe slipped out of the sling and fell on an Irishman's shoulder, badly breaking it. Although in great pain he insisted that we take him to the hospital in Manchester as he had relatives around there. We put our coats on the floor of the van, loaded him up and away we went to Manchester. We dropped him off at Manchester Royal Infirmary where he staggered into the Casualty department. Heaven knows what he told them. In today's world he would have been air-lifted to hospital by helicopter.

We also worked on a pump station near the Grouse and Claret at Rowsley and one between the railway and the A6 near the Darley Dale boundary with Matlock. We worked everywhere in Darley Dale. In time, after about a year, I had a gang of my own, five or six Irishmen, with a JCB driven by a local man, Doug, who was exceptionally handy with his fists. He maintained discipline when necessary by thumping one of the Irishmen every now and then. I learned a lot from all these men about civil engineering, and what a hard and dangerous profession it is. One of the gangers was called Joe Parsonage. He was over sixty and had spent his life from the age of thirteen working on jobs such as the Fernilee and Ladybower reservoirs, sewer tunnels and bridge jobs. At dinner-time he would tell me yarns of jobs and the men who worked on them, wandering from place to place. I also met Jack the shot-firer from Ashover again who told Harold and me a curious tale. He had married a farmer's daughter and when her father died he left the farm to his son. The only thing he left to Jack and his daughter was the old grandfather clock. Jack had the clock for several years before he found in the bottom of it a considerable sum of money, and a note which stated "Thou shall not want, Jack." He was probably pulling our legs.

My gang on Shand's had a canvas hut called an elephant tent and a couple of propane gas rings. Tea was made in a bucket, two ounces of tea, a gallon of water, a pint of milk, and put your own sugar in. I think we paid about one pound per week into the kitty and got a fry-up of sorts at dinner-time with bread and everything fried in dripping in a big, and I mean big, frying pan. We had meat, sausages, bacon and eggs, oatcakes, fried bread, all washed down with copious amounts of tea. Most of the Irishmen carried a knife and ate with it.

1962-3 was the coldest winter for years. It froze every day for around six weeks but we never lost a day's work. Shand's provided us with a good waterproof suit which we put on over our working clothes. This kept us dry and warm throughout the severe winter. Ted the foreman acquired a steam cleaner and we put the steam pipe under the sand and gravel heaps to stop them from freezing solid. We had to install a new sewer from the A6 down Station Road to Four Lane Ends pump station. We were about eight feet deep under the railway track. The trench was very wet and the sides were always threatening to fall in between the props. A new young Irishman was very nervous and on his first day there was a bit of movement on the side of the trench and some earth fell in. He scampered up the props out of the trench and promptly disappeared underneath a passing bus which fortunately was going reasonably slowly. He rolled out from under the back of the bus as it slid to a standstill, stood up and then leapt up and down screaming. We held him down on the road till we got the van to take him to the Whitworth Hospital. No wonder he shouted and screamed. When he went under the bus he was rolled up the road which scrubbed bits off his knees, ankles, elbows and his head. He was other wise unhurt. He returned to work a few days later covered in plasters.

It was now 1962 and I was thirty-five years old. I considered myself to be at the peak of fitness at this time, apart from the odd pain in my chest now and again. However, one teatime, I was driving with Barbara when I suffered a pain in my chest which became so bad that I was rushed to Walton hospital at Chesterfield, where it was found that I had had a pneumothorax, and had almost died. I was in the hospital for three weeks and unable to carry out physical work for another six months.

Insurance Salesman

Our son Andrew was at school and Barbara had acquired had a job working down Station Road for the National Savings Office when, to our delight, she became pregnant again. I had a wife and three children, soon to be four, to support, so three weeks after being discharged from hospital I bought an insurance book from Charlie Gladwin of

Birchover, who I knew from working at the Co-op. The insurance company was the Co-operative Insurance Society and they lent me the money to buy the book. I went to their Ripley headquarters for some training and spent the next four months selling insurance, doing the rounds in my ex-post office van. There was no salary with the job, only commission on sales and premium collection. Charlie Gladwin gave me a list of suspect people who were always making trivial claims, or who, when you went to collect their money, told you to come back next week. The CIS vehicle insurance at that time was quite competitive so I sold enough to get by on. One smallholder used to part-pay me in eggs. It was the easiest job I have ever had. Clean, dressed up, no manual work and very little brain work. Part of my training included the use of the prospect book. Before going to see someone, to improve your prospects of making a sale it is important to find out as much as you can about their background, hobbies, family, interests etc. so that you can relate with them. By writing down everything you had gleaned in your first visit, and reading it just before your second visit, it became easy to establish a relationship with the client. I could see that while it was a nice dressed up, steady job, the insurance life was not for me and after four months I went back to Shand's on the Darley sewerage scheme, but the job was almost over.

Brian left Shand's and set up his own building business, and Pat and Harold went with him. I left and got a job as foreman with Harry Camm on the Ashbourne sewerage scheme. This would be around August 1963. I got on well with Camm's. They employed a few Irishmen and lots of wandering men, quite a few Polish men and displaced persons from Eastern Europe. We seemed to do a lot of hand digging. The agent for the job was not the best. He vanished and was replaced by one who, in my opinion, was no better. One morning in mid-December it snowed then froze. The roads were sheets of ice. I slid down the hills to Ashbourne arriving ten minutes late. The agent stormed at me in front of my gang. I thought the general foreman, Len Nadin from Chesterfield, and I ran the job very well. I had a little mental fit, told the agent to do my job and went home.

Later that morning two of Harry Camm's bosses came to the bungalow and asked me to go back but I refused. Much as I liked the civil engineering world I had had my fill of it and was mindful of my health. I thought of going back to Wildgoose & Sons and decided to leave things until after Christmas as I had a few jobs to do around the bungalow Osiris. So ended another term at the University of Life. Each term had equipped me more for the exam. Life at Paton's and Baldwin's factory, life in the building industry, a short life in the insurance business, and life in the civil engineering industry, which I must admit I liked the best, but could not bring myself to face the lifetime of the hardships that it would entail. I was now thirty-six years of age with a wonderful wife and a lovely family I scarcely knew through always being at work. We had a very nice home with most of the mortgage paid off. I felt a bit sorry for my mother and father at Highlands who were now in their seventies. 1964 was to be the most momentous time in my life. It all began with a knock on Osiris' front door.

Factory days

My introduction to factories of all types began on 31st May 1941, Whit Monday, six days before my fourteenth birthday. The second war was not going well and Germany appeared to be winning hands down. Many of the evacuees, who had arrived from big cities and towns to live in our haven of rural tranquillity in September 1939, had returned home after the seven or eight months of the phoney war. May 1940 was the commencement of the real war, quickly followed by the evacuation from Dunkirk, and the aerial Battle of Britain. The grim, dark and cold winter of 1940/41 saw ever more frequent and widespread bombing raids. Our big cities were being blasted almost out of existence. The evacuees who had gone home returned to Darley Dale again.

All able-bodied men between eighteen and thirty and not in a reserved occupation were called up to serve in the armed forces. Food was scarce and rationed. Britain had its back to the wall. Brother Clifford lost his job at Smedley's Hydro when it was taken over by the army for use as a training base for an army Intelligence Unit. Secret passwords were part of their training and the most ludicrous one to me was the use of a secret password to establish the identity of those members who belonged to the Smedley's Hydro Intelligence Unit. When one member met another he did not give a formal greeting, ie good morning, how do you do, hello, he had to say hi-di-hi, and the secret reply was ho-de-ho. As with a lot of secrets this quickly became public knowledge and soon became a cheerful joking exchange between Matlock civilians.

When air raid sirens sounded all large factories carried on working until enemy aircraft were actually spotted on the horizon. The factory alarm was then sounded and the factory evacuated at a great rate of knots into the hopefully nearby air raid shelter. This system helped to keep production going. The factory alarm was sounded when an enemy plane appeared by a man who was posted to a vantage point, usually on the roof. These men were known as Jim Crows. They were equipped with a steel helmet, a pair of binoculars, a bucket, a stirrup pump and a long handled shovel. A good knowledge of the different types of German planes was a definite asset. How the system worked in the dark I do not know.

Paton's and Baldwin's

I never even had an interview at Paton's. I just turned up at 7.30am on Whit Monday morning. I was then sent to the engineering workshop which was right at the back of the factory. I was shown how to use a hacksaw, a file, the vice and a hammer and chisel. I was given a piece of tool steel, a screwdriver handle, and shown how to make my own large screwdriver. I still have it and use it over sixty years later. Working with the engineers I had the run of the factory, fetching and carrying, helping various men with different tasks. Three months later I knew every inch of the factory and most of the people who worked there. Because I was the youngest in the factory everyone looked after me, especially Mrs. Swift, the canteen manager, who often gave me an extra dessert. Remember food was rationed.

The workrooms at Paton's were very large, with the wool manufacturing machines powered by rotating shafts which were suspended from the ceiling. Pulley wheels were fixed to the shafts and drove a pulley wheel on each machine by means of a two or three inch belt. To renew the belts we had a device which coupled the two ends together with a type of hinge. This device enables the belt to be made to the exact length required. Every pulley on the machine had another one the same size immediately alongside it. This pulley was called the idler. To stop and start the individual machine a lever moved the belt from the fixed pulley to the idler, or vice versa. The main overhead shafts ran the length of the room and were driven by a huge electric motor. Starting the motor was an acquired skill and only carried out by the engineering staff. A lever on the starter had to be moved up a notch at a time, timed by the sound and revs of the electric motor. When the lever reached the last notch and the sound was right a quick flick of the wrist pushed the lever home. If everything was just right it stayed there, if not the lever fell down to the start position. A short wait until the motor had stopped then one began the cycle again.

What had been a brightly lit but quiet room, where the operators were talking and preparing for the day's work, suddenly became alive. Dozens of belts, mostly unprotected, thrashed about. Machinery clattered noisily. Conversation was now either by lip reading or by shouting. People scurried about bringing and taking away woollen material on trolleys. Several factories later I found what was a simple and orderly process to the factory worker mostly looked and sounded like a scene from hell to the uninitiated. Roaring, thrashing belts, whirring machinery, hasty movements of the dextrous highly skilled operatives all gelled together to astound a new visitor.

Most people think that factory work simply consists of watching a

Some of the workers at Paton's and Baldwin's factory, Matlock, after the takeover by Lehman Archer and Lane. Brother Clifford is on the back row 5th from the left

machine work. Actually you do watch the machinery work, having to stay very alert, constantly adjusting it and feeding it with material, continuously watching out for snags and breakages, imperfections etc. No let-ups, no putting one's feet on the office desk and switching off for a moment. Operating large machines means being on one's feet for hours on end. As an example, by 1942 the Paton's factory, by then Lehman, Archer and Lane's tap and die factory, was working two twelve-hour shifts five and a half days a week. On Saturday we finished early, around lunch-time, and only maintenance staff worked on Saturday afternoon and Sunday.

Some of the men were in the Home Guard and took part in training exercises on Sundays and at night. I found that factory workers had a great cameraderie. It may be the same in sedentary occupations. I do not know because I have had no experience of that type of work environment within a large workforce.

Taking out the wool producing machinery, floor by floor and installing tap and die manufacturing in its place was a poignant time.

People who had worked the sensitive yarn manufacturing machinery for years and took an enormous pride in their skill were left stranded, having to learn new skills. The men installing the tap and die machinery were mostly from the London area. Some of the machine operators also came with the machines. It was a time of great upheaval and change as the wool machinery operators learned to work drills, lathes, various types of grinding machines, and heat treatment ovens used to temper the taps and dies. By the way, taps are used to make nuts, and dies the bolts.

Several months passed. All the machinery evacuated from London had been installed. Instead of the smell of raw wool a stink of burning oil pervaded the factory. All the Paton's and Baldwin's work force had been transferred to the new company. I was told that because there was now a surplus of maintenance engineers I was to work a very simple grinding machine in the factory. Doing repetitive work, standing behind the machine, doing the same monotonous action from 7.45am to 5.45pm was purgatory and not for me. All the window glass in the factory had been painted black, doors had an internal porch with another door to stop the light being seen in the blackout. Once inside the factory you did not know if it was light or dark outside. I was really pleased to be taken ill with appendicitis and get away from my new soul-destroying job at Paton's. After the war the factory reverted back to wool production until 1990 when it closed with the loss of one hundred and forty-three jobs. Like so many of our factories it was demolished and housing built on the site. To me another small nail in Britain's industrial coffin.

MASSON MILL

During my time in the construction industry I added to my knowledge of factories by working on a variety of extensions, refurbishments etc. My first factory job came when George Twigg and I were sent to Masson Mill at Matlock Bath. It was being refurbished with new

Masson Mill

kitchens, toilets and wash hand basins throughout. Wall tiling to all the toilet areas, wash basins and the canteen kitchens was specified and George and I were sent to the mill to carry out the tiling. I remember all the tiles were a bilious green colour. Masson Mill was a very large mill and once again I had the run of the place, working on all floors. Meeting people, being assimilated into the workforce, George and I were allowed to dine in the canteen with the workforce. The job lasted about three months.

Masson Mill was a place of huge contrasts and great interest. Sometimes I had my lunch alongside the waterway which led from the weir, which was horse-shoe shaped with the open end facing upstream and which seemed to me to be facing the wrong way, to the water turbine which drove the huge electric generator which powered the factory. The channel ran alongside the Derwent at the north end of the mill. Birds sang, ducks splashed, water white with foam cascaded over the weir. After the confined noisy hurly-burly of the mill one truly appreciated the green open aspect of the great outdoors.

A ground floor room at the south end of the mill was without doubt the noisiest place I have ever worked in. It was full of machines processing the cotton, with hundreds of belts. In this room I met one of my old school mates whose job was looking after all these belts which had to be adjusted, renewed and tinkered about with, without stopping the machinery. I watched in disbelief as a lady machine operative seized the two ends of a broken cotton thread and tied both ends together with one hand. The dextrous one-handed tying operation took place in the twinkling of an eye, and would have been a credit to a magician. In order to keep the humidity at the right level and also to keep the dust down, fine water sprays were in constant use. In some rooms hand sprays were also used. These sprays had some sort of disinfectant added to the water, consequently you and your clothes smelled of this not too unpleasant perfume.

On the top floor, for obvious reasons, ie fire, cotton went through a gassing process. Small, and I mean small, lighted gas jets were on top of a machine which the cotton thread passed through at high speed, leaving the cotton thread smooth and shiny. There were lots of fire extinguishers about. The occasional very small fires were quickly put out, mostly by the finger and thumb, applied smartly to the thread. Fires are a great hazard in cotton mills. Metal-faced fire doors were everywhere and there were several escape routes from each room. At Lehman, Archer and Lane most of the women wore men's overalls or boiler suits which prevented the oil splashes and swarf ruining their clothes. Masson Mill ladies wore aprons with pockets in them.

I enjoyed my time working at Masson Mill. Thirty-two years later I was asked by the works manager, Mr. Clifford Wright, to have a look at the high main roof which was about sixty feet above the river Derwent. I went out on to the roof through a trap door and scrambled up the roof on to the ridge. The ridge was made of lead about three inches wide. I walked it from one end to the other looking for slipped or damaged slates. It was a stupid and foolish thing to do but it gave me a great feeling of elation and satisfaction. Masson Mill, one of Arkwright's cotton mills, opened in 1786/7 and closed as a cotton mill in 1988 when around one hundred and thirty workers were made redundant, some who had spent all their working life there. Today it is a historic Heritage Project, along with the original Arkwright Mill at Cromford, both mainly employing paper shufflers and retail outlets, another small nail in Britain's industrial coffin.

A few of the people who worked there in the mid 20th century are:

Manager – Mr A Stock
Assistant Manager – R Warren Walker
Office Manager – A Arthington
Copping – R Blears
Twisting – C Wright , F Wright (both became Managers)
Winding – J Davis
Warehouse – J Brown
Beaming – G Carline
Maintenance   W Wright
Electrics   L Stamps
Joiner – E Orridge
Office – Miss Biddulph & Miss Kirk, W Frost
Canteen – Mrs Station
Operatives Families – Buntings, Lugtons, Martins, Spencers, Yeomans and Bowmers

This information was supplied by Clifford Wright, who started work at 14 years of age at Masson, and retired in 1984 as Manager.

The first part of Masson Mill, built in 1771, was originally a paper mill owned by Robert Shaw of Snitterton, and George White of Winster. It was purchased by Richard Arkwright in 1780 who built his cotton mill alongside it. The mills closed around 1990.

Tor Hosiery

The Tor Hosiery factory on Dimple Road at Matlock was my next factory job. David Sheldon had the contract to extend the factory. In contrast to Paton's and Masson Mills, Tor Hosiery was a fairly small factory making nylon stockings. The factory was very clean and tidy

Tor Hosiery 2006

and relatively quiet. The ladies who worked there were extremely dextrous. I used to watch them hold part of a nylon stocking in their hand then place it on the pins on the machine, one pin to each hole. I don't know how many tiny holes there are around a nylon stocking, hundreds? To carry out this feat required a very steady hand and good eyesight. They carried out this delicate operation with effortless ease. We also shared the works canteen with them. I was sent twice more to Tor Hosiery when I worked for Wildgoose's to help build two more extensions to the factory. The factory was first called Potter's Hosiery. In the 1930s it became Tor Hosiery, manufacturers of silk stockings, and in 1945/46, manufacturers of nylon stockings. It was taken over by Courtaulds after the war. In 1983 Courtauld's were on the point of closing the mill when it was bought by the Swedish hosiery firm Swegmark. Swegmark ended hosiery manufacture in the mid-1980s.

Some of the people who worked at Tor Hosiery from 1939 to the 1950's are:

Managers – Mr Espig, Mr F Hagler, Mr Street

Office – Ellis Needham, Minnie Allsop
Stores – Jim Bagshaw
Fitters – J E Allen, Mr Ram
Canteen – Mrs Furniss
Operatives – Frances Edwards, Mary Holmes, Dorothy Brown, Winifred Coney, Greta Thompson, Winnie Smith, Marion Marsden, Gertie Edwards, Phyllis Edwards, John Dethick, Margaret Darlington, Sheila Slater, Rose Pickford, Irene Fox, Barbara Wagstaffe, Nellie Whitehead and NoraWhitehead.

This information was supplied by Irene Wilmot (nee Fox).

Tor Hosiery was originally Potters Mill, owned by William Henry Potter. It was recorded in 1930 as Manufacturer of Hand Machine Hosiery, becoming Tor Hosiery in the 1930s.

The original mill had several extensions in the 1940s/50s. Tor Hosiery was taken over by Courtaulds after the War. In 1983 Courtaulds were on the point of closing the mill when it was bought by the Swedish hosiery firm Swegmark who ended hosiery manufacture in the mid 1980s.

Ragusa

At the Ragusa Ashalt factory, which I helped to build for Wildgoose's in 1950, men carried buckets of boiling asphalt from a tar boiler to iron moulds placed on the floor which were filled by hand from the buckets. Lots of limestone dust was scattered about the floor to prevent the asphalt sticking to the bucket, the floor, one's boots or anything else. It was the hardest work in the area. It was normal to see men stripped to the waist on a winter's day with clouds of steam rising from their bodies. After a brief rest while the asphalt was setting all the blocks had to be struck from the moulds, lifted and stacked on wooden pallets. A fork lift truck then took the pallets outside on to the loading bays. Several attempts were made over the years to mechanise this energy sapping drudgery. It took almost thirty years and the help of computers to finally do away with the huge manual input required.

Enthoven's

The HG Enthoven lead smelter is at South Darley. I was sent there to help build a standby generator house in the 1950s with Fred Barratt and Henry Waterfall. I had been to Enthoven's in the wartime, helping bullets to escape from being smelted down. There were sacks and sacks of them lying about, just waiting to be put to a much better use as catapult ammunition. A list of do's and don'ts was given to us. This was in the mid-1950s when health and safety regulations were practically unknown. To go into the actual smelting works was an eye-opener. Vats of boiling lead, heat, red-hot pipes, battery acid and heaps of strange coloured materials. Metallic blue smoke, with a smell like no other, hung around.

Enthoven's is to me the dustbin of Britain as far as lead acid batteries are concerned. Old batteries are a huge environmental problem and HJ Enthoven makes the world a far better place to live in with their expertise on safely recycling them. However no one wants the lead dustbin in their back yard. The lead smelter should in my opinion be in the same place as the lead smelting works of yesteryear, preferably on the wild bleak windy moors, away from all dwellings, where the pollution can do least harm and no disturbance is caused by the constant whine of the large fans which try to suck up the deadly fumes. I believe an early start to relocate a new state-of-the-arts smelter is overdue. If it is not relocated the existing one will just continue to grow. Keep the smelter in the area by all means for the employment it produces and the good work it does, but in a more sensible environmentally friendly site where it would be away from people. Bearing in mind the wind in Britain mainly blows from the west the more distance the wind has to travel from the smelting site to a dwelling the more its pollution is dispersed. This was obvious to everyone two hundred and fifty years ago. Common sense today is often ignored.

Firth Rixson

Our stone gang was moved to Firth Rixson steel stamping factory at Darley Dale. Besides working on the roof and the huge brick wall, which I have mentioned elsewhere, we also worked inside the factory carrying out building work. The noise from the giant stamps was tremendous. When the stamp crashed down on to a billet of red hot steel a cascade of sparks flew all over the place. Just before the stamp hit the billet a small handful of sawdust was thrown on to the top of the red hot billet. This stopped the stamp sticking to the billet. One man worked the stamp, lifting and dropping the heavy stamp by means of a dangling rope. Another man had the job of making sure the billet was in the correct position with a long metal rod.

Elsewhere rows of large mechanical drop hammers forged lengths of high quality, self-tempering steel into the centre shafts for jet engines, another very highly skilled job. A good operative could judge the size of the forging to a nicety, also the strength of the hammer blows, which were controlled by a foot pedal. The jobs at the steel factory were very manual and everyone had to be very fit and alert. Knock knock went the hammers, bang bang went the stamps. They could be heard all over Darley on a still winter's day or night. These massive, mind bending bangs and knocks were encapsulated in a cacophony of lesser sounds, steel dropping on the floor, grinding machines, steel billets being sawn, finished billets being dropped into steel baskets ready for removal.

All these sounds, along with the works' standard gauge loco shunting railway waggons combined to produce a noise and sight that would terrify an office worker or academic. Again what seemed like an uncontrollable state of chaos to the uninitiated was in fact well ordered. It takes a certain type of person to work there in the strong, smoky, smelly, noisy atmosphere of a steel works. No place for the faint hearted. The work was hard, so were the men. At that time in the late 1950s a few women still worked in the factory, crane driving, in despatch, checking materials etc, a remnant of the wartime workforce when many women worked there. The size of the building is immense, a cathedral dedicated to the worship of steel.

For us, the best thing was that we were once again allowed to use the works canteen and enjoy that luxury, unheard-of in the construction industry, a hot dinner followed by a sweet, also being protected from the vagaries of the weather. Several of the workmen at the factory had been at Churchtown School with me. I well remember in 1940 going to watch the men and machines excavating the foundations, and seeing the factory take shape, rising from the LMS sports field to become the largest building in the area. The huge noisy stamps now been replaced by equally huge presses which make little noise compared to stamps.

My experience of working in factories was brief. Various jobs suit various people. I finished up by having my own factory in 1990 called TDI, manufacturing insulated damp-proof course and vehicle safety equipment. I was pleased and proud to have gone full circle from a factory fetch-and-carry boy to MD of a thriving up-to-date Darley Dale factory.

This was to be the end of my factory days, fifty-six years after starting at Paton's and Baldwin's. I found working in factories an exhilarating experience, observing and living a different way of life and being encapsulated and part of a workshop family, isolated from the vagaries of the weather and worrying about when, why and how at work. So different from the building industry where when, why and how are everyday concerns. My factory days were a very enjoyable part of my adventurous journey through life. Personally I have always found it to be a major advantage when one has actually knocked the nails in before telling other people when, where and how to knock them in. There is no substitute for experience and persistence to make things work.

In my lifetime I have witnessed a huge decline in the manufacturing industry in this area along with the rest of Britain. The lost jobs in factories appear to me to have been replaced by paper-shuffling jobs, whose day's work disappears into a computer or filing cabinet. To have no manufacturing base to a country is like building a house with no foundation. It looks good, it is nice to live in, but it will not endure.

BANDS OF BUILDERS

The world we observe and dwell in today consists of an artificial landscape, mostly fashioned by construction and agricultural workers. Construction of all types, shapes and sizes litter our world, carried out by the most enduring men, builders. They have left a legacy beyond compare, from the Great Wall of China, Stonehenge and ancient cities, to railways, canals, roads, dwellings and lowly boundary walls. Without construction workers there would be no factories, administration centres, no infrastructure. People generally are not aware of the scale of achievements by the building trade workers. We are all so familiar with them we are inclined to just accept them as the normal landscape. Building first began when primitive man decided to erect some sort of a barrier in front of his cave. This provided better shelter, safety and security, exactly what a modern dwelling supplies. Building quickly became synonymous with mankind's progress, using material at hand to build anything from tropical huts to the immense lost cities of Europe and South America. Wherever man resides builders provide the means for him to do so. Next time you go on a journey, be it down to the shop or to another continent, pause and look around. Almost everything you see is complemented by the work of a builder in some shape or form. Not all serve their original purpose. Many are ruins, monuments to past needs, but they or their vestiges are still there to be seen. To me these men who shaped and built this world we live in are special people. Men who had the ability to perceive tomorrow, men whose skills were so much in demand that kings and rulers of men sought them out, sometimes enslaving them, for their knowledge and skills.

In Europe the golden age of builders commenced around 1000 AD and lasted five hundred years or so. Rulers, to maintain their power and status, needed castles, cathedrals, churches, defence works and dwelling houses, visible symbols of their strength and wealth, essential to maintain their influence and protect them against others. Because their skills and knowledge were so much in demand builders banded together to carry out large jobs, selling their know-how and skill to the highest bidder wherever they might be. They travelled from Scandinavia to the Middle East. These travelling bands of builders were ultra-resourceful. Imagine arriving in some foreign land after travelling many miles with a few horses carrying their tools and equipment, to construct whatever they had been hired to build. These large jobs sometimes took years to build. The masons were very proud of their skills and being unable to read or write often signed their work with a mark. Almost every stone building of consequence up to the 1800s contains these mason's marks. Door and window jambs of Derbyshire manor houses of the 15/1600s period such as Haddon Hall, Bolsover Castle, Stancliffe Hall, Hopton Hall are excellent places to look for them.

The travelling bands of builders were absolutely self-contained, usually led by a scholarly Latin speaking person well versed in the art of drawing plans, mathematics, and the use in construction of the humble square and trammel. A large set-square was the most important tool in building for thousands of years. Because it is an exact right angle it has many functions. Fitted with a line with a weight attached to it, and held vertically, it ensures that with the plumb line exactly parallel with the upright, not only will it provide a vertical line it will also provide an absolutely level line. Extending the upright of the square sideways gives a consistent angle. This angle can be easily adjusted to requirements. A trammel consists of a centre point with a distance piece to the size of the diameter required. This basic device enables curved walls or arches to be easily constructed. Every band also carried its own measuring stick, divided into equal lengths by means of marks or notches. I have already described the use of the three boning rods. These simple devices provided the means to constant plumb, level, curves, batters and measurements. As I have stated all these could be easily and simply adjusted to meet specific needs. We now have the simple technical means to build our construction to a high standard.

The Building Trade

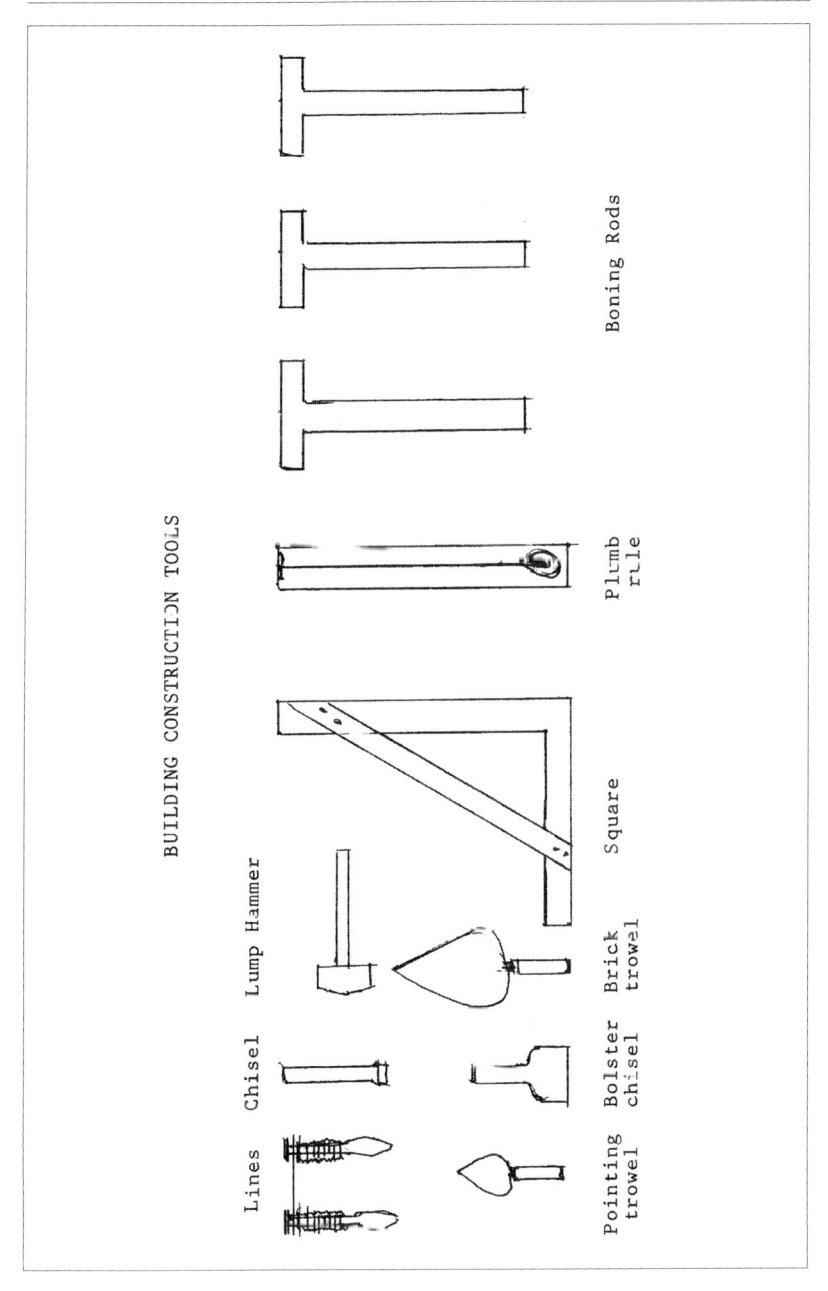

Building Construction Tools

- Lines
- Chisel
- Lump Hammer
- Square
- Plumb rule
- Boning Rods
- Pointing trowel
- Bolster chisel
- Brick trowel

Who else would be in the gang? A blacksmith with a supply of metal to fashion tools, including adzes, hammers, axes, chisels, wedges and crowbars. A cooper to make buckets, barrels and dishes. A rope maker, a leather worker, a forester, woodworkers, carpenters, quarrymen, builders, teamsters, cooks, labourers, masons, specialist workers who could erect scaffolding or build cranes which usually worked with a counterweight balance, wheelwrights, thatchers and lead workers.

Always on any construction site from time immemorial the first job concerns home comforts and shelter. Today it is to unload and erect the cabins, then it was to build a hut or lodge with a thatched or turf roof, preferably near a good water supply. The next job would be to find a suitable supply of building materials, sand, lime, stone, ashes and wood as near to the site as possible. All these materials had to be acquired and delivered to site. Stone was cut to size and shape in the quarry. All excavated material was carefully disposed of in allotted places. Roads, paths and any paved areas were constructed first to facilitate material movement. The main aspects of the building had to be considered, ie facing south, position of entrance, internal well if possible, height of defensive ditch or moat. If it was a religious building, ie church, cathedral or monastery, it usually had more detail, a lead roof, massive timbers and complicated masonry. I also believe these types of building would suffer from too many learned but inexperienced employers exasperating very experienced tradesmen with inappropriate demands (today's planners!).

Travelling bands of builders were very much in demand between 1066 and 1500, so much so that sometimes in the early 1300s these bands were held captive by their employers, kings, barons, dukes, on completion of their project. They were then set to work on another project. After many years of abuse a notice was posted that a meeting of the Master Builders of the various bands of builders was to be held in Strasbourg in 1366. At this meeting the Master Builders decided that if anyone, no matter who he may be, detained any mason or members of the travelling band of builders against their will, no building gang

The building trade

Mason's marks. Top left: *Stanton Woodhouse.* Top right: *Stancliffe Hall.* Below left: *Haddon Hall.* Below right: *Snitterton*

28 A selection of English masons' marks. Masons carved their mark to show responsibility for work done. There is no way of connecting them with named masons but they can prove contemporaneity of work

would ever work for him again. The building gangs became a brotherhood, not a secret society, more a trades union. The threat of being unable to construct any more castles, fortified dwelling houses, palaces etc., was enough to guarantee the freedom and wellbeing of those travelling bands of builders for the next two hundred years.

After that more widespread education and construction knowledge lessened the need for the travelling bands. The use of cannons rendered castles obsolete. The four hundred years from 1075 to 1475 was undoubtedly a great age for castle building on a grand scale. At that time ordinary people were still living in huts, and for them to see and visit one of these mighty buildings must have been awe-inspiring. The Victorian age saw a massive resurgence in large construction projects. Many of the building workers of that age had acquired skills and knowledge handed down to them from those wonderful bands of builders. Men who with a few tools, lots of knowledge and skill could build cathedrals, castles or huge stately homes from scratch without the vast army of non-productive people who are now solely employed to oversee and regulate today's construction workers.

When I started work in the construction industry in the 1940s some of the men from whom I acquired my building knowledge and skills were around sixty or more years old. They in their turn had acquired their skills and knowledge from previous generations who had none of today's scientific advances to help them. Any of the pre-war builders I had the privilege of working with could have constructed the pyramids without recourse to mechanical aids, quantity surveyors, structural engineers, building inspectors, safety officers, or planners. Today's forty ton articulated lorries run safely over bridges constructed for horses and carts several hundred years ago. They speak for themselves, as do mediaeval castles and cathedrals. The Industrial Revolution heralded a resurgence of the travelling bands of builders, after a long lapse, for the construction of the canals and railways. The construction of the railway and canal infrastructure became a world-wide phenomenon. Every nation had a tremendous demand for construction workers of all types, from monumental masons to labourers. It is alleged that Thomas Brassey employed over one million men working in various countries in the 1850/60s. Railway and canal building was a moving-on type of work because of its nature. Good tradesmen ensured a very high standard of work. Next time you have the opportunity to be near a railway track stop, look and consider that it was probably built between one hundred and one hundred and fifty years ago by hand. Massive embankments, cuttings, viaducts, tunnels, bridges large and small, stations of all types and sizes. Most of these structures have survived virtually intact with very little maintenance required. Part of Haddon Hall near Bakewell, Derbyshire, has been continuously occupied since the twelfth century with no major alterations taking place to the original structure. Central heating, plumbing, insulation and electricity, essential to modern expectations, have been installed superficially but the original building has survived intact. Traditional methods with traditional materials and skills handed down over the centuries ensured a long life. If these men had constructed the ill-fated Spaghetti Junction near Birmingham there would have been no need for its continuous major repairs and upgrading. Many modern buildings constructed with new materials by mechanic-type tradesmen in the 1950/60s have already vanished. Tower blocks and schools nation-wide are being condemned as unfit after a short life of forty or fifty years.

Personally I have nothing against the design of modern building. It is a shame that price and quantity are considered more important today than durability and quality of materials. My own conclusion is that in spite of huge advances in materials and construction methods, people still want to see and live in the same type of buildings as their grandparents. I call this "the bird's nest syndrome". Countless generations of birds have always built the same type of nest out of materials to hand not very differently from man. I believe it is taking far too long for people to accept that traditional building is now almost obsolete for small dwellings. People are so slow to change in their perspective of what is acceptable. Railway carriage door handles in the 1950s were still based on the type fitted to stage coaches of the 1800s.

The most modern double-glazed PVC doors and windows are made to resemble window designs of approximately two hundred years or more ago. (Bird's nest syndrome again). People, including planners and architects, the present day master builders, successors to their medieval forbears, need educating in the tremendous potential of ultra modern materials in new but sensible and durable types of building and construction methods. It has taken over seventy years for plastic materials to become accepted as normal in construction for drains, gutters, windows, kitchen furniture. Modern dwellings could still be individually tailored in size and shape to suit individual needs. They would be warmer, lighter, cleaner, healthier, quieter, maintenance-free and recyclable, and easy to transport and erect. There is, and always has been, change and why not as long as it is for the better, not what we perceive as better, ie traditional dwelling (bird's nest syndrome). Generations to come will accept these ultra modern dwellings as normal.

I have witnessed many changes in my lifetime. I remember seeing my first aeroplane, first radio and television, first electrical power to our village, first computer and the internet. Our 1800s first home in 1951 still had a stone sink with one cold water tap and an earth toilet forty feet away up the garden. An 1800s cast iron, coal fired range complete with oven and water boiler dominated the kitchen living room. The cottage had no damp course, draughty doors and windows and stone flagged floors. It was built of stone with a slate roof and is likely to last another one hundred and fifty years but can never be modern. Aeroplane and vehicle design and manufacture has evolved immensely since their inception one hundred years ago to today's sophisticated technical standards. If dwellings had similarly progressed in the last one hundred years we would now be living in self sufficient, high-specification, technically-equipped factory-built abodes. This bird's nest syndrome still prevents us from accepting the super-modern dwellings possible today. People simply cannot accept that the construction they see today is practically obsolete. The bird's nest syndrome gives everyone a feeling of "It must be right. This is how it should be". All arising from a feeling of familiarity. Do we not want to move on? Obviously not!

Conservation officers will not accept that the vast majority of the dwellings they so assiduously preserve are totally obsolete, antiques in a modern world. By all means preserve what we have, but do not condemn the generation to come to dwell in substandard, primitive low-tech, high-energy-consuming buildings. Today we have the ability and the knowledge to completely transform our abodes. I firmly believe it is now time for a building revolution.

Builders must also like to live a rough, nomadic existence to stay in the construction industry. Personally I love it as life is never settled or boring. One can be assured of a new experience every day. We are the last remnants of a bygone age when manual skills and self-reliance were king. I have had a lot of young people work for me over the last forty years, from all sorts of backgrounds. One fact I have noticed in today's young people is the lack of response to mathematics. If I ask an older, fairly illiterate person "What is nine times seven?" he will immediately respond with the right answer. Today's young person has not got that response. The value of learning tables off by heart is enormous. All the chanting of tables in the infants school is never wasted, especially when you need to do mental arithmetic in a hurry, miles away from calculators and computers. Every builder needs a thorough knowledge of tables and measurements of all types, facts that every school child of my age had thanks to chanting tables and having to solve mathematical problems without a calculator.

Building construction has changed more in the sixty years since the Second World War than in the previous six hundred years. Some of today's builders are all too often a collection of so-called specialists and sub-contractors gathered together to carry out a job under an accountancy-based management system. Today we build up to a minimum standard. Yesterday's builders built down to a very high standard. I am probably old and prejudiced and anti-plastic but yet I must admit that the JCB excavator has taken away a lot of the drudgery of building. There is not much fun in digging foundations and drain trenches by hand, especially in the rain. Even digging requires a skill and know-how only gained through years of experience and hard physical work.

CHAPTER 6:
LEWIS JACKSON (BUILDERS) LTD

About a week before Christmas 1963 a knock came on the door and there stood Brian Watkin, my old workmate Ted Lane's son-in-law. George White, Charlie, Harold and I had built Brian a house called Westleigh down Church Lane, Darley Dale, in our spare time in the 1950s. Brian worked in a bank and his wife Pat worked for Lehane, Mackenzie & Shand. Brian told me he had purchased a plot of land up Greenaway lane and had all the plans passed for a chalet bungalow. He said he had heard I was out of work and asked if I would build it for him. He said he had had two similar prices to build it and that if I could build it for about the same price the job was mine. I told him I hadn't any money but he told me not to worry about the money. He said he trusted me and would pay me stage payments up front. I replied that I would be pleased to build it, and would start after the New Year January 1964.

BREAK FOR PHILOSOPHY

Because of knowing that I could have been dead, after suffering a double pneumothorax in 1963, I realised that as long as you did not hurt other people too much it did not matter what you did in your journey through life. Treat life as a great adventure was my creed from now on.

I am not a frequenter of pubs and have never been drunk. I think that people who become addicted to drink, drugs or religion are pretty similar in character as these fulfil a need in their lives. I have found it impossible to rationalise with persons who are seriously addicted so I do not try. People are what they are. Common sense in my opinion cannot be acquired by education, experience or status. Some have it, some never will. I found out over many years as a builder, when virtually living with people while building them an extension or carrying out alterations, that people's characters are not determined by whether they are rich or poor, somebody or nobody. In all walks of life people are very similar when it comes to being either a do-gooder or a sex and violence person. I have worked with real rogues and with people who have devoted their life to helping others. It would do everyone a world of good to do this, as people are inclined to get fast in their own stratum which becomes a rut so deep they cannot see out of it. Just a few people genuinely have no conscience and can make life intolerable for others. I have no time for these sad people. Crime, vandalism, terrorism, sex and violence are all exacerbated when these sad people are in a position of power.

It is a myth that if you do good you will prosper. I have known some real rotters prosper and take great pleasure in doing so. My own views changed as I grew older and became aware of the personal issues and ambitions of others. I believe I was the youngest trade union shop steward in Matlock at the age of twenty-three. I still have my card. At seventeen I thought, and still do, what a marvellous world it would be if everyone worked together and shared out the wealth of the world. By the time I was twenty-seven I had discovered that the majority of people wanted a share of the wealth and the power but not the hard work. I became cynical. I have known people who have wasted their one and only life, working hard at not working. I am appalled at the lack of education to become good citizens. I believe my generation, compared with today's generation, are neither better nor worse as people, but have better values regarding life instilled in them. It is my opinion that some of today's younger generation, through an uncurbed onslaught of advertising bordering on coercion have become discontented as people. If as much effort had been put into instilling values and responsibilities into people and make them proud to improve themselves and the nation, life would be better for everyone.

If a person of their own choosing and free will decides not to contribute towards the state by leading a life of crime and idleness, why should I and others be penalised by this person's action. Prisons should be run as factories and made to pay. Life education classes should be held in the evening for the inmates. The good citizens should not have to pay and suffer for the rotten ones in our society. The true job of the do-gooder is to train or make the no-gooder become a viable member of life's community, and not be so stupid as not to take advantage of them as they take advantage of us. I have worked hard and long all my life and have become a very independent person. To prosper requires fifty per cent luck and fifty per cent hard work. Without one fifty per cent there is no other fifty per cent. I have been so lucky to always enjoy my work, be interested in it, and make it my hobby. If you really enjoy your work it can become your pleasure, leisure and recreation.

One change I am pleased to see in my lifetime is more opportunity for people to change their type of work, their life style and their abode. The price to pay for this is work and study. If one does not work at one's life nothing happens in it. Life is short and deserves to be sweet. This cannot always happen in the short term. The second war gave me an awareness that sometimes, mostly through pressure groups in local areas and countries, great changes take place very quickly, turning a person's life upside down and placing it completely out of their own control. In 1939 there were happy contented people living out their lives in various parts of the world. Six years later, entirely by the efforts of others, they were either dead or suffering a living death. I have learned the hard way how uncertain others can make your life. Man's several hundred thousand years of survival as a territorial, predatory and tribal animal keeps asserting itself. This instinct needs to be channelled into more constructive endeavours.

I am afraid that for all our modern means of disseminating knowledge and information it is mostly used to make people feel more discontented with their lot, whereas I believe much more effort should have gone towards making us feel more contented with life. As I have said, people are what they are. All of us need education and training to respect other people's lives. No matter what they presume their position in society is, all people have only one life. To enjoy is heaven, to suffer is hell. I don't think personally that a person's perceived aims in life have altered much in the last few thousand years, mainly health, happiness and security.

I believe a new age is now taking over. The two hundred years of industrialisation is now a way of life. A system of mass communication and a sharing of the accumulated knowledge of the world is now occurring. Not totally world-wide as yet but it will happen. It is highly likely, in my opinion, that the awe-inspiring weapons of mass destruction that are now widely available to countries great and small will be used by some country that appears to be threatened with great danger. The most powerful of our instincts is survival, whether as individuals or members of a tribe. My father gave me a good piece of advice. He said the only difference between the hunter and the hunted is in the mind. If one puts as much effort into advancing as retreating, yesterday's defeats can become tomorrow's victories.

I have found a broad range of personal experiences help create a richer and more rewarding life. Experiences are more enduring than possessions, especially when sharing them with other people. They can be called on any time, anywhere, to help fulfil a present need. The wider and more varied the experiences, the more fulfilling they become.

After indulging myself in my favourite subject, putting the world to rights, it is back to term five in the University of Life at the age of thirty-six years. On Monday morning, 4th January 1964, I went to the Greenaway lane site, armed with a pick and shovel, opened an account with Wm. Twigg Ltd., Matlock, and bought a new wheel-barrow with a pump-up tyre. I already had an old mixer from when I had built Osiris. I had a small hen shed which I took for use as a cabin. I had the blessing and support of Barbara, who by now had had our fourth child, our son Russell. I was thirty-six years old and presumed I had lived half of my life, according to averages. I was as fit as a fiddle, with no more chest pains. Ten years of tremendously hard physical work had put me in good shape. Stewart Hopkin from Wingerworth, who I had worked with at Harry Camm's, paid me a visit on the site. He had left Harry Camm, I offered him a job, he accepted and I became an employer.

Stuart and I dug out the foundations by hand and built the house up to the damp-proof course then concreted the floors. Brian Watkin gave me a stage payment. I was solvent. My life-long friend Charlie Hopkinson decided to join me from Wildgoose & Sons. The house grew daily. Eric Bennett, who had been a foreman on Harry Camm's also came to work for me, as did Tony Lee, a young lad from Hooley's Estate, and so we were soon a gang of five. I let out the joinery work to F A Gregory & Sons from Two Dales and Walter Bowler from Hackney, both of whom were also in the undertaking business. Charlie and I could put the roof timbers on any type of building, as we had both at various times in our construction careers worked with joiners, helping them to fix roof timbers.

Before we had finished the house I had an enquiry about building another dwelling on Hall Moor Road, Darley Dale, for Tony Gregory whose parents lived near Vineyard Terrace. We built that in quick sticks. We then built a bungalow for Stancliffe Estates on Whitworth Road, opposite Fircliffe Lane, in the field where Hallowes's horse lived, the first dwelling to be built on the Hawkesley Drive estate. I finished 1964 building a house off Ember Lane at Bonsall for Ramsden's. We were a happy band of builders who could all depend on one another. Barbara kept the books and looked after everything financial whilst I built every hour I could. I went to various night classes on Derbyshire and had purchased an old Austin pickup for transport in the business, and kept the old post office van for private use.

In 1965 we built another six houses on Hawkesley Drive for Stancliffe Estates, and a bungalow for Miss White at Bidston, Cavendish Road, Matlock. We also built our first dwelling for the

The first dwelling built by LJ Builders Ltd at Greenaway Lane, Darley Dale, 1964

personal use of an architect, John Smith of Smith & Roper. In 1966 I rented a building in Stancliffe Yard and bought an old Whitlock digging machine, similar to a JCB. In the same year Harold Bowler of the Walter Bowler firm, Hackney, who had been making joinery items for me in his old chapel workshop at Greenaway Lane, sold me his business, including the undertaking side.

Undertaking

I became used to undertaking and all its responsibilities. I buried friends and relatives whom I knew and loved, including my father in 1968 and my mother when she died in February 1975. I am privileged to have been able to put my father and mother, and my brothers Clifford and Jim, to rest in the very best manner available with all the dignity they deserved, sorting out any problems for the bereaved, seeing to all the legal complexities. No matter how used to undertaking I became, the death of very young people got to me, especially our god-daughter Susan, aged twelve years. To be able to help people in their hour of greatest need is very satisfying. People who have just suffered a bereavement are very disturbed and my job was to allay their anxieties as much as I possibly could. I organised the last journey of several hundred people before finally giving up undertaking in 1998.

My very first involvement in funerals was in the late 1950's. Harold Allen and I were fetched off the job we were working on and taken to see Mr Horace Wildgoose. In his office we were introduced to a Mr Fred Holmes who had a furniture shop on Dale Road at Matlock. Holmes at that time, also carried out high-cless funeral undertaking. Harold and I were taken in Mr Holmes' car to a nearby village and informed of our part. Our job was to strip the topsoil off a large grave site to locate and remove the slabs of stone from a brick-built vault, move all the displaced material well out of sight, place planks around the vault and cover them with an artifical grass carpet material. The funeral of the local industrialist was to be at 2pm the following day. He had employed around a hundred or so people at his old-established factory.

Next morning Harold and I loaded up my old Post Office van with the tools, sand and cement, and off we went. Fortunately it was a fine day, we stripped off the turf and exposed the stone flags, then with much effort, grunting and grumbling removed the heavy flags out of the way. We laid the planks around the vault and fixed the artificial grass carpet in place. The vault already contained one high-quality mahogany coffin. While we were having our lunch someone came and inspected our work, pronounced everything alright and told us to keep out of sight until all the mourners had gone and then cement the slabs back in place. Put back the topsoil and turf, leaving everything neat and tidy. One last check around the vault and Harold and I retreated to the back of the churchyard.

We were totally surprised by the large number of mourners and floral tributes. A seemingly never-ending stream of people paraded past the vault for the next hour or so.

About 3.30pm Harold and I went to the vault which now contained another lovely polished mahogany coffin with a large engraved silver name-plate on it. We fetched the stone slabs back, mixed some sand and cement and prepared to reseal the vault. An oldish man, in working clothes and working boots who had been watching us for some time from a distance, came up the open grave. Before Harold and I could do anything, he leapt onto the coffin and jumped up and down. We quickly dragged him out and asked him what he was doing. He said "I told the factory owner some years ago that I would dance on his grave if he died first and I have kept my promise!" After that unexpected episode, we put the slabs back on the vault as quickly as we could, before anyone else could scratch the coffin.

Another funeral that sticks in my mind was when another local joiner/undertaker, who had been in the forces during the Second World War, and was notorious for his range of naval-inspired swear words. He was carrying out a funeral in another local village where the funeral was arranged for the afternoon. Needless to say, it rained all morning. At the completion of the funeral service in the church, the rain turned into a thunderstorm. To avoid any distress to the bereaved at this sad time, it was the job of one of the bearers to bale out any water that had collected in the grave. A bucket of wood shavings was then sprinkled on the grave bottom. The rain was so heavy, the vicar suggested we went back into the church for a few minutes. Ten minutes later when the storm had eased off, everyone went to the graveside and the coffin was placed on two wooden 4 x 2 timbers placed across the grave so that the bearers can fix the bands to lower the coffin gently into the grave. When the bearers were ready, they lift the coffin in their hands and the and two 4 x 2 are removed. The undertaker then stands at the foot of the coffin and gives the signal to commence lowering. This very poignant moment was suddenly shattered by the sodden ground at the foot of the grave collapsing beneath the undertaker's feet, precipitating him into the grave beneath the descending coffin. A shouted swear word, followed by several others, rent the solemn moment. The bearers stood with the suspended coffin over the recumbent undertaker lying in the bottom of the grave covered with mud and wood shavings. The grave was six feet deep and by the time the undertaker emerged, with a mixture of mud and wood shavings dripping from him, the gravedigger had appeared from out of his van armed with a shovel to straighten up the grave. Eventually the coffin was laid to rest, the vicar said a few words and we all trooped back into the church except fot the mud-spattered bedraggled undertaker who was still in a state of shock after his premature trip into the grave.

As you will have gathered, despite the most detailed and careful planning, not all funerals go smoothly. I had arranged the funeral of a very popular lady in a nearby town. I visited the churchyard mid-morning to ensure the gravedigger had got everything ready, and I could see no snags. The organist, churchwarden and vicar had all been informed of the time and date. We arrived on time at the church with the hearse and several cars. Groups of people were gathered in the churchyard and church. The churchwarden informed me that the vicar was on his way.

Time passed, with no sign of the clergyman, when a man came racing down the path to the church on a bicycle. Attempting to avoid some mourners, he left the path, hit a gravestone and flew through the air and came to an abrupt halt on a stone wall adjacent to the path. It was the vicar! It became clear that he was seriously hurt and someone dashed off to telephone for an ambulance. I suggested that everyone went into the church while the churchwarden endeavoured to find another clergyman to conduct the funeral. A doctor and ambulance arrived and took away the injured vicar who had suffered a broken arm and severe bruising. Luckily another vicar arrived within half-an-hour, and the chief mourners and I gave him details of the deceased. The bearers then unloaded the coffin, and followed by the chief mourners, proceeded into the church. The rest of the funeral went smoothly with dignity – if a little late. I finally gave up undertaking in 1998.

It was also in 1966 that I built and sold my first spec. house at The Crescent, Hurd's Hollow, Matlock. Jack Crossland, whose brother gave me my first job in the building trade, came to work for me, as did my mother's brother's son Ezra Toft, then Harold Allen and George White from Wildgoose's stone gang. We were now a gang of ten capable builders. Jack Johnson from my Hall & Co days now had his own firm and carried out all our plumbing and heating work. George Allwood and Michael Strange, who had worked for Harry Brooks before setting up their own business, did all my electrical work. Duncan Frost, also from Wildgoose & Sons, became my joinery manager and ran the Greenaway Lane joiner's shop. Harold Bowler stayed on to help and teach him and I the ins and outs of undertaking, and all the legalities that go with it.

The building business was going exceedingly well. Barbara and I had about sixteen employees and found work for lots of sub-contractors. We discussed where we were going and decided not to grow any larger as a firm. Duncan Frost left us and we set on an old workmate from Wildgoose days, Errol Roose, as foreman joiner and undertaker. The undertaking business was thriving. Errol made a good undertaker. He worked very hard although he was not in the best of health. I was so fortunate to have such a great team of men who were also wonderful friends. Several of them were my friends and workmates for over thirty-five years, Phillip Taylor, David Hall, Granville Wagstaffe, Harold Allen and my son Andrew.

When I was building Osiris in 1958/9 I was wrestling with the lead flashings for the chimney when a man who had been leaning over the wall watching me said "You are making a pig's ear of that. I will make the flashing for you if you like, I am a plumber". He told me he was Dennis Gregory's brother from Birmingham and was called Bert Scott. Dennis was one of three orphaned brothers and had been adopted by Hugh Gregory, nurseryman and market gardener on Darley Hillside, and had had his name changed from Scott to Gregory. Our home, Osiris, was opposite to his home. Dennis, who was about four or five years older than me, also went to Churchtown school. Bert, who came to live in Darley Dale, and I set up a plumbing and heating business called Scott & Jackson. Both Dennis and Bert served in the Navy on cruisers in the Second World War and both saw action.

Barbara and I purchased a second-hand Ford Zephyr 6, about two years old, and went on holiday in it with all the family to Chapel St Leonard's – a great improvement on the old Post Office van. We hired a bus and took our employees, wives, and children to Blackpool, and had the firm's first annual dinner at The Old English Hotel, Matlock, near Christmas. We could hardly believe what was happening to us. We carried out work for S & E Johnson, corn millers, and they sold me one of their small lorries. Shand's sold me a diesel concrete mixer, a one ton dumper and a compressor, complete with jack-hammer. Chesterfield Plant Hire sold me a vibratory roller. Wildgoose & Sons let me have some of their surplus scaffolding, the joiners had a Bedford van and so by 1967 we had become a self-contained construction firm, capable of doing practically any job.

One of my men got married and the reception was held at a public house in Wirksworth to which we had been invited. About 10pm a fight broke out. Harold Allen and I tipped over a large table close to the wall, and got behind it with our wives. Bottles, chairs, fists were flying and eventually several policemen arrived and everyone went home. A very memorable wedding.

Barbara took her driving test in 1966, and passed. She had learned to drive years before on the 1927 Morris lorry around the grounds of Highlands. Time passed in a blur. I tried to keep up with outside interests but it was a struggle. I built all day and at night serviced and repaired vehicles and machinery. In September 1966 we became members of the National House Building Council, registered number A6662. I insisted that all the work we undertook was of the highest possible standard. This was no trouble to our builders. The difference between a poor tradesman and a really good tradesman is that a really good tradesman builds down to a good standard, while the poor tradesman endeavours to try to attain a good standard. Some have the gift more than others.

Take Jack Carter from the stone gang for example. He could build random stonework better and quicker than anyone I ever knew. He would glance at the heap of rubble, pick out the exact stone needed, knock it into shape with his walling hammer if necessary, then fix it. Whenever I see stonework that Jack built I marvel how excellently, nonchalantly and easily he built them. The only fault Jack had was talking. He talked even more than I did. One afternoon Jack and I were hard at work at Nottingham building a boundary wall to a public house. Jack had been yackety-yacking on for ages and I told him to shut up as I could not concentrate on the sneck walling. Jack said again "Hey Lew" and I said "*** shut up." A few minutes later Jack said "I really have to tell you something." I again told him to be quiet and a brief silence reigned. Jack's demeanour never altered as he said "I really think you should know that the snap cabin is on fire." I spun round and it was blazing fiercely. It was too late to save my old coat and snap-bag. Jack said "I have been trying to tell you for the last five minutes. It's too late to save it now" and calmly carried on building while the cabin burnt down. Jack rarely flapped.

DESIGN AND CUSTOMERS

Designing and building dwellings is a very rewarding and interesting job especially if you have only yourself to please. Lewis Jackson Builders Ltd. built one hundred and one dwellings, fifty of them for sale, never building more than three the same. I believe the most important time spent in planning is walking round the vacant site, weighing up the pros and cons, visualising how the finished dwelling will harmonise with the site. The best place for access, the importance of the main aspect of the dwelling being as near south as possible. Kitchen, bathroom, utility, small bedrooms to face east or north. On which side of the dwelling are the main services to run, type of materials to be used, height of ground floor level, type of windows. I learned never to choose the kitchen furniture, bathroom suite or tiles, and fireplace for a dwelling for sale. I always included a prime cost sum for the client to buy them with and stipulated where they could purchase them from. People's tastes vary immensely and if they choose the fittings they are much more likely to be happy with the finished product. Planning officers vary considerably as do estate agents, building inspectors and highway officials. At least nine months are needed to build a dwelling, three months for various planning authorities etc. and six months from building start to completion. Purchasers of my houses could have any colour decoration they liked so long as it was either magnolia or white. Never sell a dwelling until it is almost finished and ready for the final fittings. If you do people will want to change it in some way or other. This leads to disputes, missed time schedules and needless harassment. A decent dwelling, well built and well looked after should have a two hundred years life. It will need several refurbishments over that period.

We next built a house for the Derbyshire County Council's Surveyor, Gordon Race down Greenaway Lane. As I have mentioned I met Gordon Race in the late 1950s when I was sent by Wildgoose's, with Harold Allen, Jack Carter and Vic Shimwell, to build the stone facade of a railway bridge near Blyth, between Worksop and Doncaster. By the end of 1967 in three years we had built sixteen dwellings besides umpteen other jobs, large and small. I was now forty years old.

One of the brighter things to look forward to as a builder is the fact that in a short time you will have left the site, its people and troubles, and moved on to the next challenge. I won an appeal against the Peak Park Planning Board over windows and materials at Birchover. We built an extension and a large building with a first floor studio for the Keys at Middleton by Youlgrave, and an extension at Bakewell for one of the Thorntons, the chocolate people. Andrew, who has a gift for building, built his first house without supervision, Rye House at Two Dales.

When I built Isis, next door to Osiris, in 1969, again opposite Dennis

Gregory's house, Bert, the plasterer Mac, and his mate Jamieson, and Harold Allen had all been in the Navy in the war. George Allwood who was doing the electrical work also went to sea on a battleship as a civilian, fixing and maintaining radar systems for fire control of its big guns. Dennis came across to Isis and the six of them decided to have a Navy Day, running the house as a warship. I was piped aboard, they kept the time by so many bells, and went to action stations every time someone came. I thought they had the makings of an ideal crew for a pirate ship. They were the right men in the wrong age. Bert and I got on well together, as I did with the plasterers, Mac and Jamieson, having lots of fun every day. They were all superb craftsmen. Our building venture, almost by accident, was running away with us! I contracted to widen the Bentley Brook from where it runs past Huntbridge House to Matlock Green. I got the job and utilised my civil engineering skills and my Whitlock digger. We were so lucky, it hardly rained while we did the job and it came out very well. I began maintaining Stancliffe Hall Boys' School and Hinckley's KSR works at Rowsley, also Shand House, the headquarters of my former employer.

In 1970 whilst at Isis I became the owner of a Rover three litre car. I had been a Rover fan for twenty years. This was my fifth and last – I was always having to delve into the engine, fitting new exhaust valves. The engine was junk and I have never had a Rover since. One day in 1970 whilst fetching bricks with the Dodge lorry from Waingrove, Ripley, I saw a 1968 3.4 S type Jaguar for sale. It was white, sleek, and the epitome of everything a car should be. I could not resist the urge to have it. Barbara drove it everywhere. I took my mother, then aged about eighty-three, down the A38 Burton bypass in it as fast as it would go, around one hundred and twenty-five miles per hour.

Between 1971 and 1975 we built eight houses at Birchover and eight elsewhere for sale. We also looked after the building maintenance of several quarries for Tarmac, and three historic old Halls, and built houses and extensions for clients. Andrew, after a brief spell working for Derbyshire County Council and in civil engineering, came to work

Left to right: Charlie Hopkinson, Andrew Jackson and Eric Bennet
blocking Haddon tunnel 19th July 1975

for the family firm and worked on the houses at Birchover, where we had a lot of trouble with the natives over access roads, drains etc. As stated before, people are very tribal and territorial. Wherever I build people nearby do not want change. It is understandable. At Birchover I could see this coming so I purchased the private access road from Davic Thornhill, from whom I had purchased the land, to safeguard the scheme. I had learned a few lessons about "Not in my backyard" and "Have you got the right?

JINXED VAN

In the seventies we ran Bedford vans. One van was jinxed. One of our joiners, Ian Barnes, was driving it backwards down a narrow farm track at Hartington as the vicar of Hartington was coming up the track in his almost new car. The vicar drove on to the grass verge to try to get out of Ian's way, unsuccessfully as it happened. Ian drove into the side of the vicar's car, seriously damaging the front wing, taking off both doors and the centre door pillar of the four months old car. It also kinked the roof. The vicar was unhurt. I asked Ian what the vicar had said. "Plenty, but all without a swear-word" said Ian. I had previously fitted a heavy three inch by three inch piece of angle iron across the back of the van, in place of the bumper which had already been damaged by the joiners.

A few weeks later another joiner, David Helliwell, was going past Hooley's Estate in the same van behind a large Derby Carpets furniture van. David took his eyes off the road for a moment to gaze at a comely young mother pushing a pram on the elevated footpath. The furniture van stopped abruptly, David did not. He hit it so hard he almost went inside it amongst the carpets, pushing both rear doors inwards. I towed the battered van home to repair it. It required a new radiator, bonnet, sump and lights, which I acquired from a scrapyard, and repaired it. Except for being about an inch shorter than it was before it ran quite well.

They say accidents come in threes. A few weeks later I received a phone call from Andrew who was in the same van. "Bring the big Dodge lorry and a good chain to Bakewell river bridge". "Have you broken down?" I asked. "Not exactly, I've gone through the parapet of the bridge, and the front wheels are hanging over the River Wye. Come as quickly as you can. The police have closed the road and sent for a crane to lift the van off the bridge". The Dodge lorry and I arrived on the scene after threading our way through lines of stationary traffic. Despite protests from the police I fixed the chain to the back axle of the van and to the girder fastened to the back of the lorry, and snatched the van off the edge of the bridge and dragged it down the road out of the way. This relieved the traffic congestion and gave the crowd something to look at. Both front tyres were flat and the front of the van badly damaged. The police arranged for the crane to be stopped and sent back. We then dragged the van by brute force with the lorry up to the disused Bakewell railway station and on to the platform. With the help of some

The van on Bakewell Bridge 1975

onlookers we loaded the van on to the lorry off the station platform and then went home. I once more repaired the van. It was now considerably shorter than when new, but it still ran well. The police inspected it and gave it the ok. The following year this ill-fated van caught fire under the dashboard. Nip Wagstaffe, the foreman joiner, was driving it. This last disaster occurred at the top of Station Road, Darley Dale, and it was decided to scrap it. Some vehicles are lucky ones, some are unlucky. This Bedford van was definitely an unlucky one.

1978 saw us with two cars, a BMW three litre and a Fiat 850. At work I had a Dodge lorry adapted to carry a Drott five ton tracked bulldozer and a seven and a half ton Ford lorry. The Dodge and the bulldozer were purchased from Mr M Smith who ran the Darley Dale Garden Centre, now the Forest Nurseries Ltd. I extended the Garden Centre for them and both designed and built the hexagon restaurant there. The building business was still going strong. Errol Roose had gone back to Wildgoose & Sons and had been replaced by Granville

In 1990, our apprentice, Stephen Marsden gained the Gold Award in Advanced Craft Brickwork, ahead of 1,300 candidates from across the country. His workmates Andrew Jackson and Robert Gregory already held Silver Trowel awards for their skills. All trained at Chesterfield College of Technology and Art. Lewis Jackson Builders Ltd. must have had one of the most highly qualified teams of builders in the country

Wagstaffe as foreman joiner. He was exceptional both as a craftsman and a manager. I was once again so lucky to have such a splendid man working for me. I believe any firm is only as good as its staff.

Demolition

When Stancliffe Estates and the Stancliffe Stone Quarry went into voluntary liquidation in the late seventies I purchased the land between Fircliffe Lane and the A6, enough to build twelve good houses on. We did our first large demolition job for Derbyshire Dales District Council at around this time. This was the old Fire Station above the Town Hall, Bank Road, Matlock. We demolished it by clamping a thirty feet length of ten inch by four-inch timber in the jaws of the four-in-one bucket of the Massey Drott. The demolition was a great success and Derbyshire Dales were very impressed with us. This led on to other things. Soon afterwards a heavy goods vehicle ran away down Cromford Hill, damaging several properties and coming to rest embedded in a house. Cromford Hill is a very busy road with especially large lorries carting quarry products from the nearby Middleton quarries. Derbyshire Dales District Council telephoned and asked me if I could go immediately

1956 Bedford Silver Service bus

with my men and equipment to make the dwelling safe as it was in danger of collapse. We shored up the dwelling, boarded up the opening, cleaned up the debris from the road quickly and the police opened the road again.

    Going through Wirksworth one day in 1978 in the Dodge lorry, on the way to Mugginton for a load of sand, I called in at a garage and saw in a corner a stripped down car. It was a 1950 registered Healey Westland, which had been dismantled ready for rebuilding with a new ash frame. It was beyond the garage's capabilities and I purchased the remains. Charlie and I built a makeshift garage at Highlands from second hand timber and zinc sheets left over from demolishing Matlock's old Fire Station. We loaded the chassis and all the bits on the lorry and took them to the garage. I was friendly with a lorry mechanic from Johnson's Mill, David Jaina, and another mechanic from Longcliffe, John Humphrey. We three and an auto electrician, Ian Hodgkinson, from Woolliscroft's Silver Service Bus Company, rebuilt the Healey, re-braked, re-wired, engine decoked and set up. A Healey Westland won the Alpine Rally and was second in the Italian Mille Miglia in 1948. Mine has given me twenty-seven years of pleasure. I also acquired an old bus from Woolliscroft, a 1956 petrol engined Bedford and ran it for years, taxing it as a private car. I eventually gave it to a bus preservation society in 1996.

By 1982, when I was fifty-five, there had been changes. The firm of Scott and Jackson had ceased. Bert Scott had emigrated to New Zealand to live, taking with him his two sons, one of whom, John, was one of our joiners. Two more of my men, Ian Hodgkinson, former auto electrician, and Russell Cope also emigrated to Australia. I was fortunate to have them as friends as well as members of my band of builders. My old mate Tom Helliwell had also emigrated to New Zealand in the 1960s. They were all hard working, resourceful and capable men, all imbued with the will to get up and go. The undertaking business of Walter Bowler & Son was handling about twenty clients a year and employed four or five joiners.

Conksbury Lane

In 1985 we had the good fortune to be offered some building land on Conksbury Lane at Youlgrave. I was very pleased as my ancestors had carried out many building projects in Youlgrave since first being recorded there in the 1500s. We were thrilled to have the opportunity to carry on with the Toft family involvement in Youlgrave. Unbeknown to me when we purchased the Youlgrave land it had a large Severn Trent water main running through it which tops up Youlgrave village water supply in times of drought. When I had built the six houses the Youlgrave Parish Council smugly announced that it was impossible for them to supply me with water. The Severn Trent said their main was purely to supplement the Youlgrave supply in times of necessity so I served notice on Severn Trent to remove their water main from my land. A sudden change of heart took place. It was decided that it was, after all, possible to supply the six houses from their main.

I had built one of the garages on the development about one foot higher than it should have been because of drainage problems. The Youlgrave parish council asked for a joint meeting with myself and the Peak Park Planning Board on the site to investigate this grave flouting of the planning permission. A total of twenty-four councillors and Peak Park Planning Board members attended the meeting. I gave them a thoughtful speech and took a few photographs of them after which they got back into the bus and moved on to pastures new. I never heard another word from any of them. Maybe the fact that I told them I had won three appeals against the Peak Park Planning Board, and was now anxious to write to the national papers about their carry-on helped. I believed then, and even more so today, that some Peak Park and council members are not really practical, and are very biased towards the Park. There is no substitute for practical knowledge, common sense and even-handedness. After we had built the six houses at Youlgrave I wanted to call the development "The Toft", from an Old English and Scandinavian word meaning enclosure. The Youlgrave parish council insisted the development be called "The Orchard". As there was not a fruit tree in sight I planted about a dozen. The Youlgrave parish council at that time were the pettiest I ever came across in my building career.

Our building firm purchased another portion of Stancliffe Quarry land including the old Precast Stone factory, and we commenced building there, utilising the development as a back-up job when we had no other contracts. It took Lewis Jackson (Builders) Ltd. eighteen years to build twenty-six houses on the Stancliffe site. I designed them all, although I employed several architects to do the detailed plans, including my friend David Monkhouse. We also built the County Architect's (Roy Geall) house on Hall Moor Road, Darley Dale in the mid-eighties.

1990 was a very busy year. Although the undertaking business was slowly but surely declining – I had not advertised for ten years, except in the church magazine and we were down to about ten or twelve funerals a year – we were taking on our biggest building job ever, a large new three-storey classroom block at Stancliffe Hall School, built of natural stone. It was a large undertaking with special foundations and involving numerous sub-contractors. Barbara as usual handled all the paperwork, Nip Wagstaffe the joinery side, and Andrew proved to be invaluable, seeing to the myriad structural details. I practically lived on the job. As the job drew to a close decision time arrived for Barbara and me. We had the equipment, organisation and skilled craftsmen to take on large jobs, ie schools, public buildings etc. I was now sixty-three, Harold Allen had taken early retirement and Eric Bennett and Charlie Hopkinson had both died, Charlie after a ten years fight against cancer, through which he worked most of the time, Eric from a stroke. I carried out their funerals. Nip Wagstaffe was not well and was looking for early retirement, and we could see Russell had settled for a life away from the building trade. We decided to let Lewis Jackson (Builders) Ltd gradually run itself down as there was now much more hassle in running a building company than yesteryear because of the huge proliferation of rules, inspectors and forms.

Emergency work

An even worse runaway crash happened again on Cromford Hill in the 1990s, close to the site of the previous one. The runaway lorry crashed into a house and bounced off into the front of another. Once more we were sent for in a hurry. We downed tools on the house we were building at Sir Joseph's Lane, Darley Dale and dashed off to Cromford where it was a scene of devastation. Police and firemen stood on the road across from the battered building, which had a gaping hole in its three-storey front and looked to be in urgent need of tender loving care. The fire chief and police inspector told me they had sent for the Gas and Electricity Boards to cut off supplies. Gas was escaping and the electricity was clearly very dodgy, with wires hanging down. The fire chief calmly announced that the building was far too dangerous for anyone to go in until we had made it safe. My son Andrew and our men worked miracles with Acrow props, timbers and wedges. They were very amused that we would have to make it safe before the firemen or local authority workers could enter the building, or the safety officer inspect it to see if it was safe enough for other workmen to enter. We were so busy and focused on the job that we did not notice a TV crew appear. Imagine our surprise when we were on the television news that night.

Not long after this we received another emergency call to a cafe and bungalow on top of High Tor at Matlock, which they said was on fire and collapsing. When we arrived the roof of the bungalow and cafe had fallen in and the fire brigade had extinguished the flames except for a huge plume of burning gas coming out of the service pipe to the meter which had melted away. The fire chief told us he had sent for the Gas Board to cut off the supply, and there was nothing more they could do. He said the fire engine was needed elsewhere, and that they were leaving. Andrew appeared with the JCB, the huge flame was still roaring out of the pipe, and there was no sign of the Gas Board. It was late afternoon on a winter's day. Andrew swept all the debris to one side with the JCB. We then shaped a piece of wood into a round plug. One of our men went up to the blazing gas pipe, plug in one hand and a hammer in the other, and calmly knocked the plug into the pipe and extinguished the flame in an instant. The Gas Board eventually arrived and commenced to cut off the gas supply in the road. We all went home.

Next morning we went back, piled all the debris in a big heap, mostly charred timber because the roof and part of the cafe had been of wooden construction. We poured plenty of diesel on it and set fire to it again. This got rid of all the dangerous nail filled charred timbers. While the timbers were burning we demolished the remains of the bungalow, dug up the floors and foundations, carted them away and soiled the site over. We then removed what ashes remained of our fire to the tip. Derbyshire Dales, who were the owners of the property, were once again impressed. We only did one more job of this type. It was the large goods shed next to Matlock railway station which had been on fire. We found these types of jobs very exhilarating. If you have the expertise, the equipment and plenty of common sense there is little danger. Eric Bennett, who has sadly died, was at his best on this sort of job. He excelled at propping up buildings for the removal of walls etc. Whilst I had great faith in him I found it best for my peace of mind not to go near the job until he had finished it.

We carried out repairs after several minor accidents which the Electricity Distribution Board had, such as when they dropped poles on dwellings, knocked down farmers walls etc. The Board asked us to repair and service their substations around the Peak District and we worked in almost every village and town from Buxton to Ashover, though not Chesterfield.

In 1997 the Distribution Board rang up and asked if we could build them a new sub-station very quickly at Eyam in the heart of the Peak District National Park. I asked them "What about the Peak Park Planning Board, and the plans being passed and vetted by them?" They told me to ignore them as they needed the new sub-station as soon as possible. The site was near to the Royal Oak public house. We moved on to the site with a JCB and lorry and began excavating the hillside where the sub-station was to go. Officialdom soon arrived by the car load and, much to their chagrin, found that electric sub-stations are immune from all planning laws and regulations. We built the sub-station to a very high standard out of local natural stone. I believe the Peak Park Planning Board was astonished that anyone could actually construct a building without the benefit of their advice and expertise. Everything that makes Eyam such a wonderful village was planned and constructed long before the Peak Park Planning Board was thought of, but they do a very good job of preserving the village.

The company that owned the twenty-seven acre Stancliffe Quarry was called Stancliffe Park Ltd and the company that worked and sold the stone was called WIL Ltd. Barbara and I purchased the two companies outright in 1996 and leased the quarry to a company called Realstone Ltd, then to the Stirling Stone Co Ltd from Scotland.

Left to Right: *Granville Wagstaffe joiner, Phillip Taylor plasterer, the author, David Hall builder and Andrew Jackson builder.*
My workmates for around 30 years

At the Millennium I was seventy three, Barbara was seventy, and the spring was definitely going out of our steps. We were now down to four employees, including Andrew. I still worked occasionally at bricklaying, concreting and stone-fixing, and looking after my collection of vintage vehicles and machinery which I had acquired over many years, mostly as junk and brought back to life. Barbara and I celebrated our Golden Wedding Anniversary on 31st March 2001. We purchased Redlands, the bungalow at the top of Crowstones Road, Darley Dale, where I spent fourteen happy years in my youth. It was badly in need of extensive renovation as the previous owner had completely neglected it. We re-roofed it, and altered it completely internally, added a garage to it and decided to re-name it, calling it Phoenix, partly because it had "risen from the ashes", and partly because Phoenix was a sister submarine to Pandora and Osiris on which my brother John had spent so much time in China in the 1930s. The houses next door to Redlands/Phoenix, which my father and mother built in 1936, are called

Pandora and Forres. At this time we had the opportunity to purchase Pandora and we seized the opportunity. Forres was the submarine depot ship on the China station, all a long time ago.

Lewis Jackson Ltd had shrunk and now only employed six people including my eldest son Andrew, David Hall, and Phillip Taylor, all of whom had worked for us for around thirty years. Granville Wagstaffe the foreman joiner retired in 1995 after 23 years. We built our last house, which was built for, and mostly by, our son Andrew, at the junction of Bent Lane with Whitworth Road, Darley Dale, and which he named Millennium House. We sold our last building plot and this gave me time to realise my long-time ambition of building myself a large agricultural implement shed in our garden, utilising part of the old Whitworth conservatory back wall. I had been going to build myself a shed since 1970 but never before had the time to spare. When I think of all the hours I spent out in the open, lying under vehicles and machinery, getting cold, wet, and covered in oil, it is a god-send.

SOME CLIENTS

It was a joy to meet so many interesting people whilst working on their properties, and to hear a wealth of local history from them. L. du Garde Peach from Hucklow, whom I first met in 1957/8 while building the chalet bungalow for his secretary at Conjoint Lane, Tideswell, told me about the children evacuated from Guernsey in 1940 to Hucklow. Two hundred and fifty children and around twenty staff arrived at Hucklow in July 1940. Hucklow had a population of around one hundred. He told me of the trials and tribulations the children had suffered, how Tideswell and Hucklow were bombed in August 1940, and the people of Hucklow, a lonely isolated peak land village, took them to their hearts at a time of great stress. I have researched this wartime happening for around forty-five years and met several of the participants, given occasional talks to Peak dwellers, and written about it. I belong to the same age group as those children and feel for them, uprooted from their island home and parents to dwell in Peakland Derbyshire, exiled for five years from all they knew and loved. The exiled children are now in their seventies and eighties. We have worked in the Hucklow area several times. I usually go and visit the grave of one of the children, Joan Shaw, who died in 1944 aged fourteen and is buried at Hucklow, exiled for ever.

Over the years on various walks around the south side of our valley, ie Clough Wood and Stanton Moor, I had seen several deer. In the 1970/80s we carried out building work for the Thornhills of Stanton Hall, Stanton in the Peak. Nicholas Thornhill told me that Stanton Hall had a deer park with around forty to fifty deer until 1944 and when Britain was becoming short of food the Thornhills were served with an order to cull the deer and plough up and cultivate the deer park. When the dreadful day arrived for the deer to be culled Nicholas told me, with a twinkle in his eye, that somehow they had all escaped the night before and were nowhere to be found. Sixty years later their descendants are still living free on the south side of the Darley Derwent and I often visit them. I know they have had some TLC over the years by their original owners. It is fortunate that they live in an area out of bounds to the general public with the consequence that many newcomers have no idea that we have a herd of around forty deer in our valley.

Another family we worked for was the very old Derbyshire family of Bagshaws who then lived at Snitterton Hall, a large medieval building on the south side of the Derwent. One day I had occasion to visit a part of the house I was not familiar with. Imagine my surprise to see a series of paintings of Red Indian chiefs in the full traditional dress of buckskins and feathered head-dress. I asked Mr Bagshaw how they came to be there. He told me they were his ancestors and that at the time of the French/British war in Canada the Ojibway Tribe had been helped by one of his ancestors and in return they had made the eldest son of the Bagshaw tribe an hereditary chief of their tribe. Amazing to think that for many years we have had a Red Indian chief and a herd of wild deer dwelling in our valley that very few have known about.

We installed a new kitchen in a house near the Whitworth Hospital for a family who had just come to live in Darley. The man said they had come to live here in our valley because it was so lovely and so handy to both large cities and wild scenery. He went on to say he had visited our valley often over the previous twenty years and I asked him where he stayed when he visited. He replied "I have never stayed or set foot in the valley before. I was a fighter pilot for twenty years and as you know this is a low flying area. I used to fly round the valley and decided it would be a nice place to live and settle down in, and here I am".

We also built two dwellings for the Smith family from the Red House stables. I had worked in my spare time for the family, who had a concrete block factory at South Darley and a fluorspar plant at Eyam, since I was twenty-one, and also for Caroline Smith who ran the Red House Stables. I had the great pleasure of driving Caroline to her wedding with Peter at Bakewell. I have enjoyed over fifty years of friendship with her and her brother Trevor, since Trevor started manufacturing concrete blocks, facing type, in the early 1950s and I built a demonstration panel for him at Bakewell Show for publicity purposes. Trevor and his wife have had more than their share of family tragedy.

Caroline kept carriages and a stage coach for film work and hiring out, and is an expert stage coach driver. After an unfortunate accident Caroline had no one to drive the large horse box which carried the team of four horses that pulled the stage coach. I shall never forget the time I drove the horse box with four horses in it and towing a large trailer behind, with the stage coach on it. We were going to Sheffield to transport the Lord Mayor and other civic dignitaries to switch on the Christmas lights. I could see trouble ahead in Sheffield when we went round the traffic island at Baslow. The lorry and trailer was almost sixty feet long and when I looked out of the side window of the lorry I could see the rear of the trailer across the island. A police escort was waiting for us at Sheffield. They led us into a small car park already full of cars. Caroline and I were on our own and worked miracles, unloading the stage coach and horses then harnessing the horses to the coach. Caroline is very resourceful and very hard working.

I dressed, as usual when on stage coach work, in top hat and period great coat. I took my seat as postillion brakeman and we set off to the city centre, complete with the Lord Mayor and his entourage, escorted by a police car. Thousands of people had gathered to watch the switching on ceremony. Caroline detailed me to hold the horses. I had already wedged the brake full on. The Lord Mayor alighted from the stage coach with his entourage and mounted the podium to switch on the lights. Suddenly six men in uniform, all armed with trumpets about a yard long, stepped forward to blow a fanfare. Caroline gestured a warning to me as I stood between the two lead horses facing the thousands of people gathered there. I grasped their bridles very firmly and hung on. Caroline gathered up the reins and the next moment I was six feet in the air as the horses reared. I hung on for dear life as the fanfare trumpets burst forth in the horses' ears. I was scared for the children and the people in the crowd, and for me. Luckily the brakes and the horses held. We were very relieved. It could have been a disaster of epic proportions. Blowing trumpets in a horse's ears is a sure recipe for an exciting time. After the ceremony we took the Lord Mayor and his party on a tour of the lights. When at last we got back to the car park, loading the horses and the stage coach, and extracting the outfit from the small car park took ages. It took the long drive home over the moors to calm us down.

I sometimes used to go with the stage coach on Sunday mornings. One morning we went to Bakewell to take a load of tourists to Chatsworth House. The coach was being driven by a Mr Marriott. We harnessed the four horses and set off for Bakewell. The horses were very frisky. Coming to the flat stretch of road between Haddon Hall and Bakewell, Marriot decided to gallop the horses to take a bit of the friskiness out of them. To sit up high on the front of a stage coach, with the team at full gallop, the coach rocking from side to side, a noise like a continuous roll of thunder coming from the iron shod wheels and hooves, sweat blowing off the horses similar to foam blowing off breaking waves in a storm, all this plus an impression of great speed and danger produces an emotion like no other. Of course there was a down side. We had to stop, rest and clean down the horses of sweat before we picked up the tourists. There were usually about fourteen in a stage coach load. When we got to the Chatsworth village of Edensor we drew the coach off the road on to the grass near the entrance to the village where we disembarked the tourists

On board the stage coach at full gallop near Haddon

for a look round. There had been a considerable amount of rain the previous day and by the time the tourists came back the narrow wheels had sunk into the ground about nine inches deep. The four horses were ploughing up the grass in a vain attempt to pull it out. We asked the tourists and several onlookers to give us a push to help free the coach. As this was taking place the congregation of Edensor church came out. Amongst them was the Duchess of Devonshire who came over and said "Would you mind not parking on the grass in future." We were obviously in the wrong place at the wrong time. However, I enjoyed my stage coach days. They were to be very useful to me in the future.

 We extended a house at Cromford for Janet Ede. Janet and I found we shared an interest in history and we wrote and published a booklet together called "Sir Joseph Whitworth and Darley Dale" which the County Council put in their libraries. I enjoyed researching Whitworth with Janet and in the course of our travels we visited many Whitworth connections. We were invited to Manchester University and dined with the Vice-Chancellor. We also visited the headquarters of the Institution of Mechanical Engineers in London, and Tarvin in Cheshire where Whitworth's first wife was born and died.

JCB AND LORRY DAYS

Having a construction company can have many rewards. Among them is the ability to provide oneself with grown up toys. I have been fortunate to own three JCBs, one five ton and one ten ton tracked bulldozers, a dumper, two vibratory rollers, various vans and lorries and one bus. I also managed to collect five farm tractors, mostly about fifty years old, which I came across in my travels. It is marvellous what one comes across. For instance I acquired a 1956 forty-seater bus which I taxed as private, ie car tax, and ran for about ten years. It first belonged to Strange's of Tansley, then Woolliscroft's Silver Service. I then acquired a Mercedes 450 saloon in lieu of a debt. Four sets of gang mowers and two ride-on mowers also came my way. Practically all this machinery was decrepit, in need of TLC, and very cheap or less. Machinery and I seem to have an affinity, we get on well together. My oldest pieces of junk are a 1913 Amanco stationary engine, a 1929 Dennis lorry, a 1930 9.28 Humber tourer, and a 1950 real (not Austin) Healey Mille Miglia sports car. I get great pleasure out of renovating machinery and have several friends who have given me help and advice over the sixty years since I purchased my first car, a 1929 Austin Seven, for £20. I have rarely been without either a car or motor-cycle since. The JCBs have given me many hours of pleasure. IT IS ABSOLUTELY IMPOSSIBLE TO BE BORED WHILST DRIVING A JCB. I purchased my first one in 1966 from Clay Cross, a village about twelve miles and several steep hills away and drove it home, an adventure in itself.

One of my first jobs was at the Chatsworth Estate. The job entailed

Our JCB

excavating trenches for water services to outlying farms and cottages, and re-surfacing several tracks with limestone chippings. The estate manager was a Mr Cherry who told me when and where to work. I only went now and then as I had my own work to do, excavating foundations etc. for house building. The Chatsworth job proved to be a very steep learning curve in every way. One of the jobs entailed digging a trench for a water service from Russian Cottage, on top of the hill between Chatsworth Park and the Carlton Pastures road. The ground sloped steeply away from the cottage, which was called Russian Cottage because it was a gift to the Duke from the Tsar of Russia in the late 1800s.

Early morning dew bathed the grass as in bottom gear I cautiously drove the digger over the edge of the slope. When I applied the brakes the wheels stopped but the machine continued on down the steep slope, skidding on the wet grass. I quickly released the brake as the machine started to skid sideways, in order to try to get a vestige of control of it. The wheels slowly revolved giving me a chance to straighten it up. I had no time to be scared at that stage as the wheels continued to turn at a sedate pace in bottom gear. The digger went faster and faster. I was concentrating on trying to steer a straight course down the steep hill to the road and stream some two or three hundred or more yards below me. I had visions of the almost out of control JCB rolling over and over down the hill to the detriment of its driver - me. I made it down to the road, bounced two or three feet in the air, then dropped into the stream which was about four or five feet below the road. I could hardly believe my luck that the JCB and I had both escaped unscathed. I then suffered from a distinct lack of enthusiasm regarding digging trenches on steep hills.

I managed to dig my way back on to the road and drove the digger back to the nearby estate woodyard, and telephoned Barbara to fetch me home. I went to fetch the digger next day and told Chatsworth I was no longer going to work for them as I was too busy with my own jobs, which was true, as was the fact that I liked me alive and kicking not tobogganing down wet, steep hills to destruction in a three-ton digger. As a result of this episode the gear box was cracked and I had to buy a scrap Fordson Major tractor gearbox, and spend a few nights changing the gearbox over, not an easy job.

The following winter we had a heavy fall of snow. I was fortunately at home when the Derbyshire County Council rang and asked me if I would go immediately to Woodside Farm, Back Lane off Sydnope Hill, as a lady was in distress with labour pains and the ambulance could not get because of snowdrifts. I hurriedly made my way up to Back Lane where deep drifts had formed across the single track road. I dug out the snow as fast as I could to enable the ambulance to get to the isolated farm. When I had almost cleared a road to the farm it was decided to carry the lady on a stretcher to the ambulance, now near at hand. The ambulance departed. I dug out the rest of the snow to the farm and I too departed.

This was to be the start of several winters of snow-shifting for the Derbyshire County Council. After another heavy snowfall the DCC rang around 4pm and asked me if I would go up Sydnope Hill and try to keep the road open to the point where it met the Chesterfield section, about eleven hundred feet above sea level. It was snowing hard and the wind was gusting, blowing the snow off the road in places and making drifts up to over six feet high at gateways and inter-sections. Sydnope Hill itself had been well salted. I cleared the drifts until midnight when the wind dropped. I backed the JCB into a side road, Flash Lane, for a rest, a drink of tea and a sandwich, and turned off the lights to save the battery. It had stopped snowing, the stars were out, everywhere was still and peaceful on the moor. After the roar of the engine, the glare of the headlights on the snow, and the need to concentrate, to sit at peace in the cab on the lonely moorland lane, sipping hot tea was heaven. The only sounds were ticking from the engine as it cooled down and snow dropping off the branches of the tall dark pine trees which grew alongside the lane.

It must have been approaching midnight when, cocooned in my JCB I decided that the battle was over. I had won, time to go home, when out of the corner of my eye I saw a jet-black figure slowly making its way through the snow along the main road. I looked again as best I could in the dim starlight and as the figure got nearer I could not believe my eyes and went all to pieces as I saw it was a man, dressed all in black, with no head. With the JCB at right angles to the main road it was impossible to shine the lights up the road. The spectre came on slowly down the road and to my great relief I saw it was leaving a track in the snow. When the strange apparition came level with the JCB I turned all the lights on and saw, outlined in the beam of the headlights, a man in evening dress with a large white carrier bag on his head with a slot ripped in it for him to see through. He was as startled as I had been. He told me that he was a waiter at the Red Lion Inn, and after leaving the inn at midnight to make his way home his car had gone off the road and got absolutely stuck. He said he had abandoned the car and decided to walk home, despite having no overcoat, and only shoes on. I offered to take him back to the car and try and dig it out but he said he was beyond caring, wet, and very cold, and was planning to make his way to the first dwelling he came across and ask for shelter.

Finishing my break I started the JCB and went up the road towards Chesterfield, clearing a track with the front bucket. I saw lights ahead of me. It was the JCB from the Chesterfield section and the driver told me the car was stuck on the verge. We quickly dug the snow away from it then gently pushed the car to a safer place, exchanged a few words, and carried on with our job of keeping the road open from Darley Dale to Chesterfield. I went home around 2am, mission accomplished, road open.

In the next deep snow I was posted to Newhaven on the Buxton road which is really bleak, and thirteen hundred feet above sea level. The County Council's lorry-mounted snow ploughs could not break through the drifts, which were enormous where the wind had swept the snow off the fields on to the road. Some of the drifts were eight feet high and up to forty feet long. Another JCB and a huge four-wheeled loader from a nearby limestone quarry was waiting for me at Newhaven. Its four driving wheels were about seven feet high and wrapped in chains to prevent damage to the tyres from sharp stones on the quarry floor. The machine was called a Michigan and was equipped with an immense front bucket about nine feet wide. The driver's cab was about ten feet high with a row of lights on top. The plan was for the Michigan to push its way through the drifts and for my JCB and the other JCB which was being driven by a man I knew called Yates from Winster, were to clear the snow which had tumbled down from the drifts' sides on to the road, and clean the road in general. It worked like a dream. The police had closed the road from Buxton to Newhaven. Snow was still falling then but had stopped by midnight. The County Council's salt spreading lorries then came along behind us and the battle was over.

On the way home we passed by the peakland village of Winster. We cleared the road to the village, Yates went home, and I slowly made my way home down the B5057 from Winster to Darley, cleaning up the occasional deep drift, when a police Range Rover appeared. Barbara had got worried about me and telephoned the police who came looking for me. I thoroughly enjoyed my snow shifting times with the JCB especially when I was alone on the moorland roads in the night in the middle of a blizzard. I had complete faith in my JCB. The only trouble I ever had was with water freezing in the diesel filter which I soon put right, mostly by the light of a torch in a freezing snowstorm. There is something unique and exhilarating about wrestling with nature and winning.

1966 saw the closing of the railway through Darley Dale. It was a sad day. My father had spent forty-nine and a half years of his life working on the railway, most of it as an engine driver. I was hired with the Whitlock digger to load the sleepers from the line through Darley. I was particularly sad when I loaded them at the Churchtown crossing where I had spent so many years of my life watching and waiting for trains on my way to and from school. I remembered all those Jubilee class locos, thundering past, standing outside Redlands on a cold and clear night, listening to the rapid clack-clack-clack of a goods train, or the sound of an express hurtling clickety-click down the valley, seeing the rosy red reflection from the fire-box when the door was open or the trailing white steam, standing at the crossing gates, being engulfed in a cacophony of sound, smell and movement. I acquired a Midland Railway lamp-post off Darley Station and fixed it on the end of Highlands drive, as a tribute to my father. Father used to take me for

Midland Railway lamp post from Darley Dale station at Highlands

rides on the engine when I was small, shunting in Darley Dale sidings. Monday 7th July 1974 was another momentous day. This adventure started several days previously with an advertisement which stated "600 gallon petrol tank, complete with pump for sale. Blackwell near Taddington". Off I went to have a look. There was not much to be seen as the tank was underground. All I could see was a hand cranked pump standing by the side of the farm track. I purchased the outfit because at that time we had several vehicles which ran on petrol. I drove the JCB up to Blackwell, about thirteen miles away in the Peak District, excavated the tank and loaded it on to our lorry together with the pump. We then went back to Highlands and dumped the tank and the pump adjacent to where it was going to be installed.

On the morning of 7th July I began excavating the hole for the tank at the end of the drive. The pit was about eleven feet by six feet six inches by six feet six inches deep. I stood the lorry on one side of the hole and positioned the JCB at one end. David Hall, who was then twenty two, was helping me. The ground was dry and we soon had the hole excavated down to the required depth. David went into the hole with a pick and shovel to level off the sides and bottom, throwing the soil into the JCB's digging bucket. The Dodge lorry, which was almost full of excavated material was standing some distance away from the side of the hole. The ground was exceptionally hard clay. I had many years' experience of excavations and was sure there was no danger, when without the slightest warning the side of the pit where the lorry was parked fell in, knocking David to the ground and burying him except for his head and shoulders. The twin rear wheels of the lorry slid into the pit immediately above where David was buried. Poor David was shouting "Help, dig me out, get me out, help me," as the lorry slowly slid down the side of the hole directly above him. The weight of the lorry and debris began to crush him and his shouts and pleas to get him out rose in intensity.

Very little time had elapsed. I was still in the JCB. I lifted the rear digger bucket then leapt into the driving seat, raised the stabiliser legs and quickly moved the JCB to the opposite side of the pit to the lorry, squeezing the front bucket into the ground and putting the stabiliser legs down. I placed the rear digging bucket into the side of the lorry above the rear wheel and applied all the pressure the hydraulics could muster to prevent the lorry from sliding further down the pit on to David. It was not a time to panic. I scrambled out of the JCB, made sure the lorry and the JCB were stable and told David he was safe and that I would only be gone a moment to get help. Luckily the house was only fifty yards away and my wife Barbara was about. I told her to dial 999 for an ambulance and fire engine and stress it was very urgent, then ran back to the scene of the disaster.

David was in great pain. Checking that the JCB was stopping the lorry from sliding any further into the pit, I jumped down and started to shovel debris away from David's head and reassure him that he would soon be out. Meanwhile Barbara had also telephoned the joiners' shop and told them to come to Highlands. She then went off in the car to get one of our building gangs, who were working locally. David was slowly being crushed under the weight of the lorry and debris so I decided to get back in the JCB and protect David by ensuring that the lorry was securely propped to prevent it sliding any further down. After what seemed ages, but was actually only a very short time, a fire engine and rescue vehicle came tearing up the drive. The chief fireman weighed up the job in a flash and ordered the heavy fire engine into position, attached a steel wire tow rope from the engine to the Dodge lorry which took the strain. With the JCB propping it and the fire engine anchoring the stricken Dodge lorry, David was relatively safe, although still fast under the debris and the lorry. He was obviously in great pain and very anxious. My men arrived, complete with picks, shovels and buckets, and I asked the fire chief to let them take over the job of extricating David, which he did. More sirens sounded as the ambulance arrived. Thanks to the superb effort by my gang of builders David was soon uncovered. He could not stand. The ambulance men rolled him on to a stretcher and with everyone helping David was whizzed off to

Chesterfield hospital, where he was found to be suffering from a broken pelvis and multiple bruising.

The next day I pulled the lorry out of the pit then cleaned out all the debris from the pit. The cause of the accident then became apparent. When Highlands was built in the 1880s a drain trench about five feet deep, running parallel with the pit and only one foot four inches away, had been excavated. There was no means of knowing this so instead of the lorry standing on solid ground, as I thought, it was standing on the old drain trench. When the lorry was loaded the pillar of solid earth suddenly gave way, burying poor David. Construction sites are dangerous places but there are usually some resourceful men about who are fairly unflappable when accidents do occur, thank goodness.

When travelling on the road drivers of all types of vehicles treat JCBs with great respect, especially when negotiating heavy traffic in towns. I found that raising the front bucket a little increased awareness and respect immensely. No car or lorry driver in his right mind would argue with a JCB. I enjoyed driving and maintaining the machines and lorries. Around 1985 I had a flying lesson at Netherthorpe and to my delight found that I could fly straight and perfectly level almost immediately as driving a light aircraft is very similar to driving a bulldozer, with only the one control stick to adjust for keeping level. It takes months to be able to cut a level path over undulating ground with a bulldozer and it is a very similar technique with an aircraft. I also had no fears of banking the plane steeply or landing it. I was quite dismayed to find that actually flying the aircraft was only a small part of becoming a certified pilot. Navigation, wireless, rules of the air, all have to be learned and examinations passed so I decided not to bother. In 1968 I purchased a second-hand Bedford TK ten-ton tipping lorry to work with the JCB and fetch my own building materials.

One night in 1967 there came a knock on the door, and there stood Jim Slater, whom I had first known when he lived with his parents at number five Vineyard Terrace in the 1930s. Jim worked at the Millclose lead mine when he left school, which must have been in the 1920s.

After Millclose finished in 1939 he worked at several other small lead and calcite and fluorspar mines. I know he worked at the Magpie Mine prospecting for a short time after the second war. Jim was the last of the old lead miners. "I hear you have a digger" he said "and my mate and I could do with some help." "Such as?" I enquired. "Prospecting on Tideswell Moor" was the answer. "We think we have discovered a rich fluorspar vein."

I arranged to meet him early on Sunday morning on Tideswell Moor with the digger. It was a lovely dry spring morning and Jim and his mate came in a ten-ton tipper lorry. Off we went on to the moor and came to an old lead mine shaft. Jim asked me to stand on the side of the shaft with the digger and take the side out of it. As I dug out the stonework to the top of the mine shaft it became obvious that the "old man" (a lead miner's term for yesterday's lead miners) had sunk the shaft through a vein of fluorspar. The vein came almost to the surface. I dug along the vein, loading the spar into the lorry, which Jim's mate took and dumped somewhere fairly near. I went back the next Sunday and we had another good day.

I knew one or two men like Jim, including a relative of mine, who were obsessed with finding a rich vein and becoming a millionaire. I still know men who want to do exactly the same thing today but are stifled by the Peak Park rules and regulations. The Peak District National Park owes its existence to the character of the landscape and the villages which nestle in that landscape, all built from adjacent materials and in the right place, ie a reasonable water supply, shelter from the north east wind, and facing south west to take advantage of the sun. Snow stays longer on the cold north-east facing slopes so the villages were usually built on the south-west facing side of the hill to make the best of the natural resources available. One thousand years of natural common sense planning has produced a landscape which no planner could ever have developed.

The Peak District needs and deserves to be conserved and protected, especially from some of the planners. In my opinion the 1997 development of the Bakewell cattle market building by the Peak Park Board will in the future be held to be a glaring example of what not to do with our legacy, very similar to the planners' Tower Block syndrome of the 1950/60s.

Lorry driving is all right in small doses. I collected all our building materials with the lorries so that we could have them when it suited us – loads of doors and wardrobes, kitchens, breeze blocks, bricks and sand, slates from near Nantile in Wales, tiles from Cannock, timber from Sheffield. In the 1970s Charlie and I went to the Dorothea Slate Quarry at Nantile near Snowdon where all the men in the quarry spoke in Welsh to one another and English to us. We watched the men splitting the slate by hand. The slates were cut to size before being split and graded. Firsts were the thinnest, then seconds, and thirds were the roughest and thickest. I was accepted as a lorry driver when I called in transport cafes, exchanging information on road conditions, routes etc. I knew the width and length of the Dodge lorry exactly. Lorry driving is one job you cannot skive at. It occupies all the senses and demands high concentration all the time. I also liked lorry driving because no one can get at you (this was in the days before mobile phones). I relinquished my class one licence when I was seventy-two years old.

QUARRY DAYS – SANDSTONE

From being a young child I had always been familiar with Darley Dale Stancliffe and Hall Dale sandstone quarries and, along with other north Derbyshire folk, accepted them as part of the fabric of the Peak. Stancliffe, with its wonderful hard fine-grained sandstone was famous throughout Britain. I have a list of imposing buildings constructed from it.

At the time of my employment in the 1950s with Wildgoose's I spent a short time in their Lumsdale Quarry. It was absolutely fascinating to learn how to cut huge stones into pieces with a pick, a sledge hammer and a few steel wedges. Arnold Wagstaffe, George Page and a few more men, with only a crane, got and worked the stone. Sandstone quarries had a proliferation of stone cutting and shaping machines, some dating back to Victorian times. I worked alongside circular saws of various types and sizes. Some had wheels made of carborundum, others similar to wood cutting circular saws were fitted with diamond tips. They ranged in size from ten feet to two feet, all terrifying, noisy machines, shrouded with spray from the copious supply of cooling and cleaning water fed on to the blades.

Another type of stone cutting machinery was the wire saw. This consisted of two large pulley type wheels with a groove on the rim which held an endless wire rope. The wire rope revolved at high speed and was fed with a mixture of carborundum dust and water. The wheels were about eight feet apart, fixed to a vertical sliding mechanism which allowed the wire to cut through the stone from top to bottom, to a profile shape if necessary. The oldest type of saw was the horizontal swing saw. The first time I saw one in action I was amazed to see it had no teeth. This type of saw was usually about fifteen to twenty feet long and could carry several blades. They cut by the abrasive effect of small cast iron shot fed on to the blades. Water sprayed on to the blades carried the debris away. This type of saw made a very distinctive sound, a repetitive whoosh, whoosh, as the blades traversed back and forth on the large blocks of stone. I have known all these types of saw to be working at the same time in Stancliffe yard. The swing type saws were modernised in the 1950s by having diamond tips brazed to the cutting edge of the blade. This eliminated the need for iron shot and speeded up the process.

Three other types of machine were in use, one a stone planing machine, usually about eight feet long. The stone lay on a steel bed. A travelling arm carried a high quality tungsten tipped chisel back and forth over the stone. The planer, in the hands of a skilled operative, could cut grooves or flutes in round or square column stones and shape stones to profiles. The chisels were reversed at the end of each pass and so cut both ways. Stancliffe had two stone lathes, one horizontal, one vertical. The vertical lathe had an eight feet revolving bed. The stone was rough cut to shape, placed on the perforated bed and firmly wedged in position. The lathe bed revolved quite slowly. A stone cutting chisel bolted to a vertical frame alongside the bed was fitted with a mechanism to wind the chisel in and out.

Thousands of grind and mill stones of all shapes and sizes were made on this machine and exported all over the world. Besides mill and grind stones a highly skilled operative could work miracles, manufacturing fountain basins and bowls, complete with stems and embellishments, ie flutes and lips. Some of these fountains weighed several tons and after being hand finished by masons were works of art.

The horizontal lathe worked on a similar principle but manufactured much smaller and lighter things such as stone balustrades and small circular items. Sometimes the operator hand-held a long handled chisel to shape the stone as it revolved. This machine, similar to the vertical lathe, required great know-how and skill to operate.

Planing machine

Boring machines for stone have home made bits. These are of the most unlikely construction consisting of a piece of quarter inch plate bent to the radius of the hole. They had a width of four to eight inches. They also cut with iron shot until the 1940/1950s when diamond tips were fitted. The height of the plate was to suit the depth of the hole required. Boring machines cut vertically.

All this machinery is grouped around a crane with a long jib to serve them or under an overhead travelling crane. The machine mechanic has a most important part

Brian Richards, Les Holmes and Eddie Holland in Stancliffe yard 1960's

to play in setting up and servicing them, including renewing the diamond tips. Most gritstone quarries also adapt this huge diversity of stone cutting and shaping machinery to suit special needs.

Another machine is the polisher which consists of a flat revolving cast iron disc about sixteen inches in diameter which itself revolves around an adjustable centre point. This disc, which works under the pressure of its own weight, is fed with various mixtures of material ranging from fine carborundum to clays and whitening and is capable of putting a mirror finish on very hard granites and marbles. Again know-how and skill, coupled with experience, are essential as every stone has a different hardness and texture.

All stone working machinery has constantly evolved over the last one hundred and fifty years, culminating in today's complex computer guided and programmed intricate machines.

STANCLIFFE

Some of the people who worked in Stancliffe quarry from 1940 – 1960 are listed below:

Managers – Thomas Bowers, Gerard Smith and James Sharples
Office – Dennis Fearn & Reg Boden
Draughtsmen – Harry Tideswell and Keith Walthall
Quarrymen – Bill Wilson, Bill Elliott, Albert Downes, John Noton and Jack Goodwin
Quarry Foreman & Shotfirer – Bill Needham
Crusher- Joe Allwood and Ron Marshall
Planing Machines – Cyril Howes, Eddie Holland, Rex Marsden and Herbert Wragg
Wallstone Makers – Sid Quigley and Harold Cundy
Wire Saws – Charlie Jepson, Peter Crowder, Ken Barwick and Brian Richards
Carborundum Saws – Tony Welbourne and Fred Ollerenshaw
Crane Drivers – Frank Cowley, George Draper, Edgar Pashley and Les Holmes
Fitters – Bill Bell, Bill Wayne and George Bond
Swing Saws – Stanley Willers and ? Thornhill
Blacksmiths – Dick Wilson and Pat Devaney
Stone Yard Foreman – Roy Everett
Yard and Quarry Lorry Drive – Don Willers

Information was supplied by James (Jim) Taylor and Reg Street.

Stancliffe Estates came into being after the death of Lady Whitworth in 1896 and finished around 1977. Stancliffe Works was originally built as Sir Joseph Whitworth's collective Farm and Estate headquarters.

QUARRY DAYS – LIMESTONE

Decorative limestones such as Hopton Wood stone and the hard fossilised limestones found in certain parts of Dene Quarries, are quarried in similar ways to gritstone. No high explosives, ie gelignite are used as these splinter the stone, producing cracks and shakes. Similarly again to gritstone quarrying, relatively non-violent explosives are used, ie black powder, a variety of gun powder, in small directed quantities. Since 2000 our Stancliffe Quarry has been worked using a very low expansion rated, non-violent explosive in a shaped drill hole which does very little harm to the stone, and with well placed and thought out shaped drill holes, cuts the stone cleanly and safely.

I have worked in many industrial aggregate limestone quarries fixing machinery and crusher bases, constructing buildings to house them, and excavating and concreting bases for conveyors, roads and wheel washes. The first quarry Lewis Jackson (Builders) Ltd worked in was Cawdor Quarry at Matlock around 1966. We carried out construction and maintenance for Tarmac until the mid 1980s. I watched the evolution of limestone aggregate quarrying for over twenty years. When we first worked for Tarmac there were quarries at Stoney Middleton Dale (Ben Bennet's) where we installed the bases for a new conveyor system, Cawdor Quarry at Matlock where we constructed several buildings, Intake Quarry at Middleton by Wirksworth where we shuttered and cast a large concrete structure for an experimental plant to produce burnt limestone for the chemical industry. Unfortunately the method was not a success. We constructed storage hopper bases and a very large industrial shed, also a wheel washing pit, at Middle Peak. Intake, Middle Peak and Prospect Quarries were under the control of a Mr Musson based at Middle Peak. We maintained the buildings at Steeple Grange Quarry, Wirksworth, and Prospect Quarry at Grange Mill on the Via Gellia Road. The engineer in charge of plant was a Mr Arthur Reynolds.

Limestone quarrying is a brutal operation, where big is beautiful in every way. I noticed that as plant got larger smaller quarries closed first, Ben Bennett followed by Prospect then Intake and Steeple Grange. I believe these quarries each only produced under one thousand tons a day. Cawdor and Hall Dale also closed at Matlock and all production was focused on Middle Peak – eight to ten thousand tons per day.

High explosive is king in the limestone quarrying industry. In the smaller quarries with relatively small crushers and screens large stones were drilled and blasted each lunch-time. This action was called popping. A familiar sound around lunch-time was the quarry siren followed sometimes by a large blast dislodging the quarry face, and always by a series of small bangs as the "pops" went off to make the very large pieces easier to handle. Small quarries, especially those with no rail access, became redundant. In Derbyshire we now have the largest limestone quarry in Europe at Tunstead, near Buxton. The Peak District National Park surrounds it as it was left out of the designated area in 1950, a good and well thought-out judgement in my opinion.

One of the most famous quarries which I never had the pleasure of working in, but visited several times, is the Middleton by-Wirksworth underground limestone quarry. The extent of the workings is almost unbelievable, around two miles of roads passing through chambers up to seventy feet wide and high. There are traffic lights at intersections and huge trucks carrying many tons of pure uncontaminated high quality limestone trundle past, deep under the hills of Middleton. Men on ex-fire service vehicles perch on top of ladders and lifts, examining the roof and walls for loose stone. Powerful lights hang from the roof, lighting the underground labyrinth of roads and chambers. The steady drone of the extraction fans and the muted sound of machinery, along with dark unlit chambers, make this a strange world, both dark and oppressive to work in.

As opposed to today's intensive limestone quarrying sandstone quarrying has scarcely altered in the last hundred years except that large excavators, which can be fitted with lifting equipment, have replaced fixed cranes. To give an instance of how limestone quarrying has altered, when George Twigg and I were working at Masson Mill in 1947/8 we sometimes had our lunch in the canteen. We usually sat with some of the ladies. In the course of conversation about hobbies and pastimes one lady said "My husband's pastime is resting and sleeping.

He does practically nothing at home." George asked where her husband worked and she said "He is a breaker and loader at Wirksworth Quarry." I was intrigued by this statement and speaking to a fellow builder he informed me that the men at this particular quarry were paid on piecework at so much for every narrow gauge jubilee truck filled. Each truck held around one ton. Any stones too heavy to lift into the truck had to be broken up with a specially shaped sledge-hammer to enable them to be loaded. It must have been back breaking heavy work, especially on days of inclement weather, and it was not difficult to understand why the lady's husband spent so much time resting when he came home from work. The last time I was at Middle Peak Quarry the loader picked up about nine or ten tons at a time and I loaded it into a fifty-ton truck. Conversation in a limestone quarry is almost impossible because of the noise from all this massive machinery. Limestone quarries are either dusty or muddy deserts, no birds or animals, few trees. They do not grow well on limestone rock. By contrast all the sandstone quarries I have worked in have had an abundance of flora and fauna and been comparatively peaceful.

Limestone quarries require a huge investment of money and machinery. I have known several sandstone quarries run by just two or three men. A strange paradox in today's world is the ability of environmental groups to curtail quarrying while at the same time ensuring disused ones become sites of special scientific interest for flora and fauna. Lathkill Dale is a good example of this. Over the last four hundred years it has gone from agriculture to industry, and in the last one hundred years, as nature has taken over, to a delightful dale, now used only for leisure and recreation. The redundant workings and cliff faces of many old limestone quarries are now an asset to the countryside, adding interest and a haven for flora and fauna. The man-made cliffs of the old Matlock Cawdor and Hall Dale Quarry, when viewed from the A6, are now virtually indistinguishable from the natural cliffs of Matlock Dale and Matlock Bath which attract so many tourists to the area. Some of the environmental groups are what I call "today people." They can only see and appreciate the present moment, having little perspective of the past and future. However their hearts are in the right place. The environment needs to be managed long-term. Our much maligned quarries provide the basic materials for dwellings, large building projects, roads, railways and the chemical and steel industries, sugar beet processing and tooth paste and many other everyday items. Stone and coal are two of Britain's more abundant minerals but coal is now mostly imported.

Chapter 7:

Inventions, patents and manufactures – IDC and TDI

The problem

We had built many dwellings by 1982, some of them in exposed positions and at a reasonably high altitude. Insulation was becoming important and this, and the lack of knowledge of the consequences of central heating, double glazing and draught-proofing, led to many problems in the house building industry. The coldest place inside any dwelling is around openings in the walls, ie doors and windows where the inside walls abut the outside walls. This made the inside walls colder at that point than the rest of the dwelling, and caused the window and door jambs to suffer from mould caused by condensation. It was particularly prevalent on the north-east side of dwellings which received very little sun on the window and door jambs. Bathrooms, kitchens and utilities are usually on that side. All generate lots of humidity.

Experiments

I thought a lot about this problem and came to the conclusion that the interior walls needed to be insulated as well as damp-proofed where they abutted the exterior walls. I attempted to bond rigid expanded polystyrene to damp-proof course to provide an insulated damp-proof course. This proved to be an impractical and fragile material. In late

1982 we were busy building a dwelling on Sir Joseph's Lane, Darley Dale (by the way, I named the Lane after one of Stancliffe Stone's locos "Sir Joseph Whitworth", not the great man himself, because the new lane followed the course of the old Stancliffe railway). I had been pondering what I could use as an insulation backing to the dpc when an eight feet by four feet sheet of two inch thick expanded polystyrene blew on to the lane just as our lorry was going past. The lorry's twin rear wheels ran over the sheet. Picking it up I found the section that had been crushed beneath the lorry wheels would bend over without breaking. I gave this phenomenon some thought. After experimenting I discovered that by heating expanded polystyrene and crushing it very quickly it re-expanded then became flexible. This was because the crushing destroyed the cell structure and the heat and compressed gasses reinflated the material which then became flexible. Dunlop Adhesives provided me with a solvent that came out of a standard air paint spray gun in filaments similar to a cobweb. I made my first material by heating the expanded polystyrene on an iron plate, heated by a propane burner, applying the Dunlop bonding agent, then sending the polystyrene and dpc through the wringer of our old, small Hoover washing machine. The two layers became welded together and made a robust rollable insulating and damp-proofing material, the perfect material to both insulate and damp-proof the inside of buildings from the exterior, thereby stopping both damp and cold bridging and therefore mould and condensation. I could see a lot of potential in the material if I could make a machine to produce it and then sell it nation wide.

IDC AND DAMCOR

Being very busy at the time I realised I needed help. I thought back to my days at Lehane, Mackenzie & Shand and Ken Dabell, who I had first met in 1952. Ken had risen through the ranks to become managing director of the Shand empire and knew someone in most of the large construction firms in Britain. I knew he had recently retired, so on a nothing ventured, nothing won principle I went and knocked on Ken's door. I explained to him what I was trying to do and offered him a share in a company to make and sell the material. Ken accepted and we were in business with Insulated Damp-proof Course Limited (IDC). Ken and I spent 1984 tinkering with production machinery in the old Stancliffe Precast Stone factory which I had just purchased. We went home at night, covered in various glues, and gloomy with disappointments, but we eventually conquered them all. We finally perfected a machine that would produce the insulated damp-proof course which we called Damcor, at Ken's suggestion.

Patents

I wondered if my solution could be patented and became interested in patents and their history. I found that I would have to match a number of requirements if I were to be granted one.

A patent is a government grant to an inventor, assuring him of the sole right to make use of, and sell, his invention for a limited period by means of a document conveying such a right.

An invention involves an inventive step if, when compared with what is already known, it would not be obvious to someone with a good knowledge and experience of the subject. An invention must be new or involve an inventive step. It must be capable of being made or used in some type of industry. Industry is "non intellectual."

An invention is not patentable if it is one of the following:

A discovery, ie a new planet, a scientific or mathematical method, an aesthetic creation, ie literary or artistic.

A method for performing a mental act, a method of playing a game, the presentation of information or a computer programme, a new animal or plant variety.

The invention must never have been made public anywhere in the world before the date of the application.

There are now around 30 million published international patents on file at the Patents Office. Only around 1 patent in 3,000 results in a nationally-known, highly commercially successful product.

What I did not find out until later was that patents are subjected to opposition, opinions and litigation at the highest level. A Patent agent/solicitor is in my opinion both necessary and expensive. All too often litigation takes over. The 20 years of patent protection rights are soon-ended, after which the patent is open to exploitation by everyone.

A history of UK patents

The first recorded patent was granted in 1449 by Henry VI to John of Utynam for twenty years for a method of making stained glass. Fifty patents were granted by Elizabeth I from 1561 to 1590. One patent refused in 1596 was for a water closet. In 1610 James I revoked all previous patents, except for projects of new inventions. This was the beginning of our patent system and was incorporated into the Statute of Monopolies Act of 1624.

Patent number one was granted in 1657 to Rathburn and Burges for a method of engraving and printing. James Puckle's 1718 patent for a machine gun was the first required to have a specification. This led to Richard Arkwright's famous patent of 1775 for spinning machines becoming voided in 1785 because of lack of an adequate specification. Watts's 1796 patent for steam engines, after expensive and extensive litigation, established that valid improvements to an existing invention could be patented. Patenting was simplified by the Patent Amendment Act of 1852. A further Act of 1883 brought into force the office of Comptroller General of Patents.

In 1902, because of the huge number of patents granted, an Act was passed that all patents from 1855 were to be classified. This took a staff of two hundred and sixty examiners three years. The 1902 Act resulted in one thousand and twenty-two volumes arranged in one hundred and forty six classes. By 1907 the volumes had been extended back as far as a patent of 1617. The patent legislation in force today is the 1977

Tipsafe *Damcor*

Patent Act. This Act ensures that the patent system is suited to the modern needs of industry, and is flexible enough to cater for future changes in technology and operate in today's global context.

I took a piece of the material and a sketch of a machine which I thought would produce the material to a patent agent, Swindell and Pearson at Derby who on my behalf made a series of searches to find out if it was in their opinion patentable. Believing it to be so they then applied for a patent on my behalf. This did not come cheap as they were patent solicitors, and patents are the subject of many lawsuits. Good worthwhile patents usually finish up in court. Mine went to the High Court at the Royal Courts of Justice in London, where I was vindicated. Only one patent in three thousand becomes a nationally known product with excellent sales. To become successful one must have resources, tenacity and a willingness to pay heed to legal advice, but above all the patented product must be needed, necessary and better than previous products. It also requires to be made known.

In 1984 I applied for an American patent and I paid several hundred pounds for a half page letter from a QC concerning Esso Standard Oil, who decided to oppose my American and European Patent on some flimsy pretext. The QC said that Esso opposed all oil-based patents on principle, that they turned over three hundred million dollars per day worldwide, and would break my resources. His advice was not to even bother trying to oppose them as he had seen multinational firms lose millions in protracted battles. JCB patents division gave me the same advice. I still had to spend hundreds of thousands of pounds protecting the validity of my patents. There was no contest. I withdrew my patent application. Might is mostly right. It hurts, but it is a fact of life.

DAMCOR®
The Insulating Vertical DPC

BBA BRITISH BOARD OF AGREMENT
CERTIFICATE No. 03/3921

A COMPLETE AND SIMPLE SOLUTION TO THERMAL BRIDGING WHERE THE CAVITY IS CLOSED. COMBINING ADVANTAGES OF EXPANDED POLYSTYRENE AND POLYETHYLENE D.P.C.

- R' Value of 0.492
- Flexible, is Supplied in Rolls
- No Special Fixings In Use. No Special Installation Techniques
- Easy to Build as Brickwork Proceeds
- Easy Cut With Trowel or Knife
- Lengths Can be Lapped or Joined With No Loss of Thermal Efficiency
- Supplied in Various Widths
- Light and Robust
- Economical
- C.F.C. Free and Energy Efficient

Buoyed by my success in getting a British patent for Damcor I decided to improve it by introducing a similar product which was fireproof. I read in a magazine that someone in Iceland was producing a fireproof fibre material made from lava rock by an electrical process. I telephoned the British Embassy in Iceland and they gave me the name and telephone number of the firm, who said they would send me a container load for three thousand pounds. On a "Nothing ventured, nothing won" principle I said "Yes please." When the container arrived it was a standard shipping size. I patented the product and called it Stonecor.

I also, in co-operation with Honeywell and Lowe Electronics perfected a keypad operated fuel cut-off for vehicles, which was fitted to a Ford Escort. The device rendered the vehicle almost theft-proof, no fuel – no start. It proved to be non-patentable with opposition from vehicle manufacturers who, like Esso, were all major players in the patents game.

The first house in Britain to have Damcor installed was number 10 Sir Joseph's Lane, a house that I designed and built with my old mates Charles, Harold, Eric and foreman joiner Granville. I had no idea at this time of the effect my product would have on my future. I visited the firm which manufactured expanded polystyrene, Metal Closures (Rosslite) Ltd. who occupied the old Power Station at Formby near Liverpool. I took them a sample of Damcor to inspect. They seemed sceptical but gave me a sheet of two inch thick rigid expanded polystyrene to take away and process. I returned the following week with their rigid and fragile material rolled up tightly. I unrolled it on the desk of their managing director, Mr.Hart, and they were very impressed. They had been producing expanded polysyrene for over twenty-five years and thought what I had done was impossible. I showed them the patent certificate and negotiated a license for them to produce Damcor at their works in return for royalty payments. Ken and I took the machine to Formby on the lorry, set it up, and trained an operative.

I then wrote to the Department of the Environment, the National House Building Council, and the Building Research Establishment about our new product and its ability to improve the quality of building, also the quality of life for its inhabitants. The DOE and BRE evaluated Damcor and set up a series of seminars on mould and condensation, and preventative methods and materials to overcome these problems. Barbara and I travelled to places as far afield as Corby and Manchester to attend the seminars where I spoke to private, City, and County architects on Damcor Insulation. I also spoke to budding architectural students at UMIST Manchester. I was not very happy with Rosslite's manufacturing or marketing of Damcor which was in their control from 1985 to 1989, when events beyond my control changed things dramatically.

TIPSAFE

A completely different invention originated in an idea by David Jaina. I knew David well – he had helped me to rebuild the Healey Westland in 1978/80 and we had built a house for him in 1981 behind S & E Johnson's mill at Two Dales, where he worked as transport fitter/foreman. David was inspecting a lorry one night in 1988 when it slipped off the jack and smartly removed his middle finger. Another mechanic who was there rushed David to the Whitworth Hospital. When they arrived there David took off the towel he had wrapped his hand in to have a look. The driver also looked and promptly fainted and banged his head, knocking himself out. David rang the bell and the hospital had two casualties.

Around March 1988 a knock came on the door and there stood David. He told me he had been thinking about a vehicle stand which could be fastened to an anchor bolted on to a lorry chassis so that it could not slip. Eventually we came up with a design and David made a prototype. We then had the idea that the anchor could also take a prop to support the body of a tipping vehicle when it was raised, thereby making it safe for people to work under, and David and I decided it was a sound idea. I gave it some thought, drew up some plans of an anchor and prop and took them to an engineering draughtsman I knew at Millthorpe, a Mr Artindale, who had worked for a foundry at Dronfield as draughtsman designer. He produced a working drawing for me and introduced me to the foundry manager.

David and I formed a company called Tipsafe Limited and I acquired a patent in our joint names for the body prop idea. I took our foundry produced prototype to Leyland Daf Technical Services at Preston, and paid them a small fortune to have the product tested and certified fit for use. David was still working at Johnson's Mill. I did the marketing and we attended transport exhibitions at Harrogate and Telford. David fitted it to several lorries. The prop was a great success, sold well, and I am sure it has prevented many accidents. Tipsafe Ltd. was awarded the first prize for the best contribution to vehicle workshop safety, presented at the Grosvenor Hotel in London by the Minister of Transport.

Tipsafe Damcor and Insulation (TDI)

Life turned upside down unexpectedly one morning in October 1990. A knock on the door sounded the arrival of the postman delivering a registered letter from Rosslite at Formby, who manufactured Damcor for us informing us they were ceasing trading on 31st December 1990 and selling the site. Ken Dabell and I went to Formby and made arrangements to take back the Damcor machine and any stock they had. We rented a workshop in Toft and Tomlinson's old garage at North Darley, then owned by Charlie Lowe of Matlock Transport, whom I had known all his life.

I decided to amalgamate IDC and Tipsafe, under the name TDI (UK) Ltd. TDI stands for Tipsafe, Damcor and Insulation. I chose the name because it has a familiar ring to it, similar to DTI, the initials of the Department of Trade and Industry. I gave David Jaina a share in the new company, along with Ken Dabell who was also a director of Tipsafe and IDC, and we commenced trading at Darley Dale in January 1990. David left S & E Johnson to manage the firm and push the Tipsafe side.

I oversaw the marketing of Damcor and Tipsafe, and Ken masterminded the finance and bookwork of the firm. David's wife Monica

T.D.I. Damcor 1993. Unity Complex, Dale Road, Darley Dale.
Left to Right: *David Pritty, Monica Jaina, Mark Thompson, Howard Barker, Ian McKay, Sara McHale, David Jaina and Dennis Millward*

T.D.I. Damcor 1994. Unity Complex, Dale Road, Darley Dale.
Left to Right: *Lewis Jackson, Ian McKay, Mark Thompson, Liz Hughes, David Pritty, Monica Jaina, Chris Bennett, Dennis Millward, John Tayulor and David Jaina*

Damcor delivery lorries

worked in the office and became Company Secretary of TDI. We were a good team. David and I, and occasionally Ken, went to every exhibition we could and spread the word of our products. We sent out thousands of brochures to builders and architects and worked hard to get the firm off the ground. In the first year TDI made a profit of around £35,000 before tax, a very encouraging situation.

More and more architects specified Damcor, the fruits of the seminars Barbara and I had attended, and the marketing. The product Damcor was simple, reasonably priced, and what is more worked. It worked so well that the DOE made anti-cold bridging products part of the Building Regulations and then TDI really took off. By 1992 the firm employed ten people. In 1993 I invented and patented another cheap and very effective insulated cavity closure, another anti-cold bridging product. We made it in two versions, Polycor and Thermacor, part of the 'cor' family of products. I next produced a product called Inperim, a floor slab perimeter insulating material based on and covered by the Damcor patent. All five products acquired British Board of Agrement certificates and were manufactured to the BS EN ISO 9002 quality assurance scheme.

1994 and 1995 saw a rash of rival products as other firms attempted to get on the band-wagon. The award winning Tipsafe vehicle support system was selling well. The sales of Damcor were increasing dramatically, being installed in almost every new building. By 1996 we had a staff of thirteen and had up-rated the insulated damp-proof course manufacturing machine. It was now computer controlled. We acquired the European Standards Certificate 9002. Sales now averaged £35,000 a week, and TDI had become well known in the construction industry. The TDI years were very exciting, similar to Lewis Jackson (Builders) in the 1960s. Adopting my creed that nothing really matters what you do in life so long as you do not hurt other people, the TDI project blossomed.

NEC

We took a stand at the National Exhibition Centre, Birmingham, in 1990, at a total cost of around £20,000. It was to be the start of our foray into mass marketing. The weeks before were spent preparing the exhibits, having brochures printed, and building a demonstration section of a house wall, including the abutment of the internal and external walls at a window opening with the insulated dpc Damcor. I marvelled at the cost of the stand, which was twenty feet long by ten feet deep, and realised that not only was the NEC Britain's largest exhibition centre, it was also a goldmine for the owners. It was obvious to me that if people do not know of a product one cannot sell it. To make our product known we had three hundred thousand A5 leaflets printed at a very moderate price by giving the printers the money up front and giving them three months to print them when they had a slack period. We then sent the leaflets to printers of magazines connected with the construction industry on the same money-up-front system, to insert them in their magazines when they had the time and space available. This method proved to be excellent in every way.

Travelling to the NEC every day for over a week was no joke, one hundred and twenty five miles a day in November, misty and rainy, seething traffic and long queues of vehicles to get out of the place. I cracked the queue-to-get-out problem by interviewing one of the security men and thanking him with money for his short cut suggestions, which helped to bypass the nightly line of traffic waiting to get out, escape is probably a better word! Apart from the rotten journeys to and from the NEC I enjoyed my five years role of salesman, and acquired an insight of where, when and how in most things concerning the NEC and the transport exhibitions at Harrogate demonstrating Tipsafe. Most of all TDI became a nationally known and respected firm. I applied the same principle to TDI as I had done to Lewis Jackson (Builders) Ltd. We made the product as near perfect as possible and stuck to delivery dates, which were next day in the Midlands and north of England if we received the order by midday. My long-standing view that any firm is only as good as the staff it employs was once again proved right. TDI had a truly excellent team, full of enthusiasm and ideas. Damcor was exported to the Middle East and the Falklands and by 1996 total sales were running at £1,850,000 per year.

Selling up

After five years my friend Ken, who spent the winters in Lanzarote, wanted out and the manager just wanted to manage. I was sixty-nine and thirteen years had passed since the idea of insulated damp-proof course had come to me. I had several offers from large firms for TDI and Barbara and I decided to sell.

In retrospect I now know I was naive in selling to big business. I realise now that some companies are unscrupulous in their dealings, always striving to take advantage of others in business, no matter what the cost to people and places may be. I have seen men and women cry when, after working for thirty years for a firm that was taken over by a larger firm, with every assurance for the future, the concern is closed down the following year. Employees who had led a secure, happy working life were suddenly cast adrift on the high seas of life after their ship had been scuttled. In January 1997 Barbara and I sold TDI (UK)

Ltd to Polypipe Ltd from Doncaster for a goodly sum, on condition that the business stayed in Darley Dale.

I thoroughly enjoyed my patent days which made me a considerable amount of money. I could not have managed without all the help and advice I received in the twelve years from the first patent to the sale of TDI and the patents, trade marks etc. Usually the people who make the most money are the ones who manufacture a vastly improved version of the original acquiring a patent for the improvement on the original. I found that like Toyota and Ford the factory that assembles and sells the final product makes the most money, not the factory that makes and supplies the components.

Radon days

To say 1991 was hectic is an understatement. We were constructing several dwellings on Sir Joseph's Lane and had acquired share in the Stancliffe Quarry companies at Darley Dale, for which I was preparing schemes for its future. T.D.I. Ltd. had to be organised after its move from Formby to Darley Dale, and strategy planning meetings for the various companies took place on an almost weekly basis, I.D.C, Ltd., Tipsafe Ltd. and Lewis Jackson Ltd. The two Stancliffe Quarry companies, W.I.L. Ltd and Stancliffe Park Ltd. were then under the chairmanship of Roy Ince. Incidentally he was, and still is, my next door neighbour, some 300 metres further up Whitworth Road. Roy was a very capable man at running companies.

In 1990 Peter Lilley, Building Control Officer of Derbyshire Dales District Council, invited me to attend a seminar on Radon Gas detection and reduction by the Building Research Council. I had never heard of the radio active gas Radon and became very interested in this phenomenon. Lewis Jackson (Builders) Ltd., possibly because we had been working with the B.R.E. for five years on the control of mould and condensation, asked us to carry out the first Radon Gas reduction job in Derbyshire. Theories abounded on how this could be done. A dwelling at Bradwell in Derbyshire was chosen and after, lots of ideas a plan was formulated to reduce the Radon Gas. After three months monitoring it was proved to be a success.

I think the officers at the B.R.E. were taken aback to find I had no qualifications whatsoever, and asked me to do a course on Radon Gas at Northampton College. I agreed but only if it was an external course, and my eldest son Andrew did the same course. We did the course by correspondence which took from 1992 to late 1995. Andrew and I went to Northampton College in January 1996 for the examination and we were both successful in obtaining our Diploma in Radon Gas Technology (I was then sixty-nine years old).

Over those three years we had carried out many Radon Gas reductions, aided by Derbyshire Dales' Peter Lilley and the B.R.E officers. The jobs were very varied, from all types of dwellings to factories, office blocks, shops, public houses and several halls.

Each job was different, from new up-to-date properties to Halls built in the 1600s with cellars and huge thick walls which acted as a conduit for the Gas, dispersing it around the building. Gas readings varied from a few becquerels to an almost unbelievable 19,000 plus. We never did get that old Hall down to the recommended safe level of 200 becquerels but managed a very creditable 600 becquerels with three extract fans and vastly improved ventilation.

I noticed that the majority of Radon Gas problems were mostly in lead mining areas and took to researching lead veins and mines in the vicinity. I found one could almost forecast which properties in a peakland town, village or small hamlet would be affected by the location of the lead veins, We gave advice and recommendations for dwellings in places as far away as Hexham and Northampton but mostly worked in Derbyshire, from Bolsover to Dove Holes, Chesterfield and Staffordshire Moorlands areas. We had constant contact with the B.R.E. Radon Gas Department and enjoyed solving Radon Gas problems.

I attended an international seminar on Radon Gas and participants came from as far afield as Australia. The man from the British

Geological Survey team gave us a lecture on how Radon Gas was present in the rocks and subsoil. I told the audience that in my wide experience Radon Gas in quantity usually came from metallic minerals, as I had noticed that the Derbyshire Great Rake, a lead vein which runs from Peak Forest to Carsington, had very high levels of Radon Gas in its vicinity throughout its length. An added bonus was that I travelled the Peak District exploring side roads as I visited isolated dwellings, meeting people and solving their Radon Gas problems.

I researched about Radon Gas in lead mines and found the Mawstone Mine in Youlgreave had the highest reading in Britain, off the scale at around 100,000 becquerels. I could trace a lead vein across a village by the Radon readings. The man from Australia backed me up and told the seminar that he had observed exactly the same phenomenon in Australian metal mines, lead, gold, copper and silver. Iron ore deposits are also affected by Radon Gas but to a lesser degreee. It is my belief that these other minerals were extruded from the earths core, and must have been very radio-active when first produced many millions of years ago. I also came to the conclusion that in areas where there was no existing metalic mineral working and no surface trace of any, that deep down in the cracks in the earth's crust material containing radio active minerals still extruded radio active particles.

I have found that it pays to think of Radon Gas as very minute particles of smoke, capable of finding its way to the surface above the metallic deposits in the cracks of the earth's crust. I have been told that lead is decayed uranium. Derbyshire in geological times past must have been a scary place with its volcanoes, radio activity, earthquakes etc.

We carried out our last Radon Gas reduction jobs, over three hundred in total, in 2004 when we decided to retire from the construction industry because of the huge ever-growing burden of rules and regulations affecting and stifling industry.

Never mind, it helps to keep armies of people employed.

Chapter 8: Life has not been all work

Dogs and other animals

When I was eleven or twelve years old mother and I went to a farm on Conksbury Lane, Youlgrave, armed with a small wicker basket. The farmer led us into a barn, rooted about in the hay and produced a clawing, spitting, growling kitten, the progeny of many generations of wild farm cats. We then lived at Redlands next to the busy A6 where Judy, as we named her, grew up. She was road-wise, savage and had a habit of glaring at you with her very green eyes. Her fur was all black and she just about tolerated us. Judy moved to Matlock Dale with us, then up to Highlands in 1948. She ruled the various dogs we had with fear. If they inadvertently went too near her chair a scratching would be their reward. She was malevolent and seemingly indestructible.

We always had a dog. Throughout my young life on the Hillside our dog, Patsy, an Irish Terrier, was my constant companion, guardian and comforter. Patsy and all the various dogs I have had since have given me endless pleasure over the years. Patsy died in 1940, about nine or ten years old. I very much missed our next dog, a rough-haired terrier called Rough, when he was run over by the army lorry in 1943, as he always accompanied me and the lads on our expeditions and when we met at Broad Walk at night if we were not going to the pictures. I was working in Darley Co-op (now Costcutters) when someone told me Rough had been hit by the lorry. I went out and picked him up and carried him home. He died in my arms. It was dreadful, I loved him dearly. Rough was followed by another terrier, Felix, mostly white with a bit of black. He also accompanied the lads on our expeditions.

In 1959, after we had been at Osiris for a few weeks, we acquired a

Felix 1946

The author with Patsy

Solomon

Sam aged 6, 1995

Solomon with a rabbit

Rhode Island Red pullet. We called her Olive and she became friends with our current dog, a boxer bitch called Mandy. They slept together in the conservatory type rear porch. It was lovely to see Olive, Mandy and the three children playing together in the adjoining field. Olive was very inquisitive and took a keen interest in gardening, spending days scratching the flower border up. I found I could hypnotise her by putting her head under her wing then gently stroking her. Poor Olive later came to a bad end one night. As it was just going dusk a fox grabbed her and ran off with her.

On some days Mandy went to work with me but after she died about 1970 we had a bull mastiff whom we called Sheba, who was eight and a half stone of sloth and dribble. All the children loved her. Russell our youngest son was about eight years old, Andrew fifteen, Lesley seventeen and Beryl nineteen. Sheba was a huge lovely placid dog but of a very scary evil appearance. Our house was burgled while Sheba slept. It is a good job she did not wake up or she would have licked the burglar to death!

In 1979 I was walking up the old rail track into Stancliffe Quarry when I saw a fox take cover behind an old zinc sheet. Walking gently up to the sheet I could see the fox crouching down behind it. We looked at each other for a few seconds. The fox seemed unafraid and I noticed a collar round its neck. I warily took hold of the collar thinking that any minute the fox would try and bite me. As I stood, half crouching, with my hand clutching the collar, I could hear someone shouting Dennis, Dennis. A man came striding along the track carrying a dog lead. Thank goodness, you caught him before he went on to the road, he said. The man, who lived in an old house at the end of a nearby track, explained to me that Dennis was a tame fox whom he had looked after since he found him as a cub. He used to let him run free now and then when there was no-one about. Dennis was like most foxes, very wary and timid. I saw him several times in the next few years. He was eventually given his freedom. He did, however stay in the Stancliffe Quarry area near his old home which was an earth in the bank behind the cottage. After his owners moved away Dennis lived out his days in the quarry. Few people saw him but I have no doubt Dennis saw all of them.

When Barbara and I had settled in at Highlands Cottage in 1951 we had a couple of cats, a tabby and a black and white one. Neither had much character. After we had moved into Isis in 1970 Beryl brought home a Siamese tom cat. We called him Solomon, and that's how the bull mastiff came to be named Sheba. Solomon was a fantastic cat, with a duel personality, good as gold with the dog and family and death and disaster to everything else. He was a big rangy blue eyed loveable monster. We decided to have some new furniture to go with our new house. Our new cream coloured tweedy settee had its back almost up to the wall and when Barbara pulled it out into the room to clean behind it she got an awful shock. Solomon had shredded the back of the new settee with his powerful claws.

At Isis the dustbin was kept near the back door. I was in the kitchen with the door open when all hell broke loose. A large old crow had landed to investigate the dustbin. Solomon flew out of the open kitchen door and grabbed him. A ball of fur and feathers was spinning round the kitchen floor. Solomon had hold of the crow and a mouthful of feathers, and the crow was pecking hell out of Solomon's chest. I separated them and both had blood on them. The crow flew off, looking like a black moth-eaten feather duster. Several times I saw Solomon in the adjacent field riding on the backs of full-grown rabbits trying to bite them; some he killed. He lived to a very good age after he went up to Highlands with us. We also had another Siamese, a seal-point which we called Leyla. She was a beautiful cat but very much quieter and lived to the age of fourteen. After them we had another Siamese, Solomon number two, a red-point and he too was a superb cat who passed away in 1993.

Sheba the dog became ill when she was about eight and we sadly had to have her put down. She was replaced by a mongrel half chow, half collie, a neutered dog we called Boris. We all loved Boris and he loved water, swimming and diving was his Mecca. He could swim under water, and searched the river bed for stones. He was very independent and when we took him for walks we often lost him, but he never lost us. Several times I decided, after lots of searching shouting, swearing and scrambling through undergrowth, that this time he was gone for ever. I would set off for home, having decided to abandon him, only to find him walking quietly behind me. I loved all our dogs. When Boris became ill with leukaemia and died aged nine I cried, as I did with our other animals. Before he died I took Boris to Bradford Dale, which he had enjoyed so much, where he had one last quiet swim.

After Boris we had another mongrel, Sam, half collie, half something else. He is a very well-behaved, clever dog and is now seventeen years old in 2006. Sam learned to open any door with a lever handle by pressing the lever down with his paw. I taught him to shut the door after him but he mostly leaves it open. Barbara says we are two of a kind as far as door closing is concerned. We still spend a lot of time playing together. Both Boris and Sam came from Sheffield's dogs' home as very young puppies. I have buried Solomons one and two, Leyla, Sheba and Boris all together on the bank of Highlands opposite Hall Moor Road. I call them the Good Companions, for that is what they were.

You are never alone when you have a pet you love. I have walked many miles over the Derbyshire peaks, dales and moors with the dogs for over sixty years. Like people each one was different in character. It is lovely to have a treasure trove of pet memories, including pigs and Olive the hen. In 1953 Dennis Gregory, the nursery man, gave me a young pigeon. It became very tame and when I went for a ride, or to work, on my bicycle it would fly alongside. One day after about two years it disappeared, short of a mate was Dennis's theory. Recovering at home from my heart attack in February 2005 I saw a cock pheasant strutting about on the lawn and I decided to tame him if possible. I scattered bird seed on the lawn each morning for him and sat on the doorstep, keeping very still. Each day I put the seed a little closer to the doorway and sat there, completely ignoring the pheasant. After a week or two the bird would come and eat the food within touching distance.

Freddie the pheasant

One morning I held the food in the palm of my hand, keeping very still. Freddie, as I now called him, was very wary. I gave him no more seed until next morning. Freddie decided I was harmless and to be trusted and pecked up the seed in my palm. Over the next few weeks we established a routine. If I was not about Freddie did a raucous screech then stood on the garden table waiting for me to hold out a handful of seed for him. He had a disconcerting habit of suddenly standing stock still and looking me in the eye from about one foot away whilst making little chuckling sounds. After about ten weeks Freddie let me touch and stroke him then one day he did not appear. I went looking for him and found him lying dead in the road next to the house, bumped by a passing vehicle. Once again I was struck by the absolute finality of death. All pheasants have not only no road sense, they seem to be totally devoid of any sense, truly stupid, but I shall never forget Freddie and the fleeting friendship we shared.

I remember the horse belonging to the Hallowes family at Cherry Tree Farm. I cannot recall its name. I first worked with it and had a ride on it and the hay cart in the fields where the Oker Avenue estate now stands. I was about eleven years old. The Hallowes brothers used to bring a stoneware gallon bottle of cider for everyone to have a drink out of an old tin mug when hay-making. The horse lived in a field off Whitworth Road, now Hawkesly Drive. It was there throughout the war. In the winter when it was very cold and snowy it used to shelter under the hay barn at the bottom of Sandy Path, coming to look at us sledging down Whitworth Road. After I was married and ran down past the field on my way to catch the van or lorry to work, I used to have a quick word with it. I must have known the horse for over twenty years. I watched it become old and sway-backed. Sad to say I never noticed it had disappeared, never to be seen again.

Our present dog Sam, my constant companion, is sixteen years old now. We do not walk as much as we used to because we are both getting old and creaky and I miss our trips and adventures together around our beloved Derbyshire peaks and dales.

Lead mine days

In 1943-1947 as the gang explored Masson hillside from Northern Dale to the Heights of Abraham we stumbled across a place called Jug Holes near the top of Salter's Lane. It was a large natural cavern and in the cavern was a lead mine shaft. A little farther up the hillside some men were extracting fluorspar. We had noticed a ladder there. The following Sunday we went back suitably dressed and armed with a tin of paint, paint brush and two or three torches. We borrowed the ladder from the fluorspar mine and put it down the shaft which was not very deep, about fifteen to twenty feet. We arrived in what appeared to be a natural cave formation with mining passages off it. We were all amazed at the extent and formation of the lead mine. I had imagined proper shaped tunnels and walkways. The mine/cave was in fact a labyrinth of caverns, steep drops, jumbled rocks and side openings. We marked our route with painted arrows on the rock. I was enchanted with it. We found stalactites and stalagmites, ponds, signs of old workings and discarded tools. We went back to the mine several times, always careful to put the ladder back where we found it. Years later, in the 1960/70s I explored other old mines and caverns on the Matlock Bath side of Salter's Lane, finding many old artifacts of bygone lead miners, and in one huge cavern complex a date, 17-something. I loved exploring down old lead mines. A word of advice, never go alone. Take two or three torches and spare bulbs and batteries. At Tarmac I worked on quarry jobs alongside an old lead miner, Jack Beck, who had actually worked one of the mines we explored. I also worked with Bert Smith, who had worked at the Good Luck mine up Via Gellia, as well as Jim Slater who had worked at the Magpie Mine at Sheldon. They told me a wealth of stories of their lead mining experiences, and other older men who they had worked with when they were young. Lead mining is a hard and dangerous job. Not everyone has the temperament for it.

In 1978 a knock came on the door and there stood Lynn Willis, who I knew from attending lectures on lead mining. He asked if I could lend him a couple of acrow props to put across a lead mine shaft. He also asked if I would like to see where they were going and I foolishly said yes. Where they were going was three hundred and sixty feet down the Wills Founder lead mine at Winster. My friend from Two Dales, Lesley Porteous and I went to the mine the next day. I was suitably dressed for the occasion - old clothes and my waterproof suit. I sat on a four-inch wide seat, suspended from a quarter inch wire rope, and was let down the shaft, by a winch, at a speed of one hundred feet per minute. I found it was to be almost four minutes of fearsome, exhilarating apprehension before I landed on an 1819 water pressure engine fixed to a massive oak timber wedged across the shaft on the Yatestoop Sough level. I was even more exhilarated when I realised that the oak timber was ninety feet above the bottom of the four hundred and fifty feet deep shaft.

I spent a few hours exploring the old mine and the sough. The water pressure engine was dismantled in situ and lifted out of the mine. Using my building expertise we loaded the water pressure engine on the Dodge lorry and took it to Cromford Wharf. The ten feet by one foot six inches diameter iron cylinder of the hydraulic engine weighed well over one ton and we had nothing with which to load it on to my lorry. That is where my practical experience of lifting heavy stones and concrete lintels came in. We had plenty of railway sleepers, and placing two sleepers on the ground at right

The author and the water pressure engine at the Matlock Bath Mining Museum

angles to the cylinder approximately four feet from either end we rolled the cylinder on to the sleeper. Two of us lifted one end while two pressed down on the other end and two more put another sleeper under the raised end then vice versa. When we had raised it to the height of the lorry body I backed the lorry under the pipe, which was then let down on to a roller on the lorry floor. The men then held the pipe while I backed the lorry under it. When we arrived at Cromford Wharf, where we were to store the engine, I tipped the lorry up and gently slid it off on to a couple of sleepers, placed a few rollers under it and rolled it into the store.

With slight encouragement the Derbyshire Dales District Council, in partnership with the Peak District Mines Historical Society, decided to set up a Lead Mining Museum at Matlock Bath and I became its Vice-Chairman. Charlie Hopkinson and I, and one or two more of our men, excavated a large pit in the Matlock Bath Pavilion, concreted it for the installation of the engine, and helped with other bits and bobs. The date of opening of the Museum clashed with a trip to America which Barbara and I took in 1980 so I could not attend. However, because I missed the opening a picture of me looking at the pressure engine was taken and reproduced as a book cover and as a postcard for sale. I felt very honoured. The post cards are still available at the Mining Museum.

In 1993 I fulfilled one of my lifetime ambitions when I was invited to become a member of the Great Barmote Court, the oldest industrial court in Britain, if not in the world. I was appointed a juryman. The Barmote Court is a lead-mining court. It is believed to have its origins in the late 800s in the Danish held and administered areas of England. When the rules of the industry were revised in 1288 they were already ancient. They were further revised in 1851 and 1852 – as one juryman commented to me, they are always altering the rules. The lead mining area, known as the King's Field, covering a large part of Derbyshire, is divided into two sections, High Peak and Low Peak. The Barmote Court in the Low Peak is held at the Moot Hall in the Soke and Wapentake of Wirksworth. It was called by that name in 1086 in the Domesday Book. Soke men were free men, and Wapentake is a region. There were six regions in Derbyshire, five of which eventually became known as hundreds.

Originally there were many Barmote Courts, but these are now represented by the Low Peak court held at Wirksworth, and the High Peak court held at Chatsworth House. There are also two small liberties (small mining areas), one at Hassop and Calver, owned by Henry Stephenson from Rowland, and Youlgrave and Harthill owned by the Duke of Rutland. My grandfather Toft was a member of the Duke of

Rutland's Liberty. The Toft family has a recorded three hundred and fifty years of lead mining connections. I am very proud to have been selected to serve on the Barmote Court and I now have the honour of serving on both the High Peak and the Low Peak juries.

The Low Peak Barmote Court and lead royalties are in the ownership of the Crown. The one at Chatsworth is held by the Duke of Devonshire, leased from the Crown. At the 2003 Barmote Court, held at Chatsworth House, the Barmaster William Erskine retired. A new Barmaster was sworn in, the Duke of Devonshire's grandson Edward Tennant. I was on the jury. About forty people were in attendance. There was no business but a royalty was registered on the lead ore extracted in the year through quarrying and fluor spar and barytes mining. The swearing in of a new Barmaster is a great occasion which only happens at about thirty year intervals. The ceremony was followed by a banquet. Most large mineral extraction firms were represented in addition to a few experts on lead mining and its history. It was a wonderful day. We were served with bread and cheese between eleven and twelve o'clock which was traditional for the mine owners and lead miners who in the past had either walked or travelled on horseback to attend.

The Barmote Court goes into session at mid-day. Proclamations are read, the jury is counted and we kiss the bible as we are sworn in. The old Barmote Prayer is said. The Steward of the Court is Michael Cockerton, from Bakewell, in wig and gown. At the end of every session of the Court an inscribed clay pipe is traditionally presented to each member. It is all very ceremonial and quite moving, especially when you know that you are a member of the oldest continuous court in the world, over a thousand years old, which since the days of the Vikings has always been composed of men from all walks of life dispensing unbiased justice to the mineral fraternity. Lead mining in Derbyshire was first recorded in the reign of Emperor Claudius. I believe the Grace which is said at the Great Barmote Courts is a fitting reminder of the inexorable march of time and the fragility of mankind.

"Eternal and ever blessed God, who has made us heirs of many ages, and set us in the midst of many men, deepen our gratitude for Thy blessings, as we have received them from our fathers, our benefactors, and our friends. May we never forget the kindness which surrounds us in the present nor be unmindful of the treasures we inherit from the past, but having a lively sense of our debt to our neighbours, and a loving remembrance of departed generations, may we reverently carry forward the work of the ages, and daily endeavour, as faithful stewards, to enrich the same by a good conversation, and a godly life. Through Jesus Christ, Our Lord, Amen."

American Days

Barbara's aunty (her mother's sister), Alice Miriam Scriven, from Rowsley joined the ATS in 1940 aged twenty-four. She was stationed at Camberley in Surrey. Princess Elizabeth, our present Queen, was also based at this camp when she was in the ATS. Alice met a sergeant in the Canadian Army, Ernest Cyphery, and they were married at her home village of Rowsley in 1943 and Barbara was her bridesmaid. Sadly Ernest was killed in 1944 near Caen in France. When Alice was demobbed in 1946 she went to Canada as a Canadian war widow to meet and stay with Ernest's family. While out there she met and married an English man, Bob Josey, who had emigrated to Canada. Alice and Bob, who by then were living in California, came over for a holiday in the early 1970s and invited Barbara and me to visit them, which we did in May 1980, taking Russell, then aged sixteen. We had never been out of Britain or flown before. We stayed three weeks and spent sixteen days on the road in a large camper van. We travelled around three thousand miles in California, Arizona, Utah and Nevada and had some wonderful adventures.

Our eldest son Andrew took us to Manchester Airport where we boarded a huge three-engined Tristar with one engine in the tail and one on each wing. This belonged to Freddie Laker who was running a service to Los Angeles called Skytrain. The plane was full with around three hundred and fifty people and our journey to New York was uneventful. It was a lovely clear spring day when we flew over the Statue of Liberty and New York with its skyscrapers. A wonderful start to our American adventure. There were only thirty passengers still on board when we left New York for Los Angeles around mid-day. Looking down from the plane America was laid out beneath us. I spent the five and a half hours it took us to cross America marvelling at its diversity and immensity, from forested and snow-covered mountains to harsh bleak deserts. I enquired if I could visit the cockpit and was granted permission. I spent an hour talking with the pilots who pointed out various landmarks and told me which State we were flying over.

We were met at Los Angeles by Alice and Bob who took us to their home in Hesperia, about ninety miles away in the Mojave Desert. Hesperia is situated in the high desert, around three thousand feet above sea level. It came into being as a stop on the trans-America railway. Only the main street was paved, all other roads being made of treated sand, well rolled, with deep drainage ditches on each side. At the age of fifty-two, with Barbara at forty-nine, we were about to embark on the adventure of a lifetime. We had just three weeks to accomplish the journey of exploration. Early next morning I walked to the nearby open railway track. I looked down the dead straight track which ran down to San Bernadino. Two sets of highly burnished rail disappearing to a needle point of light. Gradually the light came closer; a black pall of diesel smoke hung above it. I moved from the middle of the track to the side and watched in awe as two huge diesel locos, coupled together with only one driver, laboured up to the summit. The train seemed endless and was very diverse in content, long flat trucks carrying articulated lorry trailers, others carrying shipping containers, huge closed box cars, open cattle type trucks and gas and fuel tankers. It seemed endless. After what seemed ages two more huge diesel locos, also pumping out clouds of diesel smoke, bought up the rear. Despite having spent a large slice of my life watching the trains in our valley I was totally unprepared for the onslaught of a typical American goods train with its impression of might and immensity. That train and the highway route 15 which had three or four lanes each side, from Los Angeles to Hesperia gave us our first impression of America. Incidentally we saw more police cars in that ninety miles than you would see in nine hundred miles on Britain's roads. An omen of things to come.

Later that day Bob took me to the neighbouring town of Victorville to pick up the motor home, a six berth, seven and a half litre, petrol-engined Chrysler Tioga, twenty-five feet long, almost eight feet wide and about nine feet high, weighing approximately four tons. Fortunately I was used to driving heavy lorries. I closely followed Bob on the journey back to Hesperia, getting the hang of driving on what was to me the wrong side of the road. Next morning we set off on our American journey.

Russell, who was going to be our navigator, and I had mapped out roughly where we were going. Like the best-laid plans, this one went awry, though through no fault of ours. Our first place to visit was Las Vegas. We found that route 15 went over a four thousand seven hundred and fifty feet high pass. Then we saw a sign to the old ghost town of Calico, an old long-abandoned mining town, which we visited. The main highway into Las Vegas is called Flamingo Road with three or four traffic lanes each side. I had already noticed that it was permissible to overtake on either side of the vehicle in front. Late afternoon is, as everywhere, a busy time on the road. Keeping one eye on the wing mirrors as is my habit, I saw a sports car, a Triumph TR7 zig-zagging in and out of the traffic behind me, obviously a man in a hurry. He suddenly rushed past me and smartly cut in front of me.

Not smartly enough. My huge steel bumper bar (fender in American twang) caught him in the near side and bits flew off his car, which came to a somewhat rapid stop. Two lanes of traffic also stopped. Out leapt the very irritated TR7 driver who started to berate me. I locked the motor home door while he carried on. The welcoming sound of a siren cheered me up as it was on a police motor cycle. The policeman said "Get these vehicles off the road now" which we did. He then took our particulars and I told him I was just passing through. "Not until you have appeared at court tomorrow morning," he said, and handed me a form. "This is a citation to appear at the City Hall at 9.30am tomorrow," he said. Rather facetiously I replied "In England when you get a citation you sometimes get a medal with it." "You will get no medal here" he replied.

We progressed into the heart of Las Vegas and drew into the huge car park of the famous Holiday Inn. I went to the reception and asked if we could leave the van in their car park. They said yes and told me we could use their restaurant and facilities if we wished. No charge was mentioned. After tea we walked into the town. To me one word sums up Las Vegas – "incongruous", a huge luxurious ocean liner adrift in the middle of a desert. We saw more gambling places, bright lights and ladies of the night all thronged together than we had ever thought possible. Everything was garishly decorated, from wedding chapels to amusements and shows of all types, all brightly lit up with thousands of flashing lights. It was to me a monument to the shallowness of some people's desires.

Next morning at nine o'clock I went to the City Hall in the motor home, parked it in their vast car park, and presented myself at the main desk. I was directed upstairs to another desk where my details were taken and I was told to wait in a large, and I mean large, room. There were steel cages around the room with handcuffed people locked in them, guarded by men with guns. I was told to get in the queue for a court and my details were checked again. In 1980 I was a district councillor for Derbyshire Dales, a Rotarian and the proud owner of a class one heavy goods vehicle licence. I presented my credentials for all three to the clerk who then called me sir and told one of the ushers to bring me a chair. A short time later the usher took me into court. It was very informal. The judge or magistrate wore a suit. Progress was swift with the motor cyclist policeman and the car driver giving evidence. I was exonerated from any blame.

A great surprise awaited me. The Chief of Police of Las Vegas wanted to see me. He was most interested in our police system and could not understand how anyone became Chief Constable, ie Chief of Police without being elected, when our Mayors, like theirs were elected. As we were talking it dawned on me that in America a District is way above a Town or County, sometimes covering an area almost as large as Wales. I declined a tour of police facilities in Las Vegas as Barbara and Russell were waiting for me in the van. We stayed another night in Las Vegas visiting various casinos and just walking the streets. To watch all the thousands of gambling mad people, frantically getting rid of their money, gave us an inkling of just how affluent Americans were. We also noticed the size of their bottoms – a better-fed race would be hard to find.

Early next morning we left for the Hoover Dam, travelling down route 93 to the Arizona border. We went to the base of the dam in a lift and visited the immense electricity-making turbines. Awe-inspiring is the word that springs to mind. We left the Hoover Dam, still on the 93, as far as Kingman where we turned left on to the famous route 66 to visit the Grand Canyon Caverns. We had the Caverns practically to ourselves as the visitor season was only just beginning. Being used to our local caverns and lead mining workings I was not especially impressed. Eventually we turned left at Flagstaff off the 66 then on to the 64, heading for the Grand Canyon. By one of those quirks of fate that happen from time to time we had set off very early in the morning and about five miles from the Canyon we needed to stop for petrol and a drink at a filling station. Round the back I noticed a tiny helicopter being serviced by a young man. After a brief discussion he said he would take us a one-hour trip down the Grand Canyon for the modest sum of one hundred and fifty dollars (approximately £66 at the time).

The helicopter was a steel skeleton with a perspex bubble at the front. I squeezed in the front with the pilot and Russell and Barbara squeezed in the back. There were two aluminium channels to put your feet in, otherwise the cabin and floor were mostly perspex. Taking off we flew low over a forest of pine trees until suddenly we went over the rim of the five thousand feet (one mile) deep canyon. It was breath-taking. The pilot said he would take us down to the river and would fly up it at a reasonably low level. We were totally unprepared for the almost vertical descent and the utterly spectacular scenery. When we had travelled up the river for about fifteen or twenty minutes we ascended and flew back at a much higher level, weaving our way back down the canyon, then back to the filling station. Twenty-five years later I shut my eyes and relive the marvellous experience. We then went in the van to the canyon rim. Next morning Russell and I decided to walk down the canyon to the Colorado River, a journey of about six or seven miles on rough steep paths, not a journey for the unfit or faint-hearted but not one to be missed. That evening, as the sun went down, I took a few photographs from the rim and they came out well.

Our next objective was Monument Valley, part of the Navajo Indian Reservation. We decided to go off the paved road and venture into the reservation. The Indians lived in separate homesteads, each one separated by a few miles from its neighbour. A homestead consisted of a hogan, which was just one large room made out of timber poles covered with a thick layer of clay. It had no windows, only one door and a fireplace. Alongside it was a living shack with a pitched roof and then an open shack type of building. Both these were of timber construction. I asked at one homestead if we could park our van nearby and they said yes. Next morning I came out of the van on to the sandy and scrubby land and saw a rattlesnake appear from under the van and slither away into the scrub.

After breakfast we visited the Indian family who were not most pleased with their lot. The Navajo family kept about fifty sheep which they sent out each morning accompanied by two sheep dogs who looked after them all day and returned home with them in the evening. We noticed each family had a pick-up painted in garish patterns. We gave the head of the Navajo family twenty dollars for petrol and he took us a trip to places of interest, including many locations we recognised from old Western films. He talked to us about the Navajo nation's way of life. How they clipped the sheep, washed and dyed the wool, spun and wove it into rugs in the hogan, which was nice and cool in the summer and warm in the winter. The families prefer to live apart from one another. Each unit consists of children, mother and father, and grand-parents. A pick-up truck is essential for hauling water, wood, coal, and taking the children to a pick-up point for school. All the Indians had free schooling, free medical treatment, and owned the land, some of which was rich in minerals of various kinds. On our travels through the Monument Valley we saw a small airstrip and a length of standard gauge railway. I wondered how the sheep survived on the arid landscape as there was very little vegetation. There are some outstanding rock formations and outstanding scenery.

Leaving Monument Valley we passed a place called Mexican Hat on our way to the Natural Bridges National Park. Natural Bridges is a walking job; scrambling is perhaps a better word. The bridges are spectacular. Moving on we went over the River Colorado again. Alongside the river was a very small airstrip We were fascinated to see an old bus appear with what looked like about a dozen pirates, and a dozen tourist types on board. On top of the bus were two large bright yellow rubber rafts bearing the legend Tag-along-Tours. Two light aircraft then landed and another half dozen people got out, one or two well past the flush of youth. They unloaded the rafts and set off down an almost vertical trackway to the river Colorado to have a trip down the river. I had seen the river from the helicopter – it was not really the world's most calm stretch of water. We were only a few miles from the state boundaries of New Mexico, Colorado, Utah and Arizona.

Travelling up into Utah on route 15 is wonderful. We stayed the night at an awful place called Hanksville which comprised a filling station, a camping site and a store/roadhouse with a few shacks. The temperature the last few days had been around eighty-five to ninety degrees Fahrenheit and the elevation was between five and seven thousand feet. We had seen a few snow-covered mountain peaks. We visited Canyon Lands and Capitol Reef National Parks, then on to route 24 to a most delightful place called Torrey. Torrey was very small; a few shacks, two buildings the size of large double garages which were the Town Hall/Police Station and the Fire Station. There was also a store which sold everything from guns to toothpaste, wedding dresses and food.

A notice was displayed in the store inviting everyone to a wedding. The total population of the area was about one hundred and sixty. A small delightful tree-lined stream meandered its way through the settlement and I would think it was around five or six thousand feet elevation. The van was going well and the sun shone every day. Russell navigated us well. As usual in these small settlement places only the main road was paved. Leaving Torrey we headed for Bryce Canyon National Park which has the most amazing scenery, very hard to describe. It had a fairy-tale like atmosphere, with tall pinnacles of rock eroded into strange shapes. We journeyed right through it to a place called Escalante and the road came to a dead end about twenty miles after that.

We had trouble with the van refusing to start – there was not enough power in the battery to turn the starter. Fortunately there was a small garage in Escalante run by four very obliging brothers, one of whom towed me at sixty miles per hour, in the dark, in an effort to start the engine which did not work because the gearbox was an automatic one. We stayed the night on their garage forecourt. Next morning they charged up the battery and tightened up the slipping fan belt to make the dynamo charge. They refused any payment. We found American people, in what I called the outback, very generous and hospitable.

We retraced our steps back to highway 89, then on to highway 15 to Zion National Park. We went through a tunnel into Zion, passing some very rugged scenery. The canyon was at a high altitude, cold and snowy. We spent the night there at a campsite. Our next stop was Cedar City where we turned left on to highway 56, then the 25 and crossed into Nevada, stopping at Caliente prior to setting off on the 93. We were heading for the old silver mining town of Tonopah. The area from Caliente to Tonopah was very sparsely inhabited. There were laconic road signs with bullet holes in them, and unbelievable statements, "Cattle on the road for the next one hundred and sixty miles," which turned out not to be the case. We saw no cattle and just one man on a horse in that one hundred and sixty-eight miles. It is around two hundred miles to Tonopah from Caliente. There were a few dirt side roads off to the left, guarded by two or three fed-up looking soldiers. Taking a good look at the map I found we were passing by a nuclear and missile testing site. No wonder hardly anyone seems to live there.

Nevada road sign which reads 'cattle on road for 168 miles'

We arrived at Tonopah on Saturday night, after dusk. There was just the one main street with a road leading off to the 1905 wooden shack silver mining settlement. Barbara asked at the small police station if there was anywhere we could park up for the night and was told there was no camping area and that we must not leave our van on the road. I drove a couple of hundred yards up the mountain road, stopped outside a shack and knocked on the door. A man came to the door dressed in a fur-lined leather waistcoat, blue jeans, a check shirt and cowboy boots. "May I put our van in your yard" I asked. "Yes" he replied, and shut the door. We parked up and decided to walk down to the main street to see if we could find somewhere to have a meal. Imagine our surprise at seeing a genuine early-1900s Wild West saloon, just like the ones in Western movies. We walked in through the swing doors. The interior was also like the ones in cowboy films. Men dressed in clothes identical to the man in the shack, with the addition of stetson cowboy hats, lined the bar and sat at a few tables. "Yes?" asked the barman. "We would like something to eat please". "We only have chicken on the go" he replied. "Yes please, for three." We then sat down at a round wooden table. Shortly afterwards the Chinese cook appeared with three enormous plates and half a bucket of chicken, a loaf, butter, and knives and forks. The meal was delicious and the cost was minimal. We felt like extras on a film set. Tonopah is around six thousand feet high on the side of a mountain which contained a lode of silver. This was discovered by a prospector in 1905 called Jim Butler. By 1930 the lode was worked out as far as commercial mining was concerned and the miners left. The mine opened again for a brief period in the Second World War. At the time of our visit the old waste tips were being re-processed.

After our meal we went back to the van and went to bed. We had only been in bed a short time when we heard the sound of guns being fired, very scary. Sunday morning was freezing cold but clear and the sun shone. The road we were on was dotted with old wooden shacks. At the top of the small street stood the small wooden village church, its doors wide open. People were wending their way to church still dressed in their cowboy type clothes. It was a day of celebration, Jim Butler day, the seventy-fifth anniversary of the finding of the silver lode. Down the main street there was a carnival-like atmosphere, with people dressed in flamboyant costumes and buildings decorated with flags. Americans never cease to surprise us; they celebrate all these anniversaries wholeheartedly.

We left Tonopah to go to the Yosemite National Park just over the border in California. Unfortunately highway 120, which went from a place called Benton to Yosemite, ran over a nine thousand feet high pass which, because of heavy snow falls, was closed to all traffic so we continued down route 6 to Bishop passing many high snow-topped mountains. This area was aptly called the White Mountains. We were now heading for Death Valley some seven thousand feet below Benton, through Bishop, Lone Pine and on to the 190 highway which passes through Death Valley. The Chevrolet van had now done approximately two thousand miles in two weeks. When we got to Stovepipe Wells in Death Valley we found all the camp sites were shut for the summer because of the scorching heat.

Wending our way through Death Valley we passed another laconic road sign which said we were now twenty-four feet below sea level. It is a truly desolate place which we had almost entirely to ourselves. We visited Burnt Waggon Point and the contrast with Tonopah (six thousand feet high) was tremendous, one green, cold and snowy, while Death Valley was sand dunes, hot and waterless. However we did see a few wild burros (donkeys). What they live on was a mystery to us. We turned our wheels on to the 178 in the direction of Bakersfield. I had one of my moments of madness and decided to take a short cut on a dirt road which led to a place called China Lake. When we got to China Lake the dirt road which ran across the large dried up salt and gypsum lake became indistinct and covered with scrub. To compound matters it went dark. We spotted some lights in the darkness and gingerly made our way towards them. It was a temporary borax mining camp with a few living vans and an awful smell. We asked if we could park there for the night and again they were most helpful.

Next morning they pointed us in the right direction to civilisation, which was about another twenty-five miles further across the dried up lake. This was the main highway to Bakersfield. At Bakersfield we turned right to visit the Sequoia National Park, stopping overnight at Three Rivers. The road up to the Sequoia Park is only a few miles long, but what miles they are. We ascended to nine thousand feet through two hundred and thirty curves and one hundred major switchbacks cut into the steep side of the mountain. It reminded me of Blackpool's rollercoaster. There were no safety barriers at the side of the road and it was very narrow. Travelling in the ten feet high, eight feet wide, twenty-five feet long van became quite alarming. Eventually we reached the visitor centre and walked through the snow to see the General Sherman tree, reputed to be the world's largest living thing. At the restaurant we had the worst meal we had had in America. The snow lay thick on the ground and it was extremely cold. America is truly a country of great contrasts. Against all the rules, as I later found out, near the General Sherman I picked up a small two inches high seedling and placed it in a plastic bag with some damp moss. I brought it back to England, nurtured it and the tree is now, in 2006, forty-five feet high and seven feet in circumference. Derbyshire seems to suit sequoias.

Driving back down the mountain proved to be even more scary. On the way back towards Bakersfield we parked up for the night at Lemon Cove. Early next morning just after eight o'clock we were still in bed having a lie-in when the van shook violently for several minutes. I leapt out of bed and dashed outside. The ground was vibrating violently beneath my feet, a very strange sensation. We turned on the radio to hear a news flash. Mount Saint Helen had exploded. Later that morning as we were travelling along route 58, following a large articulated lorry, the van started to wander about on the highway; so did the artic. We both stopped at a roadhouse a few miles along the road and several drivers were listening to the radio. An after-shock had occurred. Driving while an earthquake is happening is a very strange experience. The vehicle suddenly seemed to possess a mind of its own, careering about all over the road.

We stayed on the 58 to Beechers Cors where we turned right on to route 395 which ran past Edwards Air Force Base. We then crossed route 15 (which we had previously traversed from Hesperia to Las Vegas) into Hesperia and to Mission Street where Alice lived. It was to be a short visit. Early next morning we set off in the van for Disneyland at Anaheim, Los Angeles, about ninety five miles away. We threaded our way through the Los Angeles early morning heavy traffic, arriving there around nine thirty am. Disneyland is neither dirty nor shoddy. Everything is very well organised, with lots of shops and restaurants, entertainers and musicians. They even served English teas. We had to queue for some rides but not for long.

After a wonderful day we left Disneyland about six thirty pm to make our way home and, would you believe, we got totally lost in the Los Angeles back streets. We then had a puncture on a side road on a steep hill. Barbara knocked on someone's door to ask for help and they lent us some tools. They then, with typical American generosity, offered to lead us back to route 15, for which we were most grateful as it would soon be going dark. We made good time going back to Hesperia, arriving at ten pm. Next morning, Wednesday 28th May 1980, was spent cleaning the van inside and out and in the afternoon we took it back with two thousand seven hundred and sixty-eight extra miles on the clock and hired a car.

At a 1968 evening class on Derbyshire I had met John Merrill who was also a Derbyshire enthusiast and author and I used to go walking with him. He made his living by writing books on walking. He walked around the coast line of Britain in 1978. I walked two or three stretches with him, Prestatyn to Connahs Quay, Robin Hood's Bay to Scarborough, and into London where we met the Lord Mayor. Barbara and I also met him in Scotland where he met and married his wife Sheila. I was best man at his wedding at Drymen. In 1980 we met him again in California on the Pacific Crest Trail. John had decided to walk the length and breadth of America. Part of his walk was through the Blue Ridge mountains.

He was walking from Mexico to Canada when Barbara and I met him, high in the Sierra Nevada near the ski resort town of Wrightwood. John's journey from California on the West Coast to Maine on the East Coast was very interesting to me. John had arranged to call at various post offices at specific times to pick up new socks and underwear, and if possible to meet someone from the local radio station so that he could record an audio tape to send to Radio Derby. John gave me the name of the place, date and time he would be at the post office. Many of the post offices were in small villages. I arranged to ring the post offices to inform them that John would be calling that day to pick up his parcel, and asked the post-master for the telephone number of the local radio station. I would then phone the radio station and spin them a yarn about John's walk, where he was, and his need to record a tape on his progress for Radio Derby. This led to some very strange exchanges, both with the postmaster and the radio presenter. Several times I found myself being interviewed live on air, or the postmaster would ask me if I knew people who lived in Newcastle, Liverpool or London. I had to be quite firm with the postmasters who were intrigued by the phone call, and wanted to talk and involve other customers who were present.

John was a stickler for schedules, always being where he said he would be at a certain time. He told me he would be approaching Wrightwood on highway 2 about forty miles from Hesperia around lunchtime on Friday. Sure enough as we neared Wrightwood next day in the car, there was John striding up the road with his rucksack on his back. Wrightwood is a ski resort near the ten thousand feet high Old Baldy. We all had lunch together at Wrightwood. Barbara, Russell and I then returned to Hesperia and went shopping. I was unwell on Saturday and worse on Sunday so went to the local doctor's surgery on Monday morning, paying forty dollars for a health check. This included blood and urine tests and some penicillin tablets. On my return I went to bed.

On the next day, Tuesday, Bob and Alice took us back to Los Angeles airport to catch the plane which was due to leave for New York at two-thirty pm. The flight was delayed and left at six pm for a direct flight to Manchester. Every seat was taken on the DC 10. Five and a half hours into our journey home a cryptic announcement said "We have technical problems and are going back to an Air Force base in northern Canada". A further announcement told us we would be flying down the Canadian and American coast line to New York, where we landed. After another six hours delay off we went again on the same plane, bound

The Grand Canyon

General Sherman sequoia tree – the world's oldest living thing

for Manchester. We had had to buy our own food and drink at the stay in New York and were not allowed out of the airport. I was still feeling very ill.

Halfway across the Atlantic the engine sound changed, and there was another cryptic announcement. "Owing to a slight technical problem we have had to shut one engine down and are now travelling at half normal speed to Prestwick in Scotland instead of Manchester." We were really fed up by now. Andrew had arranged to meet us at Manchester Airport but by the time the plane landed, been fixed and flight-tested we were about eleven hours behind schedule. Not long after take-off we had the last and most startling announcement yet. We were told to fasten our seat belts as we were going to make an emergency landing at Speke airport, Liverpool, which we did with an entourage of emergency vehicles surrounding us.

Three hours later we arrived at Manchester by bus. Andrew had waited over fourteen hours. He had not been able to get any information as to where the plane was, or what had happened to it. We finally arrived back home at seven am on Thursday 5th June, twenty-three days after leaving home at five-thirty am on 13th May 1980. Twenty-three days that altered my view of the world, three thousand miles in twenty-two days on American roads, averaging one hundred and thirty-six or so miles a day. I had found that Arizona, California, Nevada and Utah were all larger than England. Great Britain has over six hundred people per square mile, Nevada has under seven and a half people per square mile. No wonder we saw no people or traffic to speak of in Nevada. Our best moment was unexpectedly flying over the rim of the Grand Canyon to look straight down to the Colorado River one mile below, then flying up the Canyon itself. We truly fell in love with the rural West of America, and its lovely, generous people, wide open spaces, and absolute freedom to roam through the most fantastic scenery in the world.

The three weeks we spent travelling opened a window on to a world we had only read and dreamed about. We love America, its wide open spaces, fantastic scenery and the love and pride its citizens have for it. We only know the West of America, Arizona, Utah, California and Nevada. We have stood on top of the nine thousand feet high Mount Baden Powell, been below sea level in the arid Death Valley, and I have walked, with our son Russell, five thousand feet down and up the Grand Canyon. We stood underneath the world's oldest and largest living thing, the General Sherman sequoia tree. We were almost shaken off our feet when Mount St. Helens exploded and been on a Tristar aeroplane near Greenland when one of its three engines failed, marvellous experiences! Our most optimistic expectations had been exceeded. It was truly the holiday of our lifetime.

Since our first overseas holiday to America in 1980 we have been to the Mediterranean area or the Canary Islands most years and twice more to America, in 1992 and in 1998, to stay in Hesperia with Alice. The last time we went to America in August 1998 Alice's husband had passed away the previous Christmas and she returned to England with us. Alice had lived for fifty-two years on the North American continent on both the East and West sides. She now lives in a bungalow at Two Dales. Unfortunately her sister Dinah, Barbara's mother, died two years later in February 2001.

PUBLIC LIFE
Darley Dale Society

In 1969 Ernest Paulson, John Billingham and I formed the Darley Dale Society for people interested in all aspects of Darley Dale. Membership grew to almost one hundred in the first year. The Society also became a bit like a parish council, which Darley Dale did not have until 1980. We met on Monday nights in the Whitworth Institute in the winter, and explored Darley Dale in detail in the summer. The Darley Dale Society was also a happy family, always getting into scrapes either by inadvertently trespassing, o r arriving at the wrong place at the wrong time. Our arrangements were occasionally a little vague.

The Society, of which I eventually became chairman and Sheila Slack the secretary, became the focus for Darley Dale affairs. Ernest and I led walks and gave talks on Darley Dale and district. Sheila and I organised Derbyshire village walks for twelve years and visited over one hundred villages. We usually contacted the local historian, preferably someone who had written about the village, to take us on a guided tour. Sheila is the wife of my friend Raymond Slack who I had worked with at JW Wildgoose & Sons in the 1950s. She worked for the Derbyshire Dales Tourist Information Centre and shared my love of Derbyshlre. She also had access to information on most things Derbyshire. Since the Society's beginning we had to restrict the number of members to about thirty-five from approximately one hundred. Thirty or so people are more than enough to take on a guided walk or a day's outing to such diverse places as Granada Studios at

The Darley Dale Society

Manchester, Bournville Birmingham, Calke Abbey, Rutland Water, Fountains Abbey or the tiny hamlet of Abney.

We were so fortunate to all get on well together and, similarly to the band of builders, have lots of fun. One of our members, John Riley, had the gift of becoming acquainted with people we met on our village walks. Before we or they had realised what was happening John had gained us admission to someone's interesting house or garden. Imagine the person's surprise when John asked them if his friends could also have a look and thirty or so people appeared from nowhere and proceeded to invade their property. Other times we went for walks to explore remote places of interest. One of our lady members, Eileen Paulson wife of Ernest, always asked if the walk would be on proper well kept footpaths and I always assured her it would be. Eileen took a long time to get over losing her shoe in a peat bog when we were taking what was supposed to be a short cut. After the village walks we invariably finished up at the village pub. We visited villages from Dore near Sheffield, Scarcliffe near Bolsover, and Peak Forest near Buxton, getting to know the layout and history of the village, meeting village people and local societies. These visits to over one hundred villages gave us all a deeper perspective, knowledge and understanding of our county. I can honestly say we never had a dull moment on our voyages of discovery around Derbyshire. Time marched on and the age of the members increased. We decided to call it a day in 2002 and wound it up the following year. Our Society improved all our knowledge of North Derbyshire, our Darley valley in particular. History can help to shape one's future. We can all learn from it. It is impossible to learn from the future as there is always so much speculation about what the future holds, hopes, fears and joys. I say provide for the future but do not surmise too much.

Councillor, trustee and clubman

In 1974 I put up for the District Council and lost, tried again in 1976 and won, and became an Independent District Councillor, and also a trustee of the Whitworth Institute. The District Council appointed me Chairman of the Performance Review Committee and of the Road Safety Committee. Two years later I was summoned for driving without due care and attention. I could not be tried at Matlock because I knew all the magistrates, so I had to go to Ashbourne. I pleaded not guilty and conducted my own defence, which was that I could not have been driving without due care and attention when I was stationary. The prosecution admitted that I was stationary when the accident occurred but claimed that I had stopped abruptly in the middle of a busy crossroad, ie the Bank Road and Smedley Street junction at 8.50am when all the employees at the adjacent County Offices were on their way to work. I said that it was not my fault that the speeding motor cycle ran into me but they disagreed and I was fined. I still think the accident was not my fault. I was very annoyed, especially as I had just obtained my HGV Licence with a first class pass, at the first attempt.

I am still an Independent Councillor thirty years later. One can never really get anywhere as an Independent. I was always very careful not to become a party political animal, trained to nod to order and carry out the party's wishes. I believe most Independents have their feet on the ground while keeping their head in the air. A few political party members do the exact opposite, feet in the air, head on the ground, which is inclined to give them a very limited view.

When I was invited by the Trustees of the Whitworth Institute to join them I considered this to be a great honour and gladly accepted. The Chairman of the Trustees at the time was Mr W. Horobin, no relation of my friend Brian Horobin. I believe he was Chairman for over twenty-five years. The other Trustees were Brooke-Taylor, solicitor, Herbert Kenning, of Kenning's garages, W. Walker, ex-pudding manufacturer, Ian Duff, solicitor, Herbert and Stuart Hardy, of DFS, Trevor Glossop, architect, and the Rector of Darley Dale Tim Yates. The Secretary was Leonard Geeson, solicitor's articled clerk and a former workmate of Barbara at Heny & Lovedays, and one of my childhood neighbours on

Darley Hillside. In my opinion the Whitworth Trustees were a sedate body of shrewd business men who ran the Whitworth, perhaps a bit autocratically but very efficiently. I became Chairman of the Trustees in the early 1980s.

Barbara and I attended a civic dinner at Ashbourne at the last minute in place of the Mayor of Darley Dale who was unable to attend. When we arrived we were shown to the top table, where seventeen mayors and their escorts were seated, all the mayors complete with regalia. The chairman of the Derbyshire County Council at that time was Lionel Cannon who was seated at the middle of the top table. He had been very good to Rotary events which I had organised for charity, and I had become well acquainted with him. "Hello Lewis, welcome" he said and shook my hand. Barbara and I had no regalia so they came to the conclusion we must be some distinguished guests. I never did find out how we came to be at the top table amongst the mayors from places like Nottingham, Mansfield, Chesterfield and Derby.

My funniest experience with dinners was when I was on Derbyshire Dales District Council. Barbara and I were invited by our friend Michael Gibbs to the Alfreton and District Young Farmers' Dinner at the Shoulder of Mutton, Hardstoft. I had to attend an important council meeting so Barbara went with our friends in case I was late, which once again I was. I parked the car and wandered into this large hotel. Never having been there before I asked the whereabouts of the dining hall and was directed to a very softly lit room full of people being served with soup. A waiter directed me to a vacant seat at a table and promptly served me with a bowl of soup. While eating the soup I kept looking round for Barbara or our friends, to no avail. I asked the waiter if this was the Alfreton Young Farmers' dinner and was informed that they were in the banqueting suite and that this was the Ripley Photographic Society's dinner. I finished off my soup then got up and walked out with every eye watching me. Soup was just being served as I sat down with Barbara and friends in the banqueting suite.

These friends, Joyce and Michael Gibbs, came to live with my mother at Highlands when they were first married in 1955 and have been good friends of ours ever since. They still live nearby. Michael was a salesman for S & E Johnson's Corn Mill at Two Dales and one of his customers sold him some tickets to a Victorian Evening, in aid of charity. The event was held in the Miners' Welfare at Clay Cross. Michael had assumed that Victorian dress would be worn so we begged and borrowed Victorian outfits and set forth to Clay Cross. Clay Cross and its coal miners had a reputation for being down to earth, hard working, no nonsense folk. When we walked into the Miners' Welfare the buzz of conversation ceased. You could have heard a pin drop. Michael and I, looked like fugitive undertakers from the Wild West and, dare I say it, Barbara and Joyce only needed a broomstick each to complete the epitome of a couple of witches. We were the only ones in Victorian dress. All of a sudden everyone clapped and cheered, and the manager brought us a large bottle of champagne for daring to go in our outfits. When we left at midnight I wanted to knock on the door of a lonely cottage on the moors and ask them if we could water the coach horses but my wife and friends would not allow it.

In the early 1990s the leader of Derbyshire County Council, Councillor Bookbinder was endeavouring to get Toyota to build their new car factory near Derby. In order to be seen to be very pro-Japanese he had a number of Japanese cherry trees planted around Derbyshire to commemorate the deaths of all the Japanese people who died as a result of the atomic bombs being dropped on their country. I understood his motive in doing this and indeed he was successful. The new Honda car factory was built at Burnaston near Derby. However no mention was made at the time of all the prisoners of war who died and suffered so grievously at the hands of the Japanese. My thoughts were full of Dennis Greenhough, my mate at Wildgoose & Sons in the 1950s, and what he had told me about the Japanese and their unbelievable cruelty to their prisoners of war. Dennis spent his captivity in Japan, mostly working in the docks, being beaten, starved and neglected. His mates were left to die when they became ill. A

The tree and plaque at Cromford Wharf

member of our Rotary Club, Ken Ball, had also worked on the Burma railway from start to finish. He too told me of the appallingly cruel nature of the Japanese and how lucky he was to have survived.

I became very upset that Councillor Bookbinder and his Council had made no mention of the suffering of Japanese prisoners of war and became determined to rectify this. I had two plaques made and fixed them to two pieces of Stancliffe wallstone. My grandson Mark, who was still at school, and I went to Cromford Canal wharf car park about five am one morning, dug a large hole near to Councillor Bookbinder's tree, and planted a three foot (one metre) English oak tree, then concreted the stone with the plaque into the ground alongside. The following week we went to Lockoford Canal wharf at Chesterfield and repeated the exercise. The oak tree at Chesterfield was stolen after about two years, the one at Cromford is still going strong in 2006. I believe they are still looking for those who had the audacity to put a memorial to the prisoners of war of the Japanese alongside the Derbyshire County Council memorial to the Japanese dead. I go every now and then to tend the Cromford memorial, to prune the oak tree and think of Dennis, Ken and all their mates who suffered so much. In 1978 I joined the Rotary Club of Matlock and became a founder member of the Talking Newspaper along with Tod Dakin, the newsagent in Matlock whose shop George Twigg and I had pointed in 1948. I took an active part in the Talking Newspaper for twenty years, first as a recorder then an editor. Barbara was a reader. I was now fifty-one years old

Ernest Paulson, John Billingham, my near neighbour and I, who founded the Darley Dale Society, also founded the Darley Dale Horticultural Society, of which I later became Chairman. I like to think that we laid a very good foundation for the Horticultural Society by seizing the bull by the horns and inviting some of Britain's leading gardeners to talk to us, Clay Jones, Alan Titchmarsh, and Stefan Buczacki. They all came to talk to the Society, Clay Jones twice. We also managed to get Gardener's Question Time broadcast nationwide from the Whitworth Institute. We soon had almost one hundred members. I had kept St. Helen's Church, Darley Dale, in repair for many years and had acquired a branch from the reputedly two thousand years old yew tree when the tree suffered storm damage. I had five replica Bramley apples made out of it and presented four to the famous Gardener's Question Time panel. Years later I heard one of them on the radio boast that he had the world's oldest apple. Dennis Hopkins, head gardener from Chatsworth House, whom I knew from my days of working there, became President, and the Duke of Devonshire presented the prizes for me at the Shows. The Horticultural Society is still thriving.

The late George Wardman and I from the Darley Dale Society also founded the Darley Dale Forum Club about the same time. This was latterly run by Vic Raynes, one of my workmates from those far off days at Hall & Co, a former member of the Darley Dale Society and fellow Whitworth Trustee. In 1983/4 I was chairman of the Town Council, the Horticultural Society and the Darley Dale Society, also an editor of the Talking Newspaper. Life had become very busy.

Her Majesty Queen Elizabeth visited Darley Dale while I was chairman of the Town Council. She came to open the newly-built residential home, Underhall, at Two Dales. I was invited to the opening and told to wait in a room which had been set aside in the complex. I was sitting there on my own when the door opened and the Queen, escorted by a Lady-in-Waiting came in and sat down across the room. We were alone in this room for a short time. We had not been introduced and they ignored me. I was most disappointed that I had no chance to talk to her. Barbara and I were invited to a Buckingham Palace garden party in July 2005. Again I saw the Queen but had no chance to speak to her.

The early 1980s was a hectic time for me involved with various organisations in addition to being a district and town councillor and a Rotarian. I miss not having a good academic education, but practical hands-on experience can sometimes be worth a lot more. Sometimes you find people in an important authoritative position who are brilliant academically have very limited practical common sense. This is inclined to make them slightly irrational when someone questions their decisions. How could they possibly be wrong when they have twenty letters after their name?

Talks and Broadcasts

I was also doing talks to various groups, illustrated with my own slides, on various subjects, lead mining, history of Darley Dale, Derbyshire history and another one called "The Wild Flowers of Lathkill Dale" which I did with Joy Frost of Youlgrave for whom I had built a house. Life was very hectic. Poor Barbara, on top of her own work, typed everything and corrected my dreadful spelling and appalling English. I have a wife in a million. Barbara, who kept all the books for the various businesses, tried to make sure I did not do anything too outrageous or foolish.

Having become well versed in local history I was asked to give talks on it to various groups of people. On one occasion I was asked to speak to the Forum Club of Matlock by Tod Dakin, who I first met in 1948. I noticed that the date of the proposed talk was to be 1st April, and the morning presentation was entitled "Sir Joseph Whitworth." The year before my wife Barbara had given me a most unusual birthday present, a small brass cannon with a bore of around two and a half inches (65mm). This was too good an opportunity to miss. Alan Boden from William Twigg, Engineers, Matlock, with very little persuasion once I had told him the purpose of the exercise, manufactured a square insert for the barrel of the cannon. Alan made a brilliant job of it. Even on close examination it was impossible to tell that the barrel had not been cast square. I took the cannon to the lecture.

Forty retired men, several of whom had been in the engineering line, listened to my talk on Sir Joseph. Near the end of the talk I told them the story of the square-barrelled cannon that Sir Joseph experimented with, of how a square cannon ball with sharp edges, instead of harmlessly bouncing off the wooden warship of the day, when fired at an angle to the ship, gouged large lumps out of the ship's timbers. The square cannon ball never ricocheted off the water, but easily penetrated it, holing the enemy ship below the water line. In addition square cannon balls took up less space when stacked, and did not roll around the deck. I said Whitworth kept the gun a secret because if it got into enemy hands large versions of it would render all wooden warships obsolete. Think of the effect on Britain as the world's leading maritime nation, disaster! A man in the audience, a complete stranger to me, said he had heard rumours of Whitworth's marvellous invention of the square-barrelled gun. Many questions were asked, where, when and how had I acquired the gun, which I convincingly answered. I received several phone calls about the secret gun. A week or two later Ted rang and asked me to go to the Forum club and tell them it was a joke because members were still talking about it. I gave talks, and still do, to many groups around Derbyshire and wrote a series of historical articles for the Matlock Mercury, and in 2002 published my book "Darleys in the Dale."

Around 1990 a knock came on the door and there stood a lady of about thirty-five. She spoke to me quite normally but told me she was profoundly deaf, and a BBC 2 producer of educational programmes. She was accompanied by her dog which she told me was a listening dog for the deaf'. The lady asked me if I would assist BBC 2 in making a film called "The Age of Stone." I had been on television twice before in short interviews about Sir Joseph Whitworth of Darley Dale, of whom I had previous made a study, and I jumped at the chance. I took the BBC team to various locations and introduced them to men who worked with stone. They asked me if I would take part in the film, explaining about stone usage to young people from local schools. This I did and the young people showed great interest. I got on well with the film crew and producer and the week flew by. Surprise, surprise, the BBC gave me several hundred pounds for doing something I truly enjoyed. There was another knock on the door in 1998 and there stood another lady from the BBC, radio this time. I was invited to record my impression of my life and times for the Millennium. Once again I was elated to have been asked. I was given no chance to rehearse. We sat at the dining room table, she set the recorder going, and I reminisced for ages about times past. I believe the recording has gone into their archives.

In 1984 I lost my seat on the Derbyshire Dales District Council. I was really too busy to canvass or to give it my full attention. I was still on the Darley Dale Town Council and enjoyed it, as well as being a

Rotarian. Barbara and I still played an active part in the Darley Dale Society, Talking Newspaper, and the Horticultural Society. Barbara also joined her friend Joyce Gibbs, her daughter and her sister-in-law in raising funds for Cancer Research. With other members of the group the sum of £335,000 was raised from 1982 to 2002. A substantial sum was raised by putting on Variety Shows at the Buxton Opera House, in addition to organising many other events with the help of many good caring people. Several of Britain's top variety artists gave their time and expertise including members of the cast of Coronation Street and Emmerdale. Ann Gibbs was the king-pin of the group.

Ron Duggins, who I had known from boyhood and who was a decade younger than me, and I decided in February 1998 to start a newspaper which we called the Dales Echo. One year later we had a staff of five and one part timer. We produced and distributed sixteen thousand papers a fortnight. The launch of the paper was featured on ITV news. Despite everyone working very hard the paper did not turn out to be a success financially and after thirty-four fortnightly editions we wound up the paper. It was very disappointing. One does not win all the battles but we tried.

Princess Anne was invited to come to Darley Dale to open the workshop for the disabled at Greenaway Lane, Darley Dale, which was sponsored by the Rotary Club of Matlock. I sent the Princess some information on Darley Dale and district and was introduced and spoke to her when she came. I have a wonderful slide of the late Geoff Wildgoose, who was President of the Rotary Club at that time, and Princess Anne together which appeared to show that Geoff was patting her bottom. He wasn't.

The Talking Newspaper, which was also run by the Rotary Club, was now firmly established, serving around fifty registered blind persons. Tod Dakin, Les Bowers, ex-Assistant Chief Constable, and I were now very busy. Tod repaired and distributed the cassette players, Les saw to the administration and the re-recording of the master tapes for distribution, and I was recorder and editor. When we had more teams I became spare recorder and general dogsbody. Roy Geall became re-recorder of the tapes, a position he held for many years. Tod Dakin worked extremely hard at the project. Without him there would probably have been no Talking Newspaper and such was his enthusiasm that he also helped set up Talking Newspaper in other towns.

Barbara and I organised various events for the Rotary Club, such as the Derbyshire Motorcycle Festival held at Cromford Meadows, which was a runaway success. We had spent nine months organising it. Security at the Festival was by the Derbyshire Police and the Coventry Chapter of Hells Angels. Thousands of bikers appeared and there were no incidents. We also organised the first Derbyshire Well-dressing Festival held at Chatsworth in 1995.

The year 2002 was very momentous for me as in May I became Mayor of Darley Dale. It had been decided by the Parish Council in 1995 that we should become a Town Council because of our population size, approximately five thousand five hundred. We believed that by doing this we would improve the status of our village. 2002 also became the time when the Whitworth Trustees and the Town Council decided to amalgamate but it actually took place in 2005. The

Darley Dale Millenium Stone

Whitworth Park was completely renovated in 2002/3. It was opened by the Duke of Gloucester and I had the privilege of giving him a guided tour.

In the course of conversation the Duke mentioned that he possessed a Whitworth rifle that was left to him by his grandfather. He told me he had no idea how the rifle came to be in the family. Because of delving into Sir Joseph Whitworth's history I was able to inform him that Sir Joseph was invited to Osbourne House by Prince Albert and Queen Victoria for a few days just before Christmas 1856. Whitworth took one of his new rifles with him to show Prince Albert. I was sure that Whitworth would have presented it to Prince Albert, and the Duke agreed with me.

Hospital Days

At the end of what proved to be my last day at Paton's and Baldwin's, in 1942, I cycled home from work suffering from appendicitis, cured by a quick operation by Mr. Rose at the Whitworth Hospital, and a month's convalescence. I spent June 6 1942, my fifteenth birthday, in the Whitworth, recovering from the operation. I remember it as a crisp, white, ordered time, full of do's and don'ts. My birthday in the Whitworth Hospital was spent with another local youth, Ken Ward, who had had a motor cycle accident on his way home from work on the railway, where he had been unloading a wagon of coal. He was as black as ink and despite his cries and groans the Sister made the nurses scrub him clean before being treated for his injuries and put to bed. He said that was worse than the accident. I returned to the Whitworth briefly two years later to have my right hand put in plaster. I was indulging in some horseplay with the gang when I broke it.

In spite of working in the dangerous construction industry it was another twenty years before I became hospitalised again. In 1962 I was in the old post office van with Barbara, waiting at some temporary traffic lights on the A6 near the junction with Hackney Road. A pain came in my chest which grew in intensity. I had a struggle to drive the van as the pain worsened. We decided to drive to Barbara's mother's house at Rowsley, where we had left the children while we went shopping. I managed to struggle into the house then collapsed. A doctor appeared quickly in response to Barbara's frantic phone call, an ambulance was called and I was taken to Walton hospital, Chesterfield. Walton had been a TB hospital and now specialised in chest complaints.

I remember being rushed along a passage on a trolley, then someone knocked something like a big nail into my chest. An hour later I lay in bed in a cubicle where my two brothers and my wife came and stood at the side of the bed all grim-faced and quiet. I knew I was ill but not that ill. The doctor told me next day that I had had a double pneumothorax, collapsed lungs, and was lucky that I had got to hospital in time for them to fix me up. After three weeks in Walton I was sent home and told not to get out of breath or work for six months. Walton hospital was more of a hospice than a hospital – very easy-going. I found out that five out of the six of us in the cubicles were not expected to survive. They had various cancers of the respiratory system. I knew one of them. His wife used to come and sit with him all day – very disturbing. It altered my way of thinking about my life. I had a wife, three children, a new bungalow to pay for. I came to the conclusion that life could be very uncertain so I should make the most of it. Nothing one does matters as long as you do not hurt other people. Very few happenings are much more than a few days' event in the end.

My next episode in hospital was around twenty-six years later in 1988. I had a persistent sore up my nostril. The doctor said it was a rodent ulcer and must be removed ASAP. A plastic surgeon at Thornbridge Hospital, Sheffield, removed it and made a wonderful job of rebuilding my nose. It was only a three-day stay, the hospital was very good and I had a private room. I made a good recovery and was fit and healthy until 1994, when my legs and arms began to ache. I went all to bits when the doctor said it might be leukaemia. I also had short, sharp, violent headaches. I went to Sheffield for tests, one of which entailed drilling a hole through my skull.

This was closely followed by a trip to Chesterfield Royal Hospital for a two-day stay to extract some bone marrow from my leg. A green-clad figure came to the bedside and told me he was the surgeon who would operate on my leg the following day and extract some bone marrow. He then went on to say that I would be put to sleep and have absolutely nothing to worry about. In my years in the building industry I learned that when someone tells you it is quite safe and there is nothing to worry about it is usually a white-knuckle job which no one else is daft enough to do. I was very apprehensive as I was wheeled down to the operating theatre, frightened and twitching. The complete coward. I was laid unceremoniously on the table and put to sleep. I woke up back in the ward and my first thought was to examine my legs for bandages and signs of grievous irreparable damage. I slowly and thoroughly examined each leg in turn; there was no sign of damage to be found. When the nurse came I asked why I had not had the operation. He looked at my chart and said that I had. He pulled the curtains round the bed, pulled down the bed-clothes and told me to pull down my pyjamas and feel at the very top of the inside of my leg, near the groin. I felt a small plaster the size of a 10p coin and the nurse told me that was it. I felt a fool. I had been expecting a hole an inch across, with buckets of blood.

The result of the tests was that I had polymyalgia, a fancy term for not enough red cells in the blood, a condition which starved the muscles of oxygen and made them ache and explained why my legs had ached so horrendously. The cure largely consisted of large doses of steroids, with the result that three years later I had type 2 diabetes. No cure for that! It took me nearly four years to get over the polymyalgia and off steroids.

In 1994 my wife Barbara had a heart attack and has had a pacemaker since then. Eleven years later it happened to me too. At 6.45 a.m. on 3rd February 2005 I woke up as usual, and summoned up the courage to leave my nice warm bed. Sitting up in bed a truly magnificent pain appeared in my chest. I put my feet out of bed and tried to stand up but failed. Unbelievably the pain increased and Barbara rang our next door neighbour and friend Dr Macfarlane, who told her to ring 999 immediately. Lying back on the bed I was bewildered and pain and anxiety overcame me. Minutes later Dr MacFarlane appeared and told me I was having a heart attack. Up to then I had no idea what was happening to me – I was beyond caring anyway. The ambulance appeared about fifteen minutes later and two paramedics, a man and a woman, dashed upstairs and, with Dr MacFarlane nearby, injected me and put tubes in the back of my hand. They then loaded me into a fancy wheelchair, strapped me in and wheeled me down the sixteen steps of our Victorian staircase, transferred me into the ambulance, and away we went at breakneck speed. Barbara had hastily got dressed and followed the ambulance as best she could to Chesterfield Royal Hospital. When I arrived I was whizzed into the hospital where a team of medics were waiting.

All I can remember is the wail of the siren as we sped through Chesterfield's busy morning traffic. I was beyond caring, but strangely the thought of dying never entered my mind. After being resuscitated I was put into the coronary intensive care room and festooned with drips, wires, machines that blipped and showed signals. A nurse and Barbara stayed with me till dinner-time. Then, to me, a wonderful happening occurred. The young lady paramedic, who had helped to resuscitate me and drove the ambulance, came to see me. This simple and caring act by her moved me to tears whilst at the same time filled me full of joy to know that a complete stranger who had probably saved my life really cared about her patients and I thanked her. I spent two more days in intensive care, giving me plenty of time to reflect on what might have been. Another of life's jolts. I eventually finished up at Sheffield Northern General Hospital having an operation on my heart.

After being moved out of intensive care at the Royal Hospital into the Ashover Ward it was ordained that I would have an injection in my stomach every morning and night. I used to pull the nurses' legs, asking them which darts team they were in and would they paint a bull's eye on my stomach. We had lots of fun with the nurses over the daily routine of injections. After a week or so the doctor said on his morning round that as from then my injections were to be discontinued. Imagine my surprise when at the usual time for my nightly injection two nurses appeared in the ward and said they were going to give me one last injection. I insisted that the injections had been discontinued and I was not having one. The other patients in the ward became very interested in this episode when the two nurses produced a huge syringe with a needle like a six-inch nail. I gasped, the nurses roared with laughter and so did everyone else in the ward. The joke was on me!

I arrived back home at Highlands fourteen days after my early morning heart attack on 17th February. To say I was pleased to be back home is an understatement. Sam and my family were very pleased to see me. I kept a journal of my heart attack. I believe I am not the world's best patient.

2005, February 3, heart attack, survived! I was seventy-seven years old and had almost packed up work. I no longer build but did the surveying work for radon gas reduction jobs, which involved travelling around Derbyshire and drawing up plans and specifications, and pricing. The heart attack put an end to work in the construction industry but I still drive the old Ferguson tractors mowing our four and a half acres of lawn and service my old vehicles. Growing old is a slow process but finding that you really are old and fairly decrepit comes as a shock and you realise that while most other illnesses can now be cured the cure for old age is quite drastic and long lasting.

In the early 1970s I joined Matlock Rifle Club, a gentle sport where one spent most of the time either resting or lying down. I told my doctor, James MacFarlane, that at last I had taken up a sport. "I hope it is nothing too strenuous and energetic," he said. I replied "It is one of the few sports I know where you can go to sleep between action." "Fishing?" he inquired. "Rifle shooting" I said. "It just suits me. I have to sit in a chair for ten minutes to lessen my heart beat rate, walk very slowly to the firing position about three metres away, and then lie down. Take another short rest. Take aim at the target, gently squeeze the trigger and rest a moment or two before repeating the strenuous exercise."

Friends

One of my oldest friends and colleagues was Brian Horobin. I had great respect for Brian. We had some great times together. One great time we had together was a trip to Farnborough Air Show in 1952. Brian, Charlie Hopkinson and I went down the night before in the old 1933

Rover 14. We three slept in the car in a wood near Farnborough. Three six feet people crammed into a car is not the perfect way to spend a night and by six o'clock next morning we had lit a fire, boiled the kettle and had our breakfast. We arrived at the airfield gates bright and very early, looking forward to the day's flying display. We parked the car and sauntered on to the airfield.

The first thing we came across was a Martin Baker ejection seat training unit. The unit was dominated by a sixty feet (20 metres) high lattice mast with an ejection seat fixed at the base. The attendant asked "Would you like a go? Just sit in the seat and I will strap you in. Pull the hood over your head firmly and away you will go. Which of you is to be first?" Brian said he would have a go and the attendant asked "Are you in good health, no problems of any sort? It is quite safe, not dangerous." As I have said before, statements like that call for a lot of thought. We decided that someone else should be the guinea pig. An innocent office type of person volunteered to have ago. After much tightening of straps and many instructions all was ready. By this time a queue had formed. "On the count of three" the instructor said "pull the hood firmly down over your head." We all watched intently. There came a colossal explosion, a huge cloud of smoke, and the man vanished. This was immediately followed by loud cries from forty or fifty feet up the mast. The queue, including us, immediately dispersed as the man was wound down the mast, unstrapped, and sat in a chair to recover before he wobbled off.

We saw and heard the De Haviland 110, with John Derry at the controls, go through the sound barrier, listening in awe at the double sonic bangs. After the Air Show we drove back home to Darley. Next day the plane broke up approaching the airfield after breaking the sound barrier. John Derry and his observer Anthony Richards were killed, along with over twenty-five spectators, most of them where Brian, Charlie and I had been standing the day before.

I remember one November night in 1962 when Brian Horobin and I were in Lehane's van about 7pm going round the Darley Dale sewerage scheme, making sure that all the red paraffin road lamps were lit and placed in position. We arrived at Churchtown crossing as a goods train was going past. A crowd of youths from the local estate were lighting fireworks and throwing them into the wagons of a passing goods train. Brian wound down the van window and told them to stop as it was a very dangerous thing to do. The gang leader aged about eighteen or nineteen and well built informed Brian where to go, in builders' language. He had definitely picked on the wrong man to tell him where to go. Brian, who had done his National Service in a Guards Regiment and was six feet two inches and sixteen stone, had had a hard day. He opened the door in a flash, shouting "come on Lew" and tore into action, seized the stupid youth by the throat, threw him to the ground and stood on him. I, being not so worked up and more prudent, took a shovel with me and announced I had plans to kill them if they did not go away (or similar), which to my relief all but two of them did – the one Brian was standing on and his friend who was leaning on the wall, winded. Brian, trying to calm him, had hit him in the stomach. However they quickly recovered and ran off. I offered to remove bits of them with the shovel for good luck.

Brian, who I had worked with off and on since he left school, also ran a thriving building business which he had built up since leaving Lehane, Mackenzie & Shand in 1963. After I commenced with my building business in January 1964 we only lived one hundred and fifty metres apart, both in bungalows we had built for ourselves. Brian and I did large rush jobs together. We enjoyed over thirty years of friendship until his sudden death in 1982. Only a few days earlier we had been discussing a building job together. It was a great shock to me, and his wife and three children. Barbara and I tried to help his widow Valerie and her three young daughters as best we could. I gave his daughter Denise away at her wedding in 1990 and we still visit them.

The Darley Dale Society was going well and I was taking more interest in Darley Dale affairs in general. I also got to know the Derbyshire writer, Crichton Porteous who lived at The Cottage, Two

Leica Photographic Club friends

Dales. We both loved Derbyshire. We did quite a lot of work for him on The Cottage. Leslie, which was his real name, taught me how to use a camera, and the art of composing a picture. He had three close friends, two of them part-time preachers and the other a church steward. All were Methodists, David Monkhouse, Michael Strange and Norman Taylor.

David, a Methodist steward, worked for a firm of architects called Smith and Roper at Bakewell. Smith and Roper were excellent architects. John Smith had a very strong character. After a slight dispute he asked me if I knew what the letters RIBA after his name stood for. I said "The Royal Institute of British Architects." "No" replied John "as far as you are concerned it means 'Remember I'm the bloody architect'." Two of my men, Granville Wagstaffe, foreman joiner, and Charlie Hopkinson, foreman builder, had found a small discrepancy in one of his plans. Charles drew the short straw and was elected to point it out. Charlie had as much tact as John Smith, announcing to the startled architect that as far as the staircase was concerned his plan was no bloody good. It would not fit. It was a brave statement to make to the redoubtable John Smith who promptly exploded, with good cause. The mistake was negligible.

David Monkhouse was born and raised in Darley Dale and attended Churchtown school. After leaving Smith and Roper he went on to become project manager of a large housing association who built hundreds of dwellings a year. Michael Strange who originally worked for Harry Brookes of Darley Dale and helped to put electricity in Highlands Cottage in the 1950s, eventually set up his own electrical business at Tansley. Michael was also a Methodist lay preacher. Norman Taylor from South Darley was a school teacher and also a Methodist lay preacher. Leslie Chrichton Porteous was a strong Methodist and a journalist. He became northern editor of the Sunday Dispatch and then sub-editor of the northern edition of the Daily Mail, and was author of many novels and books on Derbyshire.

In the autumn we all went out together by car to somewhere, usually in Derbyshire, armed with our Leica cameras and a twenty-four picture slide film. Around Christmas we all met at Leslie's house and displayed all our twenty-four slides, then, in company with our wives, had a party. It was twenty years of comradeship, friendly competition and shared pleasure. The diversity of subjects, even though we all went to the same area was astonishing. I had absolute faith in my four Leica Club friends. I know any one of them would have done anything to help me. Michael, David and I still keep in touch. Sadly Norman and Leslie have passed on. The Leica Club met for the last time in 1990. Leslie

The Porteous bell

died on 4th January 1991 aged eighty-nine. His wife Ruth had predeceased him in 1983. I undertook both their funerals. David Monkhouse designed Leslie a house which I built for him in 1974 in the grounds of the former James Smith & Sons Home Nursery at Two Dales. Leslie named the house "Clam Danel" after the name of the bell which was rung at starting and knock-off times at the nursery. I acquired this bell and mounted it on Leslie's house. When passing by I look at the bell and think of Leslie and all those long-gone nursery men who worked to the bell's toll.

One of my most memorable outings with Leslie was when he and I went to Chesterfield in the old Healey Westland to watch the opening of the new Chesterfield bypass by the Minister of Transport. We arrived a little late, as was my wont. A policeman waved the car through the crowd and directed us on to the bypass behind a Rolls Royce Silver Ghost carrying the Minister of Transport, and a vintage Bentley carrying the Mayor of Chesterfield and his entourage. A few more classic and vintage cars lined up behind us and off we went in convoy. After travelling two or three hundred yards Lesley said "Stop and I will take a photograph of the car with the crooked spire behind it." When we stopped the rest of the cars behind us stopped. Leslie took a few photographs and off we went at the head of the rest of the cars. By now the first two cars had gone from sight. Crowds lined the route, television cameras and press photographers were there, and Leslie and I waved to everyone. They all waved back and cheered. Arriving at the Whittington Moor roundabout at the end of the new bypass we retraced our way back, only to be stopped near the Lockoford Lane roundabout,

1950 Healey Westland setting off on a rally from Chatsworth

where the Minister (who by the way was a woman), was waiting to shake hands. The Mayor also shook hands with us and thanked us for taking part. A council official told us where to park and make our way to a nearby hotel where refreshments had been laid on. Leslie and I, who had after all only gone to watch the opening, decided not to push our luck any further and went home

After his wife Ruth died Leslie came to our house for Sunday lunch until his death. I undertook both their funerals. I was very pleased that at my instigation a housing development at Park Lane, Two Dales, near where they had lived, was called Porteous Close.

One of my friends and previous neighbour, Dennis Gregory, the nurseryman, and another, Steve Moorby, a landscape gardener, gave me lots of help and advice. Dennis died in 1983. Shortly before he died he gave me a prunus tree and I planted it next to the Midland Railway lamp-post at the end of the drive. Both are in full view of our lounge window and are a constant reminder of Dennis and my father and of the happy times we spent together. Steve Moorby with whom I have worked for many years still comes and cuts the long yew hedges every year and gives me the benefit of his gardening experience. Incidentally he is the brother of Edward of the river barge episode. One of the great advantages of living in one village all your life, and leading a varied life, is that many of your contacts and friends, in business and pleasure, go back a long, long way.

In the 1980s I became friendly with a fellow Rotarian called Alf Gregory. Alf was the photographer on the successful 1953 Everest expedition. At one lunch-time meeting Alf arrived with a companion and introduced me to him. "Meet my old friend, Tensing" said Alf. Two more ordinary unassuming men, in view of their extraordinary and brave feats, would have been hard to find. Tensing spoke very good English and was most interesting, telling me of the thrill of standing on top of the world's highest mountain. Alf eventually emigrated to Australia at the age of eighty to start a new life. He is now ninety-three (2006) which just goes to show if one has the will it is never too late to have an adventurous change to your life.

Barbara and I still went on our expeditions around Derbyshire with various groups studying its history and geology. The steroids I was taking in 1994, after my bout of polymyalgia, gave me lots of energy and I put on a stone in weight. From being barely able to stagger, one year later I walked over Kinder Scout from the Snake Pass to Edale with our dog Sam. We also walked all over Bleaklow Moors, searching out old aircraft wrecks, and I felt marvellous. Sometimes we walked on the wild, lonely moors by compass. It is a bit stupid going over dangerous moors on your own aged sixty-eight but I had Sam with me and we both enjoyed every mile. I also walked the old Roman road called Doctor's Gate, over the Snake. The Roman soldiers walking to Hadrian's Wall must have been very disillusioned in winter with the Derbyshire moors and their weather. It must have ranked as the worst posting in the Roman Empire. Sam and I also walked the Caldron Canal in Staffordshire, cadging occasional lifts in narrow boats. In 1995 Lewis Jackson (Builders) Ltd. won a contract to repair all the electric sub-stations from Buxton to Ashover and from Hartington to Wirksworth. Surveying these sub-stations I got to know nooks and crannies in Peakland villages that after all my years of exploring Derbyshire I had not previously found.

From my late teens I had always been interested in industrial archaeology in Derbyshire as well as continuing to explore and learn more about our great county. I had several expeditions down disused lead mines, always very dicey and dangerous efforts. I thoroughly enjoyed them. I was very familiar with the Peak District, having roamed it from the age of seventeen with the milk lorries, the Co-op vans, and latterly with the construction industry. I missed having a motor-bike but still had a car or a van. I started going to night classes on things connected with Derbyshire. I had always read avidly about our wonderful county. The night classes were at Matlock in the Charles White School which I had worked on for Wildgoose & Sons. While working on the school we had uncovered an old lead mine shaft there.

I met lots of people at these classes, with whom I became well acquainted. Barbara and I went out together on some of the field trips of the Derbyshire geology class in the summer.

Among our acquaintances at the geology class was a couple who I thought were prosperous Irish farmers. One night while waiting for our tutor we discussed the merits of our car engines. He had a 3.8 Jaguar and at that time I had a 3 litre Rover. I plied him with the benefits of my mechanical knowledge and he seemed duly impressed. At the next lesson I asked the tutor Roger Hartley who he was and he told me he was Sir David Huddie who was a director of Rolls Royce, and who had received a knighthood for the development of the RB211 Jet Engine! A few years later I explained in general the geology of Derbyshire to a stranger on a bus. When I had finished he informed me he was a professor of geology at some university or other and had enjoyed the free tutorial! One never knows with strangers who you are talking to.

My building friend Brian Horobin's wife had a baby girl who is nearly the same age as Russell. Joanne was born with spina bifida. She now lives independently in her own flat, and we have remained friends right up to the present time. Geoff Sellers who, like me, had left school without any qualifications at fourteen years old, had risen through the ranks at Lehane Mackenzie & Shand's and became chief service engineer and site organiser. He travelled extensively overseas, from China and America to Africa and Alaska where he worked on the Alaskan pipeline. We stayed close friends and until his death in 2003 visited one another. Geoff's wife Ann came from Rowsley and they had three daughters. Reg Parks worked at the steel factory when the Derwent Valley Co-ops closed in 1968 until he retired in the 1980s. We are still close friends.

To live in the county, as many Peak families, including my own, have done for generations, is a privilege. On my mother's side of the family, the Tofts, lead mining and building has been their way of life for over three hundred years. The Tofts took part in the lead mining dispute with the Manners family in 1657/8. A partner of one of the Tofts at that time was called Sellors, from Bakewell. I worked with the same Sellors clan in 1969 for the Duke of Devonshire on a public house in Chatsworth's Pilsley village. I also worked with members of the Bland family, the plasterers, whose forebears worked with my grandad in the late 1800s on Haddon Hall's restoration. Many old Peak families have an interwoven history, going back centuries, that most newcomers are completely unaware of. Derbyshire is steeped in history, folklore and traditions, full of magical landscapes and happenings like well dressings, village carnivals, village fetes. I have been so fortunate to have had such a good life up to now. My being Mayor for the year made me very proud. The years I have spent in our beautiful valley of Darley have been good. I can honestly say I am familiar with all its nooks and crannies. Everywhere I go in Darley I have deep-rooted memories of working, playing, visiting, exploring and delving into its past. I stand at the top of my garden at Highlands and gaze over the valley. Everywhere I look evokes a memory of people, now mostly gone, of my school friends, some of whom died in their early twenties, and places, some now altered out of recognition, some by me as a builder.

I am now approaching the end of my journey in Darley and beyond. My sun is setting on the highways and byways which I have traversed for so many years with my fellow travellers. My life has been one long exhilarating adventure with my wife Barbara by my side.

My Darley and beyond

*"Welcome to Number 10 Downing Street.
The vacancy has been filled."*